Rivers I Have Known

WILLARD PRICE

Rivers I Have Known

WITH MAPS AND SKETCHES BY THE AUTHOR

The John Day Company
New York

To my wife, my friends up and down many rivers, and the National Geographic Society which has helped to make these explorations possible

Contents

Rivers I Have Known

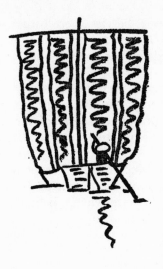

I

Why Rivers Are Important

IT WAS THE year 2000 B.C. or thereabouts when an artist of Babylon sat down with a clay tablet on his knees and carved a "map of the world."

Across the very middle of the map he cut a great river. To him it was the center of the universe.

"The Euphrates is shown," runs the museum description, "not merely as the largest and most obvious detail; it is a huge slash extending from one point on the circular, all-enveloping ocean to the opposite point, bisecting the round disk of the known world; the central fact in the setting of the human drama."

In all lands and all ages the river has been one of the central facts in the human drama, if not *the* central fact.

Early man was a hunter. Hunting was best along the rivers, for there the animals must come to drink. Man too must drink —and the water must be fresh, not salt. So the river was preferred to the seacoast.

Edible roots, fruits, berries, were found in most abundance in river valleys. When some man, or more probably woman, dropped a few seeds on the ground and they grew, agriculture was born.

The river was now even more important. Without water there could be no crop. Rainfall could not be depended upon. Too often all the prayers of the medicine man could not produce a shower. Sudden deluges might alternate with weeks or months of drought.

A river was more dependable. Except in arid regions where streams sometimes went dry, they kept flowing year in and year out. Gourds, shadufs, waterwheels, bamboo pipes or canals carried the water from river to crop.

Even the vagaries of a river could be put to good use. The annual flooding of the Nile spread new soil over thousands of square miles of cultivated fields. The flooding Amazon expanded into a lake three hundred miles wide, leaving rich deposits. The overflowing Mississippi fertilized a stretch eighty miles wide. The swelling Tigris and Euphrates joined forces to make a paradise so lush that man had no difficulty in believing that the Garden of Eden must have been located here.

Agriculture revolutionized man's habits. It was hard work—but easier than hunting at random for animals or berries. He no longer needed to search. He had food at his door.

Now he could give a part of his time to some specialty. One man took to boat building, one to carpentry, one to devising fishing tackle, one tinkered with metals, one undertook reducing spoken words to written symbols.

The river had made hunting possible, then made agriculture possible, and agriculture made civilization possible.

Groups of artisans, traders, scholars built towns and the towns became cities. Most of the cities grew up on the banks of rivers.

There water was always obtainable. There the produce of the countryside could be brought to town. The interior could be explored.

Often the river was the only road. Cairo needed its Nile, Babylon and Baghdad their Tigris-Euphrates, Shanghai its Yangtse, Rome its Tiber, Paris its Seine, London its Thames,

Buenos Aires its Plate, New York its Hudson, New Orleans and St. Louis their Mississippi.

Where a river was not available, a lake or great bay had to do —as in the case of Athens, Venice, Tokyo. It was only later with the development of road systems, railroads and waterworks that inland sites became acceptable.

But even today the tonnage of traffic on the Mississippi outdoes that on any road in the world, the Rhine is far and away the chief highway of Europe, and the Amazon is the *only* through road in an area equivalent to that of the three-million-square-mile U.S.A.

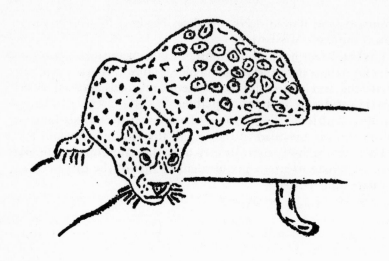

2

Mighty and Mysterious Amazon

THE STEWARD PASSES down the aisle, announcing, "We are just beginning to cross the Amazon."

Thirty minutes later: "We have just finished crossing the Amazon."

It's enough to make the most blasé passenger look up from his magazine! What's this? A plane going four hundred miles an hour takes thirty minutes to cross a river?

Right. The Amazon, greatest stream on earth, is two hundred miles wide at its mouth. It is a river to end all rivers. In fact, here is a river that is not a river. It is a moving sea. It resembles the Mediterranean more than the Mississippi. It has been called the Mediterranean of South America. Early explorers dubbed it the Mar Dulce, Sweet Sea, or Freshwater Sea. Brazilians call it the Sea River.

Once upon a time, say the geologists, it was an arm of the ocean extending all the way from the Atlantic to the Pacific, dividing South America into two great islands. Then the Andes rose to shut off its western end. Rains descended upon the mountains and flowed down the flanks to start the sea moving toward the east.

The Sea River has eleven hundred known tributaries. Ten of them are larger than the Rhine. The Madeira is three thousand miles long and collects ninety tributaries of its own before it joins the Amazon. The Rio Negro, fifteen hundred miles long, reaches a width of twenty miles before it pours its black waters into the brown Amazon.

This great sprawl of rivers, all combining to make one, drain nearly half of the entire continent of South America.

Go Up the Amazon? Why?

The plane stops at Belém on the southern lip of the Amazon. Most passengers do not leave their seats, for their destination is Rio. Belém is no tourist resort and the Amazon jungle no playground.

But who would presume to visit the world's great rivers and pass up the greatest? Besides, we are under some compulsion in the form of commissions from a museum and a geographical society. So, with keen anticipation mixed with some misgivings, we disembark, find a hotel, then begin to make inquiries about transportation up the Amazon.

We get no encouragement. Travel agents are interested only in selling tickets to Rio or Miami. As for the Amazon, they say it is hard to get up and harder to get back.

We wish to go by plane in order to get a general view of the Amazon basin, and return by slow boat with many stopovers to have a closer look at the river, its jungles and its people.

A small hydroplane makes the trip. It doesn't fly too regularly and it carries only eleven passengers. It is booked solid for the next three weeks. True, someone might cancel.

Inoculation against yellow fever is necessary because we will be invading that dread dragon's particular domain. As for malaria, the chances are heavily against us. And an attack of the Amazon brand of malaria can be more serious than a few days of chills and fever.

"You might as well shoot yourself if you get it," cheerfully remarks an old-timer (who *did* get it, but hasn't shot himself yet). "There's a special variety that kills you promptly. That's not so bad. The regular kind is worse because it keeps recurring, without any new bites, and you're just no good the rest of your life."

We take these warnings with a grain of salt, for we have learned from experience that the tall tales of travelers are as nothing compared with the tall tales of old residents.

But the American consul is not an old resident and he earnestly advises us to skip the Amazon.

"There is no hotel for hundreds of miles. If you come down by boat it just possibly could be a freighter but more likely one of the small woodburning riverboats, and they are impossible. There's no telling when one would leave—they sail when they get loaded. They are filthy. They may break down at any time. Last week one got twelve hours into the jungle and the boiler blew out. They are frightfully overcrowded. Mr. and Mrs. Hardy, missionaries, went up recently and had to share their cabin with fifteen people. Hammocks are hung on deck one slanting under another so that sometimes they are three or four hammocks deep and you must crawl on your hands and knees to get under and through them. The food is ghastly. Malaria mosquitoes swarm. It's hot. Bugs of all sorts share the ship with you and snakes crawl on board."

But, having delivered himself, he proves cooperative. He lends us two mosquito nets to drape over our hammocks, and radios a British friend in Manaus, George Browne, to expect us. Someone cancels plane reservations and we are suddenly booked and off.

It seems strange to set forth overland in a flying boat. Those pontoons would make a poor showing on a landing field. But there will be no landing fields. This is really more of an ocean voyage than a land journey. Wherever we wish to come down there is likely to be some water to receive us. This mighty Amazon system contains one-tenth of all the world's running water. It drains an area equivalent to all Europe outside of Russia.

We get an impression at once of its immensity when, rising over that part of the Amazon's mouth known as the Pará, we look north and cannot see the other shore of the river. What we see is only an island, Marajo. Only an island, yet it is the size of three Belgiums! It is held comfortably in the mouth of the Amazon like a nut in a squirrel's jaws.

We are flying now over the staggering network of rivers, the score of Amazons, through which the Amazon finds its divided way to the sea. For the Amazon, over much of its length, is not one river but many, sweeping through a swath of country from ten to a hundred miles wide. It is odd to see from our flying window many rivers running parallel within a few hundred yards of each other.

We come down on the whitecapped Amazon beside the island of Gurupá, eighty miles long and twenty wide. Merely an island in the Amazon!

Manhattan, held in the embrace of the Hudson and East Rivers, is considered by Manhattanites to be no mean island. Its area is thirty-one square miles. There is room in Gurupá for fifty-one Manhattans.

And yet Gurupá is only one island among the Amazon's tens of thousands. No one has ever had the patience to count them, and it would do little good for old ones disappear and new ones appear annually.

Greatest River on Earth

What a giant, this river! The longest, according to corrected surveys, slightly exceeding the 4,160-mile length of the world's second river, the Nile.

Place the mouth of the Amazon at New York and its arms would reach up into Canada and down into Mexico and almost to California. Straighten out the kinks, and the small end would stretch twelve hundred miles out into the Pacific. (It seems unbelievable, but figure it for yourself. The breadth of the continent is twenty-eight hundred miles; the length of the Amazon, four thousand.)

In all this length, not one bridge, not one place where man has dared to span the broad and unpredictable flood! Not a dam, not a dike, not a levee. It would be a brave man, and impertinent, who would presume to check the flow of one-tenth of all the world's running fresh water.

It pours from the continent with a volume of twenty Mississippis and continues with such momentum that its current is felt two hundred miles out to sea.

In these far reaches, well out of sight of land, a freighter ran out of drinking water and appealed to a passing ship.

"Drop your buckets where you are," was the answer. The buckets brought up fresh water.

As the rainy season comes on, the river grows in majesty and terror. It uproots great trees and sends them thrashing downstream, or riding concealed just below the surface, a dire peril to shipping. It forms great *igapos,* flooded forests, dismal wastes

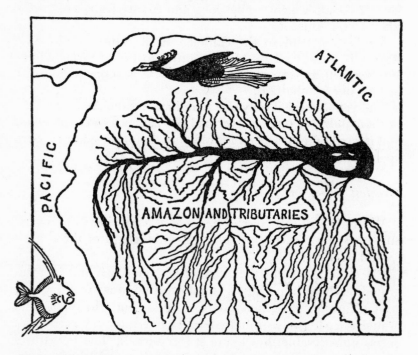

deserted by animals and birds. It spreads out to make swamps as big as Texas. It broadens to incredible proportions. At some places it becomes three hundred miles wide.

"At its peak," says Earl Parker Hanson, engineer and geographer who has made detailed surveys in the Amazon basin, "the river increases hundreds of miles in width at many points, flooding thousands of square miles of forest-covered land."

The sea is dotted with islands—uninhabited—for who would dare to live on an island that may be submerged at any time?

Boatmen must have a keen sense of direction to find their way through this maze. Experienced air pilots get lost.

Ocean liners can ascend the Amazon to Iquitos, 2,400 miles. There the river is still 120 feet deep. But seagoing ships may also ascend many of the great tributaries. Altogether, thirty thousand miles of navigable waterway are open to them in the Amazon spiderweb.

Light draft vessels can go fifty thousand miles. It means that one can sail twice the distance around the earth without leaving Amazonia.

No other continent on earth has so much nature-made highway. The interior of no other is so easy of access without recourse to the building of roads or railroads.

The watershed of the Amazon system is three million square miles, roughly equal to the area of continental United States.

Roadless Wilderness

We descend for lunch at the town of Santarém behind which lie the rubber plantations begun by Henry Ford but now carried on by the Brazilian government.

Down again at Óbidos. Again at Itacoatiara, a great logging center.

In rolls the mighty Madeira or "timber river," so called for the quantity of its half-submerged logs which tear holes in ships' hulls. One of its tributaries, the famous River of Doubt, was explored by Theodore Roosevelt and now goes under the name of Rio Teodoro.

We look down upon no roads, except within the towns. Even Iquitos at the end of the 2,400-mile flight is inaccessible by road.

Isolated Iquitos is a surprisingly modern town of some eighty thousand inhabitants. It is really two towns, one on land and one afloat. In the latter the houses rest on rafts which sit placidly on the ground much of the year but during the months of high water rise as much as fifty feet.

Iquitos is a town of startling contrasts—Bata shoe stores and chicle processing plants, smart hotels such as the Cosmopolitan, Malecon, Palace, Parisien, and houses built of poles and thatch

tied together with vines, Englishmen dressed for dinner in tux
and black tie, yes, even white tie and tails, and Americans in
sport shirts, Portuguese and Spaniards scorning each other's
language, neatly dressed mission Indians selling insurance or
automobiles and naked Indians fresh from the jungle selling
shrunken heads.

Headhunter's Heaven

The shrunken head industry has suffered a decline. But John
Dos Passos, visiting Iquitos, goes too far in saying, "Shrunken
heads are a thing of the past." True, most of the offerings in
Iquitos and Quito are simian, not human—monkeys' heads that
needed only drying without shrinking.

But a few months previously I had flown down from Quito
to the jungle villages of the headshrinking Jivaros on the Santi-
ago River, Amazon tributary. There the old art still flourishes.

I had supposed that a tribe with a predilection for smoking
heads would be wild and primitive in the extreme, so it was a
surprise to find, locked away here behind the Andes, a handsome, clean, intelligent people living in good wooden houses,
using platform beds instead of the usual jungle hammock, culti-
vating bananas, corn, and beans, and weaving their own cloth.
In peace, they wear shirt and trousers; in war, they strip and
paint. To tone themselves up for each morning's work they
take a strong emetic! They make war frequently, and great
drums transmit warnings through the jungle. They shoot their
enemy, or game, with a poisoned dart from a blowgun eight
feet long.

Technique of Headshrinking

In a cabin where heads hung from the roof an old chief
showed us how a head is brought down to the size of an orange
and treated so that it will last indefinitely.

First, the lips are sewed shut with a leather thong. This is
done so that the soul will not escape and harry the living. Then
the scalp is slit up the back and the entire skull removed,
leaving only flesh, skin and hair. A preservative of herbs is applied.

Hot stones are placed inside, and replaced as fast as they cool, the process going on night and day for several days. When one worker tires, another keeps the head turning. The longer this goes on, the greater the shrinkage. In the later stages, hot sand is used to fill out the features. The only part that does not shrink is the hair, hence the surprising contrast between the long black locks and the dwarfed head. The heads are hung near the roof, and the smoke from the fires further cures them.

"I understand that you use only the heads of enemies," I said. My companion translated.

"Not true," said the chief. "We use our friends too."

He had already told me that the tribe accepted me as a friend. I glanced at my companion, pilot of the small plane that had brought me.

"Only after they have died of natural causes," he assured me.

Of course that made it all right. After one has died of natural causes, what could be more amusing than to be perpetuated like a bust of Caesar on a shelf?

"And our relatives," the chief added. "That is my brother. And there is my grandfather." He indicated a head no larger than a pingpong ball that hung in a place of honor over the doorway. "He was a great chief and a very good man," he said affectionately. "We worked on his head a long time."

A little ashamed of the traffic, Ecuador imposes a fine upon anyone caught selling or buying a mummified head. This has resulted in black-market prices—also in spurious imitations. The authentic article may still be had for about thirty dollars, which is probably more than the first owner of the head ever earned while alive. Smuggled to London or New York, it may be sold for any price from one hundred dollars to five times as much depending upon the eagerness of the buyer to decorate his apartment with this grisly trophy.

We return downriver to Manaus, chief city of Amazonia. A thousand miles of jungle still separate us from the sea.

In Manaus the cars merely go round and round. There is no road going anywhere more than a few miles outside the city limits, nor a railroad. Manaus is as isolated as if it were on a desert island in the middle of the ocean.

Its only paths to civilization are by water and air. The jungle girdles it closely, and Indians guard the jungle. Their bows are eight feet long and they dip their arrowheads in curare. North, west and south of Manaus back from the river courses are thousands of miles of territory not yet explored by white men. But as for Manaus itself, the apartment we rented looked out upon a surprisingly modern city glorified by the dome of one of the western hemisphere's finest opera houses.

Take 'Em Alive

To collect facts and artifacts of possible interest to the museum I made a number of jungle forays out of Manaus. The most interesting was in the company of Roderick Campbell, one of several animal collectors devoted to the capture of Amazon animals for zoos, menageries, circuses and laboratories.

Amazonia has been called the world's greatest zoo. Its animals are the most fantastic on the planet. They might have been designed by a cartoonist. They are in a way more interesting than Africa's animals, because less well-known. While Kenya and Tanganyika have been the stamping ground of ardent hunters, much of the Brazilian jungle remains untrod, even by the Indian.

Animals grow far larger than those of the same species elsewhere. The armadillo, which may be six inches long in Mexico, attains here a length of three feet. The capybara, largest of the world's rodents, is as big as a sheep. The giant anteater has the size and strength of the great black bear. The otter, a foot or so long in the Canadian woods, is a ten-foot monster in Amazonia.

As you ride along a jungle trail the wheeling of a butterfly with a span of half a foot startles your horse. The jabiru stork stands up to eight feet high and has a beak a foot long. The condor of the Andean slopes is larger and can fly higher than any other flying bird, puts away eighteen pounds of meat at a sitting, may have a wingspan of fourteen feet, and is so heavy that, like an airplane, it must have a runway to take off. The world's largest non-flying bird, the ostrich, is represented in Matto Grosso by the rhea.

The jaguar and puma are the largest of their kind. There is a beetle as big as your hand nicknamed the "flying mudturtle," and a spider so large that it catches birds. Another spider suspends its webs between telegraph wires and the ground and builds cables so heavy that when wet they short-circuit the wires. The centipede is a foot long. The giant tree snail is as big as a man's fist. The tucandera ant grows up to two inches in length and its bite may be fatal.

Anyone accustomed to the small, harmless lizards that crawl over the rocks of the Riviera or the sands of Southern California is horrified upon his first encounter with the five-foot iguana or the savage-looking basilisk.

In the water is the pirarucu, the world's largest freshwater fish, the great swordfish, the sawfish that could cut a man in two with one sweep of its blade, the vicious nine-foot-long catfish, the half-ton manatee, the greatest living crocodile, and the big acara which rears its young in its mouth.

Giant among the giants is the anaconda, the world's greatest snake, usually twenty to thirty feet long, but in some cases attaining a length of from fifty to sixty feet. It belongs to the boa family, other members of which are the boa constrictor and python. But the latter two are land snakes and must be slim to squirm through brush and climb trees. The anaconda is a river snake and being supported by water, may grow as fat as he pleases. An adult anaconda has the diameter of a barrel and may weigh five hundred pounds.

Animals Designed by Walt Disney

Roderick with his seven men and myself as a working guest probed jungle waterways in a most curious craft called a *batalao*. It was a hybrid of boat and barge, shallow draft, almost keelless, motorless, propelled by paddles or poles. Amidships was a thatched *toldo* that served as a cabin. Cages occupied most of the rest of the deck. They were all empty, but Rod had no intention of returning to civilization until every cage had a tenant. Space was kept clear along each beam for the men to work, paddling in deep water, poling in the shallows.

Our first guest came at night. The Indians were sleeping in the boat but we had strung up our hammocks on shore between the trees. Something came crashing through the underbrush, evidently on the way to the river for a drink. Rod turned on his flash.

Peering into the light was a creature straight from the drawing boards of the Walt Disney studios. It seemed to have been put together with spare parts of other animals. It had the trunk of an elephant, the eyes of a rhinoceros, the mane of a horse and the body of an overgrown pig. Its trunk was very short but evidently used just as an elephant uses his, to gather food and tuck it into the mouth beneath. Perhaps the tapir is the elephant's American cousin—science has never been quite sure.

Fascinated by the light, the elephant-rhinoceros-horse-pig stood quite still. It was about as long as a horse but not so tall, its heavy body supported on half-length legs. It might weigh four hundred pounds.

"Let's get it," whispered Roderick.

The proper way to catch a tapir is to dig a pit and let the animal fall into it. There was no time for that. Another way is to snare it with a lasso. Not expecting to do any animal collecting at night, Rod had left his lasso in the boat.

The beast might easily have been shot. But the job of the man who brings them back alive is much harder than that of the hunter. A dead tapir would have supplied us with good meat for several days. But taken alive he could be sold to a zoo for a thousand dollars.

Tapir in a Hammock

"Keep this on him," Rod said, handing me the flashlight. I kept the beam in the creature's eyes. The tapir is a stupid animal—at least it seems stupid as it stands waiting for trouble. Its sense of smell and hearing are acute but as for eyesight, it sadly needs spectacles. It takes a long time to make up its mind. When it does move it goes like a locomotive.

Rod was advancing into the light. In his hands was—his hammock!

"Never saw this in a manual," he said. "But it just might work."

He flung the hammock over the animal's head and hung on to both ends as the bull, letting out a sound like a steam whistle, came to life and plunged for the river. Rod tried in vain to get his ropes around a tree. In vain he dug his heels into the ground. The beast towed him pell-mell toward the river. As the twosome shot by, I seized a strand of the hammock and wedged myself behind a tree. There was a terrific jerk on my arms, my face was rammed against the trunk which happened to be that of a javary palm covered with sharp spines, and the rope broke. There was a resounding splash as the bull and Rod hit the water.

Another sound made me go cold. It was the angry grunt of an alligator, evidently disturbed, perhaps struck by the tapir or Rod in their dive.

The alligators, crocodiles and caymans of the Amazon are an unpredictable lot. Sometimes they behave with the utmost docility and even timidity; at other times they will not only strike when struck, but will attack without provocation.

Painfully, I picked myself up and ran to the water's edge and on board the batalao. The men, aroused by the splash, were emerging from the toldo. I told them what had happened. We played the beam of the torch over the water. If any fight were going on, we could spot it by the turmoil. But the river flowed smoothly by.

A young Indian, Xingu, who was an excellent underwater swimmer, dived in. We cast off the dugout canoe that always trailed behind the batalao, and three of us combed the surface for a thousand yards around, watching for a disturbance in the water, or at least a few bubbles that would betray the presence of tapir, alligator, or man.

Now it was some ten minutes since Rod had gone under. No man could stay down that long and live. I began to think of Rod in the past tense. He had been a gallant adventurer, a great animal man, and a good friend. There would be no stone for a monument; I mentally erected a pillar of mahogany on the riverbank and was occupied in composing something to put on it, something simple but beautiful, when I heard his voice from the shore.

"What're you doing out there, boys?"

I turned the light on the shore. Seeing him there, dripping, laughing, and alive, made me angry.

"What do you mean by scaring us half to death?"

"I was unavoidably detained."

We joined him on shore.

"What happened?"

"Nothing much. He towed me about a hundred yards downriver. Then when I felt that 'gator nipping at my pants I let go and scrambled ashore."

Was I fated to trust my life for several weeks to this foolhardy adventurer?

"You're a nut," I said. "All you did was lose a perfectly good hammock."

Rod laughed. "Don't worry about the hammock. I'll use yours."

Luckily we had a spare hammock. Luckily too, Rod soon had another chance at a tapir, and this time had a pit ready for it.

Giant Ant Bear

Our next quarry was a giant ant bear, seven feet long from nose-tip to tail-tip. This anteater holds the world's record for size and strength. When standing erect on its hind feet it is taller than a man. In this position it attacks anthills which rise to a height of ten feet or more. The hill is made of clay almost as hard as cement, but the bear easily slashes it to ribbons with the four-inch-long razor-edge claws of its front feet.

Then a red snake shoots out of the creature's mouth and down among the ants in the ruined hill. The snakelike tongue is two feet long and is covered with a sort of mucilage. The ants adhere to it and are flicked back into the mouth. Back and forth like lightning goes the red tongue, for it takes many ants to fill the giant body.

The ant bear does not ask for trouble, but meets it fearlessly when it comes head on. It kills hunting dogs by slashing them with its scythelike blades. It vanquishes the jaguar in the same way, or by hugging it to death in its powerful arms.

After our specimen had been lassoed, it turned upon one of the men, gripped him around the waist, and wrestled with him exactly in the fashion of the black bear of the north. But this was a more serious encounter since the anteater's claws were far more dangerous than those of the black bear or even the grizzly. Before the man could be freed by his companions his back and arms were so badly lacerated that it was feared for a time he would die from loss of blood.

With two men hanging onto each struggling foot, the beast

was wangled aboard and into a cage. An Indian was delegated to the task of keeping it supplied with ants.

Vampire Bat

Another cage was presently occupied by a sloth which hung upside down from the cage roof and asked for nothing but to be allowed to sleep. It was big as sloths go these days, but only a trifle in comparison with its ancient Amazonian ancestor, the ground sloth, which was as large as an elephant.

It soon had as a neighbor a fine specimen of the famous basilisk. It is a lizard some three feet tall that walks erect like a man and is so light of body and large of foot that it can run on the surface of the water. What a sensation it would make sprinting across the pond in some zoological garden!

Night-loving vampire bats were usually fended off by the mosquito nets that hung over our hammocks. Rod had the good luck to be visited by one that managed to squirm in under the net—good luck, because he succeeded in catching it. A darkened cage was provided for it and, so confined, its habits could be conveniently studied.

Contrary to popular belief, the vampire is not a bloodsucker. After cutting a round hole in the flesh with its sharp teeth, it laps up blood as a cat laps milk. The blood continues flowing long after the vampire has finished its meal, and the animal or man may be seriously weakened. Cattlemen lose more cattle to vampires than to jaguars. Blowflies deposit their eggs in the wounds left by the bats and the resultant screwworms kill the cattle.

The Cannibal Fish

Among Rod's most prized trophies was the famous cannibal fish, the *piranha* (pronounced pee-RAHN-yah). This little ball of fury is more dreaded by the dwellers of the jungle than any other form of animal life (except man, and the mosquito). The anaconda and the jaguar are greatly feared, but are not so frequently encountered. In this watery world where man must be amphibian, his chief concern is the danger that lurks in water.

He naturally fears the shark, which though a salt-water denizen has adjusted itself to fresh and may be found even in the far inland reaches of the Amazon two thousand miles from the sea! He has reason to dread the giant catfish, the dogfish, the swordfish, and the red dolphin. But these usually attack things smaller than themselves. The piranha will take on an adversary of any size. Nor does it wait for its fellows. It will attack alone; and the smell of the blood it draws will promptly bring thousands of others to the feast. They will appear by magic from water that a moment ago seemed entirely free of them.

Though only a foot long, the piranha has the face of a bad dream—malevolent, staring eyes, the undershot jaw of a bulldog, or a pugilist, a mouth several times too large for so small a fish, and two rows of large wedge-shaped teeth tapering to needle points.

Like the shark and the crocodile, it is temperamental. Sometimes it will pay no attention to a swimmer. But usually the bather is in imminent danger.

A common mistake is the supposition that splashing will keep off the piranha. The contrary is the case. Splashing will attract it. Campers vigorously scrubbing the hands with soap invite attack. Indians wading into the water to launch a boat do so with a slow slinking movement to cause as little disturbance as possible.

Another favorite legend is that clothing will discourage the piranhas. It is far from true. They have no taste for clothing, but will slash through it or go under it to get at the flesh. General Rondon, famous Brazilian explorer, tells of a member of his party who went off by himself on muleback. The mule returned to camp alone. The man's companions followed the mule's tracks to a ford and there discovered the man's skeleton. The clothes were not injured. The fish had gone under them and stripped every particle of flesh from the bones.

A member of an American scientific expedition going up a river in the Chaco let his hand trail in the water while he was taking a brief nap. The hand was attacked and the flesh stripped off before he could wake. The shock he experienced when he drew out the skeleton of his hand caused him to faint and fall into the river. The swift current made it difficult for his companions to rescue him immediately; when they did a few minutes later there was nothing left except his suit and his bones.

A cattleman in Paraguay, Thurlow Craig, was startled to see, placidly floating alongside his boat, about six inches under the surface, a dark blue suit and bright yellow shoes. From the collar of the suit projected a white skull. Craig and his companion got the clothed skeleton ashore and buried it. They observed that not only all the flesh had been eaten, but the small bones as well.

Certain Indian tribes make use of the piranha in their funeral rites. Rather than allow their dead to become disgustingly putrescent under the equatorial sun, they place the body in the river where it is quickly divested of all flesh. "It is then customary," records Algot Lange, "to take the remaining skeleton and let it dry in the sun, after which it is rubbed with the juice of the urucu plant (the *Bixa orellana*) which produces a bright scarlet color. Then it is hung up in the hut and the Indians consider that great reverence has been thus bestowed on the deceased."

Our piranha was caught with nothing more than a piece of rope. Not wishing to injure them with a hook, Rod simply soaked the end of the line in monkey's blood and tossed it in. It was immediately seized by a piranha, with such a grip that the fish was readily hauled ashore. A school promptly gathered and when the line was again dropped into the water we witnessed a bloodcurdling struggle as hundreds of churning fish fought for the privilege of biting a rope end!

The Pasted Jaguar

King of the forest, the wily and beautiful jaguar, defied all capture attempts whether by lasso, net or pit—but was finally subdued by library paste!

Paste made of the viscid fluid that oozes from the breadfruit tree or the bark of certain varieties of holly is used by the Indians wherever and whenever a strong adhesive is needed. In English, it would be called birdlime because of its value in catching birds. The bird that lights on a branch that has been smeared with the stuff cannot escape, and yet is not injured. So it is a valuable means of taking birds alive.

One day Xingu was preparing some of the stuff for this purpose, half listening at the same time to the remarks of his companions on the difficulties of snaring a jaguar. Suddenly he stopped stirring and his jaw dropped. He had an idea.

"This will do it!" he cried. "This will catch him."

Rod was incredulous. "Birdlime? To trap a four-hundred-pound jaguar? You might as well try to stop him with a bottle of mucilage."

"We get many *tigres* this way," insisted Xingu." "It is good."

He turned to the other Indians for corroboration. They nodded emphatically, all jabbering at once.

"I have a suspicion they're kidding me," Rod said. "I'll call their bluff." He told the men to go ahead.

We had already located a jaguar's cave and the trail it followed to the river. The men spread a net on the trail, daubed it thoroughly with birdlime, covered it with leaves and plastered them also with the paste. Just off trail hidden in the bushes a cage was placed.

Now came the tedious part of the job, the waiting. All day, all night and half the next day constant vigil was kept by the trail. An agouti stumbled into the net and was glued fast. Xingu advised that we let it be. It might help to attract a jaguar.

It was close to noon before thirst brought the jaguar from his den. A beautiful apparition in black and gold, he made his leisurely way toward the river.

Then he saw the agouti. He was suddenly galvanized into action. While still ten feet away, he sprang, seized the rabbit-sized animal, crunched and swallowed it.

The jaguar now lay squarely in the middle of the bed of lime on the concealed net. Rod and I, still skeptical, expected to see him rise from his light breakfast, flick off any lime that might adhere to his feet, and trot away to the river for a drink.

The jaguar stood up. He lifted one foot. It was whitened with lime, but it came loose without difficulty. So the Indians were wrong. Birdlime, as any sensible person should have known, would not hold the Amazon king.

The jaguar lifted his paw to his mouth and tried to lick off the sticky mess that adhered to it. He merely plastered his muzzle with lime and leaves. Pawing his face to remove the stuff, he got more on. He pawed more desperately, spreading the lime into his eyes. He sat down in order to use both front feet. He turned to bite at the stuff sticking to his hindquarters, and succeeded only in getting one whole flank plastered. He became more and more distraught and preoccupied.

Cats Are Cats

It was all clear now. My mind flashed back to one day in my grandmother's house in Canada when a new cat had just been acquired. Grandmother had plastered the cat's paws with butter. The cat which had been highly excited by its new surroundings was now so busily engaged in licking off the butter that it no longer worried about anything else. It was an age-old method of accustoming a cat to a strange home.

Apparently it worked just as well with big cats. We could now speak and move and the jaguar paid no attention to us. He spared us a few growls, then went back to licking and biting his fur. He made no move to run off. The inbred cat-instinct to be clean dominated even his fear.

Xingu gently drew on the lines leading to the two far corners of the net. The edge of the net slipped over the jaguar's body. Now the beast seemed suddenly to realize his danger and began to thrash about wildly, thrusting his feet through the meshes of the net and completely entangling himself. The cable from the net ran in the door of the cage and out through the back slats where six men laid hold of it and, upon a shout from Xingu, pulled with all their might. The gyrations of the animal helped rather than hindered his progress toward the cage. He batted the doorjambs with his pugilistic paw, but they were stout bamboo posts four inches in diameter. His roar was something to hear and remember. It took a half-hour struggle to get him inside the cage and lock the door.

With the net still draped around him—to be cut away later—he gradually took notice of his untidy condition, stopped growling, and went to work on his fur.

"That will keep him busy for a week," said Xingu.

The Great Snake

Rod's crowning acquisition was the giant anaconda. These huge serpents lie submerged near shore with only the eyes above the surface and snatch any animal that may come to drink. Rod used a small deer as bait, drawing it by a line away from the water's edge and thus enticing the anaconda up onto the bank and into a cage. There the snake devoured the quarry whole and, with a huge lump in its midriff settled down to a long sleep.

He might awake six weeks later in a European zoo. He might sleep on for as much as a year. The anaconda, having elastically extensible jaws, not hinged like those of most animals and man, can swallow an animal much larger than its own head, even a good-sized bullock, and then go into a long dormancy while an extremely slow process of digestion takes place. During that period it is dead to the world.

This is a blessing to the animal collector. He need not worry for fear the cage will be thrashed into kindling wood by its superpowerful prisoner. The jaguar, though far inferior in strength to the great snake, needs a cage many times as strong.

Two weeks later at Manaus the chattering, grunting, crowing, squealing menagerie and the silent giant were hoisted aboard a cargo steamer bound for New York.

Life as an Indian Lives It

After briefly enjoying the rather limited fleshpots of Manaus, I ventured with some anxiety into Indian country. The anxiety was needless.

The courtesies of the city were cold compared to the hospitality of Indian tribes on the upper Papuri (which flows into the Uaupés which flows into the Negro which flows into the Amazon). Once there, I could dismiss my guide. I was treated with a kindness and generosity rarely experienced in this brittle age. Sick a part of the time, I was cared for like a beloved son instead of as one of the horde of destroyers guilty of unspeakable atrocities against Amazon Indians. No payment was accepted for food, lodging and native medicines; and I met with frank unbelief when I tried to explain that where I came from it was customary to pay for such things. To these folk, the idea that a host should charge for his hospitality was rather shocking.

There is always room for one more in the *maloca,* the typical multi-family house of many Amazon tribes, particularly in the northwest. When I first entered the Betoya maloca that was to be my home for a short time, I was carried back to a previous errand for the American Museum of Natural History that had taken me to a similar dwelling in a village of the ex-cannibal Bataks of Sumatra. There too the building had been a huge one-room affair and as dark as the inside of a boot. In each corner had been a fireplace, and on each side of each fireplace lived a family, making eight families altogether. Strangers could sleep in the open space in the middle of the room.

But the Amazon structure far outdoes its Batak counterpart. Instead of eight families, there are ten, twenty or even thirty families housed in one maloca. The average maloca accommodates fifty to eighty people. The building may be a hundred feet long, eighty feet wide, and eighty high. On ground subject to flooding, it is raised on posts. The dead are wrapped in their hammocks and buried under the building. You sleep with the consciousness that there may be a hundred dead men beneath you, and their ghosts seem to hover in the black void in the peak of the building.

The colossal thatch roof slopes to within a few feet of the ground. There are no windows and only a small opening at each end. The perpetual darkness has distinct value—it discourages insects.

Along each side of the great hall is a row of fires. Each fire means a family. Their hammocks are hung to posts that support the roof. There are no partitions, but each compartment is separated from the next by a single beam. Each space is precisely the same size as every other space—no one is given preference, no one can put on airs. The chief and the medicine man have no better quarters than the common run.

Privacy Belongs in the Forest

Of course there is no privacy. Privacy for undressing is scarcely necessary where there is no undressing. The propagation of the next generation does not take place within the maloca. Man and wife retire to the woods, not only because they wish to be alone, but probably because cohabitation in a hammock would be decidedly precarious.

Birth too is confined to the forest, the mother being considered unclean. Since the spirit of the newborn is supposed to be that of the father rather than of the mother, the father lies in his hammock groaning with the pangs of childbirth while his wife, alone in the forest, bears the child.

As for sanitation, the maloca is usually a model of cleanliness. The stench and disorder common to the homes of poor whites and near-whites is not found here. The maloca has no plumbing, nor the sins that go with it. Natural functions are performed in the forest and are the subject of strict etiquette. When the necessity arises, whether by day or night, one does not slip out quietly; one is expected to stand ceremonially and announce his intention. Whereupon all who are awake should reply, "May you do so mightily." Upon his return he must formally announce, "I have done so mightily." Which brings the refrain, "It is good that you have done so."

This may amuse the stranger, but there is a reason for it. The danger of attack by other tribes is always present. A person slinking furtively out of the maloca might be plotting a conspiracy with enemies of the tribe; and it is even more essential that no one should enter the maloca without being publicly noticed.

Equatorial Night Is Cold

The family fires are kept going all night, for the Amazon night is distinctly chill. Every hour or so some representative of each family must slip out of his hammock and put more wood on the fire. He may then sit by the fire a while, smoke a home-made cigarette of homegrown tobacco, gossip with the neighbors, and climb back into his hammock.

Thus all night long there is movement and conversation, rather disturbing to the stranger until he gets used to it. Those who do not dismount to tend the fire stretch a hand toward it to absorb a little of the warmth, and one of my most persistent memories is of the immense, gloomy hall, dotted with fires, each illuminating one or more outreaching hands.

At four in the morning, with sunrise still two hours off, the cold reaches its maximum. It is the hour when folk in civilized beds would simply draw up an extra cover. The Indians, having no covers, let alone extra ones, rise and make for the river to take a cold bath! For the water of the river, though by no means warm, is not as chill as the air. Then they go back to bed.

The comfort of the bath sustains them until sunrise when they take another bath! This time it is in the name of cleanliness. In the middle of the day there will be more bathing, this time for relief from the noonday heat. Late in the afternoon there will be another bath just for the fun of it, men, women and children playing and rolling like sportive sea lions. Now and then a crocodile or piranha takes its toll, but the bath is too precious a thing to be given up on this account.

Women spend the day caring for the children, preparing food, and tending crops. Mandioca, Indian corn, yams, sweet potatoes, peanuts and tobacco are cultivated. Also there may be some banana plants.

"Why is it that your farming is done only by the women?" I asked the chief.

"Because only they know how to bring forth."

The men do not live in lordly idleness. They do the hunting and fishing, and any explorer who has tried to keep his camp supplied with fresh meat will know that this is no small task.

Down the Amazon by Hammock

We visited as many other tribes as time would allow and what we saw is noted in another book.* There is no space for it here.

Our crowning experience was the return journey a thousand miles down the great river by woodburning riverboat.

We could have returned by small plane. But having already seen the river from the air, we wished to get the more intimate view from the ship's deck with frequent stops to explore the shores. Such stops are not afforded by the few cargo steamers

* *The Amazing Amazon,* by Willard Price. The John Day Company, 1952.— *Publisher's note.*

bound for North America and Europe. But the local riverboat stops everywhere, and in between.

The Manaus–Belém trip had taken six hours by plane. It took six days by boat. That is quick time. Some boats take a month, some two months, delaying to run up various tributaries on the way.

Our ship was gloriously named the *Belo Horizonte,* Beautiful Horizon. Upon first sight of it moored to the Manaus dock Mary could not suppress a look of dismay as she remarked, "It ought to be called *Perdido Horizonte.*"

The riverboats are survivors of the last century, some of them having served out their usefulness on the Mississippi before being transferred to the Amazon.

The age of coal is passing, the age of oil is here, the age of atomic power is dawning—but Amazon riverboats still burn wood! Some are equipped with a screw, some with an immense paddlewheel at the stern.

Birdcage Afloat

The craft has three decks, all unwalled, the doings of all passengers being completely open to view—giving rise to the Brazilian name for this type of vessel, *gaiola,* birdcage. Certainly no bird ever led a more public life than the passengers on *Lost Horizon.*

The deck was a crisscross of hammocks, suspended one above the other from deck to ceiling. Sleepers in the upper hammocks must descend by way of the lower ones, and it was practically impossible to step on a hammock without stepping on its occupant. Persons belonging in the inner hammocks must crawl on hands and knees under the intervening ones.

Beneath the hammocks large turtles wired together in groups of six wandered here and there. Hens were confined in crates but the roosters were allowed freedom and perched on the hammock strings. Geese were tethered to the posts. Hogs and goats stood in pens, hammocks draped above them. Monkeys, curassows, parakeets and parrots added animation to a scene that had no need of it. Large cockroaches skittered from one hiding place to another. A rat put out its nose from under a hand of bananas and then retreated, bewildered by the confusion—it would gain courage after nightfall. Cattle stood tied to the uprights, their tails switching over reclining passengers.

We were assigned one of the few cabins but found it stuffy. We soon realized how sensible the north Brazilian is when he abjures bunks and beds in favor of hammocks, and we slung ours on deck with the others.

The ship had scarcely left the dock before all passengers began undressing. Since most of them had no cabins this operation had to be performed on the open deck. Then they donned pajamas—a puzzling procedure since the sun was still high.

The pajamas were worn night and day for the six days of the journey. They are accepted ship attire. We as the only non-Brazilians on board felt painfully conspicuous in shore clothes. Now we understood the inspiration for that ancient ditty:

> *Floating down the Amazon*
> *With my pink pajamas on.*

The pajamas began to smell a little musty before the trip was over. The Brazilian when at home is one of the cleanest of humans, taking one or two baths daily. But the ship afforded only a single bathtub for her three hundred passengers—and it was so suggestive of athlete's foot and skin affections that it was shunned by the judicious. However even the judicious could not completely avoid an occasional trip to the water closet, an acutely distasteful experience. On a ship rolling violently in the grip of a hurricane one could understand it, but on the rock-steady deck of a river steamer there was no accounting for the Brazilian's hopelessly poor sense of direction.

We dined in the open air on the afterdeck. The tablecloths, unchanged during the six-day voyage, deteriorated from a dirty gray to a mottled brown-and-black from spilled gravy, mushed beans, coffee stains and wiped lips.

The food was truly amazing. In a land where experimental farms have demonstrated that two hundred varieties of fruit do well, fruit was never served on board except on one single occasion—and then it was a finger-sized banana. The caboclo brought up on jerked beef and farinha considers it almost as absurd to eat fruit as it is indecent to drink milk. There was not a green vegetable of any sort. No salad. No "protective foods"—no eggs or any other dairy products. There were some

black beans. There was one sliver of beef a day. There was
imported white rice, ground free of its vitamins, and the noto-
rious cheat food, mandioca. Almost pure starch, devoid of vitamins and minerals, mandioca spells bad teeth, low vitality,
and susceptibility to disease.

In spite of the predominance of starch, it proved to be a
reducing diet. Mary lost eight pounds, I nine.

To be sure there were compensations. The pageant of the
jungle was a constant delight. The ship stopped several times a
day at small settlements to put off cargo or take on wood for the
boilers. Nearly half of the time the boat lay tied up to the shore
and we had plenty of opportunity to roam the jungle and visit
Indian villages.

The Pioneer from Abilene

Most amazing were the farms. Yes, farms—where one would
expect to find nothing but unbroken jungle. The men who ran
them were real pioneers, most of them Brazilians, but not a few
adventurous and ambitious Britons, Americans and Japanese.

We stopped to see Tom Harrison from Abilene, Kansas. On
his farm outside of Santarém he was fitting props under the too
heavily weighted branches of an orange tree.

Kansas is a good state. Why did he leave it for the wilds of
the Amazon?

"I don't know," he said. "Sort of got the Go-West-Young-
Man fever. Only I heard California was getting too crowded. A
fellow from down this way told me there was plenty of room
here. So I came."

"Do you regret it?"

He grinned. "Not me. Let me show you what I got."

He parted the leaves and took out an orange. It was plainly a
Washington navel, but three times as big as the ones I grow in
my California garden.

When I said so, he replied, "I understand California got it
from here. Brazil is its real home."

Everything seemed to be at home on Tom's farm—bananas,
mangoes, avocados, figs, cocoa, coffee, Brazil nuts, cream nuts,
vegetables in bewildering variety. There were rubber trees, oil
palms, bamboo, cedar, mahogany. He had healthy cattle, pigs,

chickens and a pet boa constrictor that slept in the rafters and kept the house free of vermin.

"It's not all roses," he said. "Things grow *too* fast. It keeps you hopping. You have to be forever fighting back the jungle. Heavy rains leach the soil. You gotta richen it up with leaf mold and fertilizer. But then, whish!—things grow like magic."

The World's Last Great Frontier

Room. He's right, there is plenty of room in the Amazon basin. Three million square miles. Population, less than one man per square mile. More still unexplored country than anywhere else on earth except Antarctica. It is the world's last great frontier.

No young man should pull up stakes and rush down to the Amazon wilderness without enough money to get back if he doesn't like it. There are insects, and there is heat, and humidity, and isolation, and the language difficulty. But there is also opportunity.

This virgin territory, equal in size to the United States and even more highly favored in natural resources, may some day come to be the chief granary of a plundered planet. This belief was voiced by a distinguished agronomist appointed by the United Nations to make a survey of the possibilities of the region. He reported:

"If the Amazon can be brought into production, the world will be able to support its population."

3

Misadventure on the Nile

IT WAS ALMOST dawn. We were ready to start. Houssein came up the gangplank with the provisions. Instead of supporting the bundle underneath, he dangled it by the string. I had an uneasy premonition. Could one trust oneself on a two-month journey to a man who would carry a heavy bundle by the string? Then the string broke, and all of our food for the next three days was in the Nile.

But this accident which began our voyage was only a mild suggestion of what was to come at the end, when not merely the supplies would go into the Nile, but everything and everybody.

Houssein, still helplessly holding the string in his hand, lifted his black face to the stars and lamented—but did not dream of getting his feet wet. The captain whipped off his long Mother Hubbard of a *galabieh,* dived in, brought up cans from the bottom, and corralled floating loaves, oranges and carrots.

Two months later the little scene was to be reenacted. But then lives, not carrots, would be at stake.

"All Egyptians Are Thieves'

We came to know our men well before the trip was over. They were both Nubians, black as coalholes, and proud of it.

"We are not Egyptians," they would insist. They remembered that their ancestors had once ruled Egypt and that Nubians had been among the staunchest fighters in the Egyptian army. They considered themselves a cut above the palefaces of the Nile Valley.

The captain had courage and Houssein had a mustache. It was a brave affair and he could use it to give his face an appearance of great resolution under his piratical turban. He knew how to handle a boat, if he could just remember in emergencies, and he was a good cook, valet, and lady's maid. He kept the decks shining.

Captain Abdul and Houssein had about twenty English words between them. They did not understand our Arabic, but would never admit it. They would nod and immediately do something—and since the something they did was usually just as good as what we had asked for, if not better, there was no real cause for complaint.

Their skirts seemed a bit unsailorlike, particularly when it was necessary to climb the mast or to wade ashore. But you can do a lot in a skirt if you catch up the edge of it in your teeth. They wore no shoes and the soles of their feet were cracked and seamed like rhinoceros hide.

Our Nubians were not too easy in their minds about the trip. Leaving Shallâl in lower Nubia, we were to go a short distance south, then turn and travel nearly six hundred miles down north (there is no "down south" in Egypt, for the river flows north) to Cairo. Including tacks against the prevailing north wind, the actual distance covered would be easily a thousand miles. With stops for study, it would take two months.

But it was not the distance nor the time that worried them, but the strange country that must be penetrated. They knew their Nubia and were familiar with the Nile as far as Luxor. Below that, they must have triple money—for, believing firmly that civilization means sin, they regarded the modernized part of Egypt as a den of thieves.

They could not understand why we should wish to go in a small boat such as the felucca *Arabia* when we could travel in comfort on a steamer.

But the steamer puts in only at the important towns. The real Egypt is in the villages. These the steamer disdainfully chugs by. Some of them have not been visited by travelers from Europe or America in a century.

The Hidden Egypt

It is in these back eddies of Egyptian life that one finds the Egypt of the Pharaohs, almost untouched by the outside world, one of the most ancient civilizations persevering today upon the face of the globe, and still very much alive. We wished to visit this hidden Egypt.

The gangplank was drawn in. The captain and his aide used it as a rowing seat, and we moved out upon a mirror of black marble. The mid-February moon was beginning to show its age by a little moldiness along one side of its round face.

Dawn is impatient in Egypt, and before the moon could retire gracefully from the sky the eastern horizon flamed red and the sun came up.

One quickly understands why the sun has dominated the history, religion and life of Egypt. Once it is up, it is everywhere, all-pervading, tremendous.

We retreated under the awning and, through dark glasses, looked upon as weird a panorama as the world offers. Out of the water towered black, rocky islands like castles with their corners worn off. A goat could not have clung to those castle walls. Contrasting with the black was the golden-yellow of the desert, coming to the river's edge.

Here and there the heads of palms projected from the water. In the fruiting season one needs merely to sail up to them to pick dates, for the trees are alive though neck-deep most of the year.

Sailing over a Drowned Village

But the strangest sight was beneath us. We were passing over a village. We looked down upon narrow streets, the flat roofs of houses, walled courtyards meant to protect women from the public gaze, the marketplace, the mosque whose minaret almost grazed the keel of our boat. The building of the mighty Aswân Dam held back the waters and so raised the level that scores of villages were submerged. The Government expropriated and paid for the drowned land. The homeless Nubians were offered fertile fields in Egypt, but they preferred their own grim country and proceeded to build new villages higher up in the desert.

Here the villagers raise a few goats and pigeons, come down to the shore to tend small patches of vegetables, and go out by boat to the palms still growing on old islands now submerged. The dam has turned the river above into a lake, the backflow reaching at times more than two hundred miles upstream.

But this is only a preview of the much greater lake that will be formed, drowning more villages and temples, when the new dam to be known as the High Aswân is completed.

In the meantime the present Aswân is impressive enough.

Mysteries Below

A strong breeze came up, drawing a veil of ripples over the mysteries beneath us. The big lateen sail was unfurled. All day we sped up the strange lake.

The next day we tacked briskly down again, and climbed out at sunset upon the crest of a temple. Beneath us now, invisible because of the waves, was the island of Philae with its lovely Temple of Isis. Only the tallest part of the temple was high enough to overtop the Nile.

We stood upon it, looked down, and tried to imagine. According to those who had measured it, this part was sixty feet high; now it was sixty feet deep. If one wished to go down, there was a stone stairway that descended through its heart—but one would need a diving suit.

How desolate the goddess Isis must feel now with the slime of the Nile cloying about her, she who had formerly been honored by emperors and visited by tens of thousands of pilgrims every year!

It is only between August and December, when the dam releases its store, that the muddy gray ghost of Isis emerges, looks about upon the world that once acclaimed her, and then retires like a disappointed mermaid beneath the waves.

Now we come to the villain of the piece—the Aswân Dam—but a villain only to the regions above, a benefactor below. Egypt formerly alternated between flood and drought. There is still flood, sometimes excessive, but there is no longer a period of drought. Crops now may have water all the year round. Perennial irrigation came in with the Aswân Dam. As the population increases, still more water will be required.

Stronger Than the Pyramids

As we tried to sleep that night in the *Arabia*, still moored to the Temple of Isis, the roar of the dam filled our ears. It had a compelling personality. Early the next morning we sailed to it.

There it was, the savior of Egypt—but all we saw was a long wall, as impassive as the Sphinx. It seemed very immobile to be capable of so much. "They also serve . . ."

The dam, made of granite, even firmer stuff than the limestone of the Great Pyramid, is prepared to stand and wait a long time. It may be one of Egypt's chief antiquities several thousand years hence. A mile and a quarter long, ramparted like a castle wall, punctuated by 180 sluice gates, it rules the river that rules Egypt.

At the west end of the dam are locks through which boats are let down to the lower river. The enormous iron gates groaned open, and our tiny craft, dwarfed to a speck by its surroundings, entered the huge cavern of the first lock.

When the gates had closed, the water flowed out, dropping us forty-eight feet. The bottom of this manmade chasm was as cool and dark as a cave. The lower gates opened and we passed into the next lock; then a third; a fourth; then out into the sun and fast water.

The thunder of the excess flood escaping through the sluice gates was deafening. Rapids boiled among black rocks. The worst of the cataract was to starboard, yet there was commotion under our keel.

We reminded ourselves of the comforting words of a travel pamphlet: "Steamers make the trip through the cataract in safety." But how about a small felucca?

The men were at the oars, yet the boat darted and twisted this way and that as if gripped from beneath. Waves went in circles. Whirlpools, lathered with foam, swirled about funnel-like centers. We were being pulled toward the main torrent on the right. But our men did not worry—until an oar cracked. Then there was sudden shouting.

The captain, quick-wittedly sensing the direction of the breeze, ran up the sail. Mary hopped to the tiller. I seized the good oar to stave us off the rocks.

A few feet to the right the water plunged down into the big race. The boat hesitated, as if trying to make up its mind whether to commit suicide. Then, as the strong breeze filled the sail, she eased off to port.

We came into quiet water before another lock. The cracked oar was bound up while we were descending through the lock to a lower level of the cataract. Then there was more unruly water as we raced down between black, glossy rocks to Aswân.

Once It Was Elephant Land

Aswân is the southernmost important town of Egypt. It was once regarded as the limit of civilization, or a little beyond the limit. Hardy explorers from Egypt called it Elephant Land, probably because here they looked for the first time upon the African elephant. One sees this animal no longer, but its name is perpetuated in Elephantine Island.

We climbed the steep shore to the high street of Aswân then looked back.

It is a view to make you catch your breath. This globe offers few panoramas more lovely: the blue-green of the river accented by white sails; the rocks of the First Cataract, so glossy black that they look as if they had been freshly enameled this morning; idyllic islands like gems; and, as a backdrop to it all, a curtain of golden sand hung upon the slopes of the Libyan mountains, which are crowned by a sheik's tomb blazing snow-white against the blue sky.

On Kitchener's Island here, Lord Kitchener hoped to spend his years of retirement (which death forbade) and the government honored his memory, not with a statue, but by turning

the island into a perfumed bower of roses, Bougainvillea, poinsettia, and flowering trees.

At Aswân we laid in additional supplies for our expedition
to Cairo: canned goods, blankets, a gasoline stove, a 200-candle-
power gasoline lamp, cooking utensils for the galley, unbreaka-
ble dishes.

The governor furnished us with a letter that was to prove
magical when unfolded before the mayors of villages along our
route. Taking an interest in our proposed study, he offered to
provide us with a 50-foot dahabeah for less than we were paying
for our 20-foot felucca. But we stuck to the little boat.

The dahabeah is the luxury craft of the Nile. It is a houseboat with sails. You live aboard it as comfortably as at home. If
you wish to go south, the prevailing north wind will take you
there.

But we were going north. The only way the broad-bottomed
dahabeah can go north is to wait for a calm, then drift with the
current or be towed. It will not tack against the wind.

That does not matter to the vacationist who is on the Nile
just to enjoy the Nile. It did matter to us, with scores of villages
to visit and a destination to reach within two months.

We managed to pack considerable comfort into twenty feet.
The ten feet aft were enclosed in a canvas cabin, the walls of
which could be removed by day, leaving only the roof as an
awning. In this compartment our beds were rolled out at night
and rolled back under the stern in the morning. A folding table appeared when needed, for meals or for writing, and disappeared when not wanted.

Forward of this cabin was Houssein's domain, a four-foot galley, where he peeled vegetables, plucked chickens, and performed feats of balancing pots and pans on the primus stove
while the felucca boiled along.

The rest of the boat was a six-foot forecastle with a little door
through which the two boatmen wedged themselves at night,
pulled the door shut after them, and did not emerge until there
was a call for hot shaving water in the morning.

The captain rarely stood watch at night, for the nearest village would appoint armed guards. They sat on the bank above
us from dusk to dawn with huge guns held upright between
their knees.

There are many sights worth seeing at Aswân. The place is a delightful swirl of the barbaric and the civilized and enjoys the equable and sunny climate of paradise.

Ancient Egypt still Lives

We set out for Cairo. It would be eighteen days before we should reach the next metropolis, Luxor, with its world mixture of races. In the meantime we were to see the people of ancient Egypt, alive and in the flesh. The first we found were on the island of Bahrif. Fifteen hundred people live there. Isolated, they have kept their blood pure and their courtesy uncommercialized.

A boy came running to us across the wide beach. He did not ask for *baksheesh!* Then came four men. They did not try to sell us anything! Instead, they escorted us ceremoniously through the palms and the mud village to the mill.

On its pleasant porch, they served date wine. The mayor and his friends came and sat about us in a solemn circle.

The group was, of course, entirely male with the exception of Mary. The women gathered behind a wall and peeped over the top at this doughty female who dared to sit with the men. She must have seemed a brazen hussy.

I was interested to know how the people of an island live.

"Where do you get your supplies? Luxor?"

"We are a world alone," said the mayor. "Nearly everything we need we make here, just as our ancestors always did."

"And your ancestors, who were they—Arabs?"

"No, no." He shook his head emphatically. "Our ancestors were Egyptians. The people of Rameses."

"But when the Assyrians, Greeks, Romans, Arabs, Turks, came into Egypt?"

"They stayed mostly in Lower Egypt and in the larger towns. There is no foreign blood here." He was very proud of the fact.

"But where do your young people go to find mates?"

"They find them here, among their own cousins."

The fifteen hundred people of the island are practically one family, and this is true of most of the small villages of Upper Egypt, whether isolated on islands or on oases along the shore. Marriage takes place within the community. Even large villages are homogeneous. We were to find a village of four thousand people consisting of only three families.

Interbreeding Is not always Bad

Egypt perpetuated many dynasties by marriages between half-brothers and half-sisters. Common people intermarried only a little less closely and the existence of a sturdy race today indicates that, upon this race at least, the physical effect has not been disastrous. The mental effect has been to continue to the present day much of the mold of character and the habits of thought and action of five thousand years ago.

The chief change has been the adoption of the Moslem religion.

One fine old man in our circle had dust on his forehead and the end of his nose. He had just been praying, bowing his face to the earth. But on the neck of a woman peering over the wall was a charm identical with some found in tombs of the Eighteenth Dynasty.

Under the front of Islam, the real religion of the village is a religion of amulets and magic, superstitions and folk beliefs that have persevered for thousands of years.

We spent two days exploring the village and farmland of Bahrif Island. Life there was much the same as that of the men and women pictured on tomb walls. It was harder to find differences than similarities.

Then we zigzagged on to the village of El 'Aqaba, which, although on the mainland and near the railroad track, showed us a custom ages old. An important man had died. The street was full of wailing women, raising their hands to heaven, screaming distractedly at the tops of their voices (it is common for women to be unable to speak above a whisper for days after such an orgy), disheveling their hair, tearing their clothes, soiling themselves with dust.

It was a relief on the wall of the tomb of Ra'mos at Thebes come to life. Even in the days of the Old Kingdom, five millenniums ago, death was mourned in exactly the same way.

"Don't you feel as if you had stepped back into history?" asked the young Egyptian engineer at the Binban Pumping Station.

"Well, this looks modern enough," I said, nodding at the spruce little powerhouse that raises Nile water to the level of the fields.

"Yes, but look at the village. I am an exile here. Of course I come from Cairo. I am a graduate of the Royal School of Engineering. Cairo is modern. Here I feel as if I were on another planet—an older one; in some ways a better one, perhaps, but not the one I'm used to. Come through the village and I'll show you."

Three Thousand Years in Thirty Feet

From the powerhouse to the village it was only thirty feet, but easily three thousand years. The houses were made of Nile mud, the immemorial building material of the Nile Valley. Some of the best were of mud bricks.

We saw men making the bricks; stirring mud, pressing it into a wooden mold, scraping off the surplus, dropping out the wet brick on a board to dry in the sun. Exactly the same method is depicted on many tombs; for example, that of the vizier Rekhmi-Re' who lived a millennium and a half before Christ.

On every side we saw life going on just as we know from the reliefs it did go on in ancient Egypt: the potter turning a water jar; an old man sitting under a palm tree pulling fiber from the palm trunk back of him and twisting it into rope; women making baskets of the Third Dynasty or weaving on a Twelfth Dynasty loom; a dyer working in the old way; girls putting out the same old sun bread to rise in the same old sun.

A barber, working outdoors, was shaving a small boy's head, all except a few tufts left for religious reasons. A carpenter was sawing a board, not placed horizontally but vertically, as in the old paintings. And on the fringe of the village farmers were using plow, mattock, fork, and sickle that might have been copied straight from tomb pictures of Kha'-em'hēt, superintendent of the royal granaries under Amenophis III.

Here is most remarkable persistence of a racial type; and what makes it more extraordinary is that even in towns where Arabs, Turks and Greeks have mixed their blood with the old stock, the final result is not composite, but Egyptian. There is

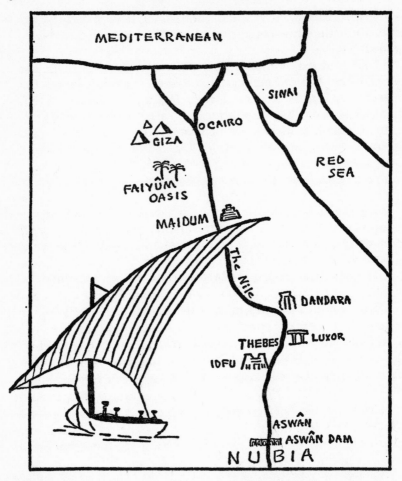

something about this land ruled by the river, the sun and the desert that stamps all men with the same brand.

The lonesome engineer, who had not seen anyone from the outside world in the two years he had been at this station, entertained us kindly, then saw us off for the camel market at Darâw.

Crocodiles Mummified like Kings

The camel survives in a land that used to abound in animals. In prehistoric times Egypt had enough rainfall to maintain forests where roamed the buffalo, lion, hyena, bear and elephant. In the Nile the hippopotamus wallowed and the crocodile slithered after its prey.

At our next stop we peered into a dark chamber of the Temple of Kôm Ombo to make out the forms of mummified crocodiles, for these animals were sacred to Suchos (Sobk), the crocodile-headed god, worshipped in this temple.

Doubtless these crocodiles, now mummified like kings, were taken from this part of the river. Two months before our trip a crocodile had been killed near Luxor. But this was a rare exception, for the animal has been practically exterminated in Egypt since religion ceased to protect it.

We scrambled up the sandy cliffs of the east shore to visit the quarries of Silsila. I felt as if I had come from Lilliput into a land of giants. Surely only giants could have cut away stone enough to make such dizzy cliffs, caves and abysses. But Rameses II knew how to make men work that his name should be remembered.

These mighty quarries, now almost forgotten, are fully as impressive as some of the temples built from their stone.

It is not far from here to the beautiful and well-known Temple of Horus at Idfu, marred only by the zeal of early Christians who felt it their duty to chip the faces of the Egyptian gods magnificently carved on the walls.

Digging into the Past

A rich discovery awaited us at isolated El Kâb. We were lucky enough to find the famous Egyptologist, Jean Capart, digging down through the centuries. An extraordinary figure is this lively little Belgian with his yellow whiskers and tiny amber glasses, his boundless enthusiasm and his disregard of dust when he practically stands on his head to see an inscription under a stone.

"Do you realize," he said, "that this is in some ways the most important spot in Egypt?"

Here was the ancient capital of Upper Egypt. Its tutelary goddess, Nekhbet, also identified as the vulture goddess, was honored as the patroness of birth and the protector of kings.

Time after time invaders of Egypt destroyed her temple in

order to destroy Egypt's kings. Time after time a new temple
was built upon the ruins of the old. The result is that here you
have, in layers, the history of Egypt.

Capart was probing down through the strata. He had just
unearthed the entrance to a chamber filled with exquisite reliefs. Only he and a few of his aides had been inside. He allowed us to squirm down into it through a hole in the stones.

"You are the tenth and eleventh persons to enter that room
in two thousand years."

It was the day when his hundred or more workmen were to
receive their fortnightly wage. A table was set in the open air
on the Nile bank. Behind it sat Dr. Capart and his assistants,
coins arranged in piles before them. Near the table was a large
rock.

Each man stepped up to the table, received his coins, and
immediately rang each one on the rock to see if it was good. If
its ring didn't satisfy him, he was given another. Dr. Capart sat
smiling into his beard.

"We have to humor them," he said. "We had the rock put
there on purpose—so they could have no grievance."

The next day we got a soaking. In a stiff breeze, the felucca
heeled too far and shipped about four gallons of the Nile. We
arrived before the great dam of Isna (which with its open
arches looks like a silver chain necklace across the bosom of the
river), our mast and shrouds festooned with wet bedding. It
did not dry before night and we slept in our clothes.

How enchanting, the early-morning sounds of the Nile! The
lark goes up, spilling bubbles of song. There is a cheerful bird
babble in the growing wheat on the bank to which we are
moored and in the tops of the palm trees.

The crew of a *gyassa* (blunt-bowed cargo boat) chant as they
row against the current. There is the rapid monotone of someone praying. There is comic relief in the fantastic "Squee-
squaw! Squee-squaw!" of the donkey, sounding exactly like a
saw going through a hard knot.

Pipe Organ of the Nile

Then, as the sun rises, the great pipe organ of the Nile begins. There is nothing like it, nothing in the world. It sounds as

if mighty chords were being played, with all the vox humana stops out.

Yet it comes only from the axles of a thousand *shadoofs* raising water from the Nile. The shadoof is a sort of well sweep with a bucket on one end and a weight on the other. The bucket is let into the Nile and fills, the singing workman lifts, the bucket rises and empties into a trough which carries the liquid life to the fields.

Where the sweep rubs on the horizontal bar that supports it, a sound is emitted. It is a creaking sound, but rather musical, and is sometimes emphasized by attaching an empty gourd or can to the bar to give resonance.

Since each outfit is a little different, the air is filled with octaves of sound for miles up and down the river. Bass notes are provided by the *sakieh*, the waterwheel turned by an ox or sometimes a camel. To the accompaniment of these instruments rises the mournful song of the workman.

This concert has been a daily feature for a long time. The sakieh dates back to Roman times. The shadoof is far more ancient.

Many a tomb picture shows a toiler at the shadoof, and parts of the apparatus have been found in graves of thousands of years ago.

Power pumps are coming in, but it will be a long time yet before the shadoof and sakieh cease to make music on the Nile.

Storm held us up in the village of Nawâsir. The mayor took us to his home for coffee. Children crowded the windows. The mayor excused their curiosity by explaining that they had never before seen an Anglo-Saxon in all their young lives.

Pursued by "Brigands"

When we returned to the felucca, we found our black boatmen very nervous. They did not know this village and were suspicious that its people were brigands. They were for putting off immediately, storm or no storm.

Put off we did, and the two men rowed. Presently there was a shout from the bank. A dozen piratical-looking men of the village were calling after us.

Our men bent to the oars. The pirates leaped into a small

light boat and dashed after us. When they came alongside, we saw that one of them was the mayor. He handed a huge turkey in over the gunwale.

"This is for your dinner," he said.

It lasted us and the crew five meals.

To come from the land of mud villages to lovely Luxor with its magnificent palaces and temples and its hotels overflowing with comfort and good food was an exciting event, particularly since we had been without butter for a week.

Here we enjoyed long talks with Mohammed Pasha Mahmud, Premier of Egypt, whose private steamer was stopping at Luxor on a trip upriver; with Sir Robert Mond, archeologist; with the scientists and artists of the Metropolitan Museum and the University of Chicago at work preserving and publishing the breathtaking discoveries made in the golden cliffs across the river.

Ancient Thebes was not only a world metropolis, but became the world's greatest graveyard. Here are the Tombs of the Kings, including that of Tutankhamen, the Tombs of the Queens, gorgeously decorated with reliefs in full color, the Tombs of the Nobles, on the walls of which men plow, harvest, winnow, broil meat, pound grain in mortars, bake bread, tan leather, carry geese by their wings, build houses, build boats, and do a hundred other things just as they are done in Egypt today.

Here are the Colossi of Memnon (Amenophis III), gazing stonily out over the plain, and the great temple of Queen Hatshepsut, so wily and human that it is hard to believe that the little minx is really dead.

Here is the Ramesseum, containing the statue of Rameses II, largest statue in Egypt. It weighs about a thousand tons (not pounds). The ears are $3\frac{1}{2}$ feet long and the feet $4\frac{1}{2}$ feet broad.

On the east bank are the stupendous Temple of Amūn at Karnak and the Temple of Luxor, exquisite by moonlight.

What Is a Copt?

The "pirates" got us again when we left Luxor. At Qamûla village the mayor took us to the police station, gave us coffee, guavas, cucumbers, figs, cigarettes, flowers, and practically everything except his daughters in marriage. Then he handed us over to the Copts.

An old white-whiskered Coptic priest took us to his home, introduced us to his sons, daughters, and grandchildren to the third and fourth generation (thirty relatives lived in the one house) , and then placed eight broiled pigeons before us.

It was Lent; our hosts were fasting. Twenty of them sat about the room watching us eat and asking intermittently in English learned at a Luxor school, "Are you happy from our village?"

We would reply that we were. And they would respond warmly, "We are very happy from you."

We slept there. Eleven brothers and sisters accompanied us into the bedroom to point out its conveniences. It belonged to one of the girls, and she took her pretty dresses out of the wardrobe to show us. The pity of pretty clothes in Egypt is that they can be worn only inside the house. On the street the long black *tob* must cover all.

Feminine jewelry was brought out for our inspection. There was a lot of it, for the priest was wealthy. His importance in this town was reminiscent of the ancient wealth and power of the Egyptian priests when they ruled Egypt.

The Coptic Church, although Christian, is older than Islam and much nearer to the Egypt of the long past. The Copts are the most direct descendants of the ancient Egyptians. Their blood is purest and their customs most like those of antiquity. The word "Copt" comes from the Greek word for "Egyptian," and the Coptic language, now extinct as a spoken tongue, is the last relic of the language of the pharaohs.

Beauty Hints from Cleopatra's Day

For a time we were living the life of the ancients. One of the girls took out her cosmetics, such as Cleopatra had used before her, and offered to make up Mary's face in Egyptian fashion.

From a small white bottle she drew a glass spatula. The end of it was smeared with a black substance. It was *kohl* (antimony) used to darken the eyelids.

Mary took it and dabbed on a couple of black rings. She looked as if she had been up too late the night before.

"No, no," said her teacher. "Let me show you."

She wiped off the kohl.

"Now, close your eyes."

She inserted the spatula between the closed lids and ran it back and forth.

"Look in the mirror."

Mary looked, and two snapping Oriental eyes looked back at her. Then came rouge, powder, perfume—all like those known to have been used of old. In fact, it is doubtful if the modern girl could have taught Queen Nefertiti anything about the art of improving upon Nature.

Two delightful days were spent in the home of the priest. Then, with a hearty exchange of "We are very happy from you," we sailed on down the colorful Nile.

Although during summer flood the river is a chocolate brown, it was now a lovely "Nile green." The sky was a deep blue, the love color of Egypt. Against it often were the white sails of twoscore boats at a time, and the gleaming iridescence of birds' wings. The hoopoe, the kingfisher, the crested lark, the little green bee eater, the kite, the egret, the pelican, flashed against the blue sky, green oasis, golden desert.

And the mountains of the Nile! We perhaps think of Egypt as flat, but it is not. The river is bordered for many miles, sometimes on the right bank, then on the left, by lofty cliffs which run through a gamut of color as the day advances. They are cream at noon, gold in the afternoon, rose later, vermilion at sunset, lavender at dusk, then a rich purplish black by the light of the innumerable bright stars.

It was like sailing down a one-sided Grand Canyon.

We donkeybacked to lonely Dandara to see the Temple of Hathor, the Egyptian Venus. It is a very youthful temple, only about two thousand years old. Therefore it is one of the best preserved in Egypt. Its walls show Roman emperors sacrificing to the gods of Egypt. The Roman rulers were willing to pay homage to any gods who would give them power.

At Abŷdos, in the Temple of Seti I, we looked upon the most superb color reliefs we had seen in Egypt. They were painted some three thousand years ago, yet they might have been done that morning. Will our works live as vividly three thousand years hence?

We lingered at dozens of smaller temples and scores of villages, so it was April before we reached Asyût.

A Lucky Misfortune

If Mary must have an attack of jaundice, it was best that it should come on here. In this progressive modern city there were good doctors to set her right and friends with whom to stay while she convalesced. Unable to see ahead, we thought it the worst of bad luck that she should have to quit the expedition. Later, as we looked back, it seemed providential.

Going on alone, I hurried now to reach Cairo before hot weather. We clipped off thirty, forty miles in a day, and one day we covered forty-eight, a noteworthy distance in a felucca tacking against the wind. Considering tacking mileage rather than river mileage, we must have traversed nearly a hundred miles of water that day.

The river was still beautiful, with startling barren mountains on one side and expanses of farm and forest land on the other. But the villages and towns were becoming larger, factories more numerous. Contrasting oddly with this modernity was the Pyramid of Maidûm, older than the Great Pyramid, and built in setbacks like a skyscraper.

One evening we moored within view of the fairylike oasis city of Helwân, raising its minareted head from the desert. Over it hung a great orange balloon of a moon. The Pyramids of Dahshûr in the opposite direction were misty, like pyramids of moonlight. They could not, it seemed, be made of stone.

Sandstorm and Shipwreck

That was our farewell to the beauty of the Nile. The next morning the air was filled with sand. The fairy city had vanished. So had the pyramids. The wind had changed; it was from the south.

"A *khamsin?*" I asked.

The khamsin is the only meteorological curse in the otherwise divine weather of Egypt. It is a hot, terrific sandstorm from the south.

The men were eager to get to Cairo. With luck we should arrive before night. This wind (if there was not too much of it) would help us there.

"No, no," they said. "No khamsin. Good."

The sail was furled down to a scrap. We went at a tremendous clip, the following waves making the boat yaw from side to side so that we corkscrewed down the river.

The gale increased. The flying grains stung our faces. We coughed sand, spat sand, wept sand. We could barely see the shore half a mile away.

Then it happened. A sudden squall struck, the boat broached to, turned over, and we were in the Nile—in a gale that blew the shouts out of the men's teeth and made the waves stand up like walls.

Only the port gunwale of the boat remained above water. Houssein immediately clambered up astraddle of it. The captain struggled in the buffeting waves to retrieve oars and gear.

Dress Shirt a Distress Signal

I clung to the boat with one hand and with the other tried to arrest six floating suitcases which were evidently of a mind to go on to Cairo without us. I was surrounded by miscellaneous bobbing articles—shaving brush, bottle of boiled water (how much of the unboiled Nile had I already drunk?), various edibles, a dress shirt.

I laughed. After all, this was an amusing experience, nothing more. I did not know then that my $300 color camera had gone to the bottom like a stone and would never be found, and I assumed that we would be picked up in a few minutes.

It was not so diverting after we had been there three hours. Boats calmly sailed by. We shouted and waved (Houssein his turban, I my dress shirt) but to no avail. Perhaps the crews of passing boats had all they could do to navigate in the storm without taking on the troubles of others. Perhaps they did not see us through the cloud of flying sand.

We could see people walking along the shore a half-mile

away. They were to leeward—the wind should have carried our shouts to them. But all the noise we could make was nothing in comparison with the roar of the waves and the grinding of the sandstorm.

Finally one man stopped, turned, and stood looking straight toward us. We brandished our signals and split our throats. He gazed steadily in our direction and we felt sure that he saw us. After standing there for a full minute he slowly turned and resumed his stroll.

The cold wind on wet clothing set me to shivering as if I had the ague. I suggested swimming—the captain scoffed at it, gesturing at the wild sea. If even an expert swimmer like Abdul would not attempt the half-mile to shore I concluded that our best chance was with the boat; but the forecastle and lockers had broken open, the boat was filling and promised to disappear entirely.

The men were saying: "Khalas! khalas!" (It is finished, it is finished.) Cairo seemed far away.

Suddenly two fishing boats loomed out of the sand fog. Our hopes rose—then sank when we saw that they were not coming to us but to a sand spit about a half-mile upstream. There they beached the boats and several men went ashore. We yelled and waved—I used the technique Indians in the Canadian woods had taught me—patting the open mouth with the hand while calling. Finally a boy ran across the sand spit toward us, looked, then ran back to tell his companions. The men indulged in excited conversation for some fifteen minutes while we shook and waited. Then they boarded the boats and began to row toward us. It took them a half-hour to make that half-mile.

We were hauled on deck and stood shaking like wet dogs. One of the fishermen gave me a woolen *galabieh*. I stripped off my things, draped them over the poles to dry, and donned the long, skirtlike robe. But I continued to shiver until I feared I would shake seams in the boat.

The men worked on the *Arabia*. After about an hour they got it righted and the water bailed out—all of this in a blinding storm and a tumbling sea—and towed it to the sand spit. But they would not take it or us over to shore until they had argued out how much they were going to get for salvaging. This was the part of the proceeding they all enjoyed most—the argument. It went on for a full hour. Lines draped with hundreds of hooks hung from poles above the deck and Houssein, arguing angrily, managed to get himself caught on a hook every time he grew too emphatic. Then our opponents would get the better of the argument while he pulled out the hook.

At last the bargaining was concluded and we were transferred from the island to the main shore. We went to the *merkaz,* police station, to report the accident. The police had me write out a long paper on what had happened. After it was done they brought the paper back.

"Is your father's name here?"

"No. My father is dead."

"Never mind, we must have his name and address."

So I wrote his name and appended the address, "Heaven."

The officer peered at the address. "Heaven. Is that in the United States?"

"Yes," I said feelingly.

I changed back into my wet clothes, piled six soggy suitcases into a taxi, motored the remaining five miles to Cairo, and arrived at the home of friends looking like something cast up by the sea. I shouted at them and they had to shout back, for I was still deafened by the roar of the khamsin. Yes, it was a real khamsin.

My wife joined me in Cairo. From the airport at Heliopolis we took off for Palestine. As the plane mounted a mile above Egypt, we got a new view of our old companion, the Nile. It stretched like a spinal column, the vital core of Egypt, with a narrow strip of green life on each side of it—just a few miles of green, then desert.

How could so much in life and culture come out of so little? Because here a mighty river shaped a mighty race. The Nile took up the dry earth into its wet hands and moulded man.

And, since the Nile remains essentially the same, we have in Egypt the phenomenon of a civilization that has stood fast (which is different from standing still) for five thousand years, and promises to keep its basic character for thousands of years to come.

4

River Wonder of the World

AN ANGRY OSTRICH blocked our path. This bird, which looks so innocent at a distance, can be terrifying in a close-up. Contesting with the ostrich in guardianship of the scenic marvel were hordes of impertinent baboons.

But it is worthwhile to press through these self-constituted defenders to see the treasure that they guard.

Lord Curzon, gazing for the first time upon Victoria Falls, exclaimed, "This is the greatest river wonder of the world."

Perhaps he was right. Certainly we had never before seen anything like it. Twice as high as Niagara and one and a half times as wide, it hurls the Zambezi over the edge of a cliff at 75,-000,000 gallons per minute. The mean height is 304 feet, and the height of the greatest fall, 355.

These are all impressive facts. But the unique thing about this waterfall is its behavior after it falls.

The Rain that Falls up

Wearing oilskins and sou'westers provided by our hotel we walked through the Rain Forest along the edge of the cliff facing the fall. There can hardly be another walk like it in the world. Most waterfalls you view from one end or the other. You see Niagara from the American end or the Canadian. But suppose you could walk through the air in front of the falls from the American side to Canada, close enough to get the full impact of the thunder, the winds and the spray; what a sensation that would be!

That is what one does at Victoria. Facing the waterfall is another cliff equally high with a chasm about a hundred feet wide between them. Into this chasm the waterfall thunders. And you walk along the edge of the cliff for a mile, past the various parts of the great spectacle, the Eastern Cataract, the Boiling Pot, Rainbow Falls, Livingstone Island, Main Falls, Cataract Island and Devil's Cataract, all of them within a short stone's throw.

It is not an easy walk. A drenching rain is falling, the winds set up by the waterfall seem determined to rip the oilskin from your back, and in many places on the path the water from the everlasting rains is ankle deep, deeper in the mudholes.

But what a sight! At Niagara, or Iguassu, the water crashes into spray which spreads forward down the river and dissipates. Here the action is quite different. The water after crashing on the rocks is blocked by the facing cliff. The downrush has made a strong downdraft of air. There is no place for this air to go except up on the other side.

So up it comes, carrying the spray with it, an upgoing rain. It not only rises some 350 feet to the edge of the cliff but keeps right on going up for another five thousand feet, making the famous pillar of cloud that is the distinctive feature of Victoria. These lofty columns of rising rain can be seen fifty miles away. Interlaced with them are brilliant rainbows.

Deluge from a Blue Sky

At last the uprush loses momentum, and down again comes the water on the heads of observers in a torrential tropical downpour of oversized drops, the conflicting winds from the chasm tossing them about. So at one moment you have rain rising straight into your hat, at the next moment coming down, and at every moment sailing in laterally from any angle.

The perpetual rain makes the Rain Forest a jungle of matted trees and vines, contrasting sharply with the brown sunburnt landscape roundabout. The Rain Forest lies along the cliff edge for a mile and is roughly an eighth of a mile wide. The sun is shining brilliantly upon the waterfall and this terrific downpour comes from a perfectly blue sky.

At the end of this memorable mile we stood with thoroughly soaked feet and wind-shaken bodies (though the day was windless) before the statue of Livingstone. It stands on the spot where the explorer first looked upon the phenomenon that he chose to name after the great Queen but which the inhabitants of this land had long before named *Mosi-oa-tunya,* The Smoke That Thunders. We felt like explorers ourselves, discoverers of a brand-new and never-to-be-forgotten experience.

"Sell Niagara"

On the edge of the gorge, only a few thousand feet from the Falls, stands a hotel one might expect to find in London but not in the heart of Africa, a magnificent structure with enormous lobby, extensive lounges, smoking rooms and terraces, an acre of dining room with smartly dressed black waiters and enough food on the menu to stuff an ox, most rooms with private bath, and, best of all, a stunning view of the Zambezi Gorge to the bridge and the tremendous columns of spray rising from the Falls.

This thundering tower of "smoke" jeweled with rainbows has evoked eloquent but quite different responses from various observers. David Livingstone waxed poetic and wrote that "such loveliness must have been witnessed by angels in their flight."

According to a popular but not very authentic story, one American had a less poetic reaction. He rushed to the telephone, called the United States, and exclaimed, "Sell Niagara!"

Lest the luxury hotel fool anyone into supposing that he is as safe as in his own hometown, the sign "*All* wild animals are

dangerous" confronts him just where the path across the hotel
lawn enters the woods. This warning applies even to the baboons, which crowd curiously around the swimming pool to
watch the bathers. They are usually docile, but some old rogues
are mean. Lion spoor is found near the kitchen door and elephants knock down the telephone wires between the hotel and
the town of Livingstone.

The Zambezi Zoo

The best way to see the animals of the Zambezi River region
is by the daily flight known as the "Dawn Patrol."

It is necessary to rise at 5:30, go by car to the small airfield,
and by 6:30 we are in the air. The craft is a twin-engine bi-
plane for eight passengers. The sun is not yet up. Passing Victoria Falls, we fly over a beautiful forest of big trees, open and
free of underbrush. We can see clearly between the trees.

But there are no animals.

Oh well, if I see just one elephant or giraffe, I shall be
satisfied. Anyhow, the trees that we are nearly shaving with our
lower wing are handsome. There is no jungle; it looks like a
well-ordered park. But it is not a game preserve or national
park, but completely wild veld. Its parklike appearance is due
to the fact that it is kept cleaned by fire and animals.

Now a stretch of treeless veld, crisscrossed by a network of
game trails—but still no animals. The horizon is a vivid blue
topped by a rose band. Now trees again, some green, some gold
—no, it is just the rising sun that strikes the taller ones and
gilds them. Now all are topped with flame, like thousands of
torches, just the crests glowing, the lower parts mysteriously
dark.

And suddenly, in an open stretch, two kudu dash away. Then
there is a herd of a hundred or so. But in numbers there is
confidence and only a few of them take flight. What looks like a
gray field turns out to be a huge herd of buffalo. They go lumbering and teetering away. We circle several times to get a better look at them. Ten zebras trot a few feet, then turn to look.
They are painted like barbers' poles. Then a herd of fifty or
more zebras mingled with some brown animals similar to antelope.

Bucking Bronco of the Air

The pilot doesn't have a care on earth: he flies as if he were riding a bucking bronco in a circus. We twist, roll, dive—anything to get a close look at the animals. We make sure that our safety belts are tight.

Surprise—a flock of ostriches. Somehow I had thought that all the ostriches had long since disappeared into ostrich farms. They fluff away like ladies waggling big bustles. Then a walking beanpole, a fine lone giraffe.

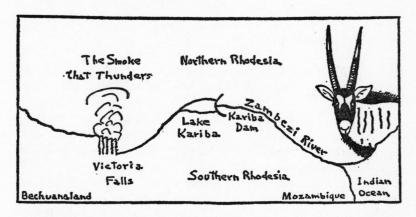

That does it. We can fly home now; I am more than satisfied. But we come upon a dozen more giraffes. They don't run— just stand and look.

Elephants! I don't believe it. But there they are, a good hundred of them, lazily flapping their big ears and ignoring the plane as if it were only an oversized fly. We skim so low it seems we must scrape the tickbirds from their backs. They still pretend that we do not exist. Now we're dipping and plunging like a sailor on leave. All the cameras are hard at work. We circle back and forth over the great beasts. They could be stuffed elephants in a museum, except for the lazy flapping of the ears.

Then one big bull decides he has had enough. He raises his trunk, spreads his ears and probably trumpets, though we cannot hear him over the roar of the engines.

Borders don't bother us any more than they do the animals,

and our 240-mile, two-hour flight takes us over parts of four countries, Southern Rhodesia, Bechuanaland, South-West Africa and Northern Rhodesia. On the return trip we fly within twenty feet of the surface of the Zambezi, following the river for fifty miles until it suddenly drops beneath our plane and the clouds of spray of Victoria Falls temporarily blind us. We rise and circle the waterfall to get a good view of it as it thunders down into the chasm.

Sometimes lions are seen on these flights, the rare variety with black mane and black tail; also hippos and crocs in the river—we see them later on a trip by launch above the Falls. Black cormorants and blue herons fly over the river. There are bulbous baobabs on the banks, and native villages of circular huts with mealie fields nearby.

The river is full of islets, trees perched on rocks, foaming rapids, sandbars. Then it widens into a lake around large islands and gathers strength before hurling itself over the precipice.

Mary didn't go because she doesn't care for dips and swoops. By the time I get back I don't care for them either, and walk rather unsteadily through the hotel to our room—to find her ready for breakfast!

Only breakfast time, but because one is inclined to confuse the intensity of an experience with its duration, it seems that a day or a decade must have passed since the take off of the Dawn Patrol.

Largest Lake Man ever Made

The trapped waters of Victoria Falls finally escape from the chasm at the extreme left end into a rocky gorge and tumble down towards Kariba where they have again been trapped, this time by the artifice of man. The just-completed Kariba Dam, built to supply power and irrigation, has backed up the great river to form the world's largest manmade lake storing 130,000,-000 acre-feet of water—more than the combined capacity of the Shasta, Hoover and Grand Coulee Dams.

But the land that would become a lake was occupied by some fifty thousand people of the Batonga tribe. The Batonga were used to trouble. They had had plenty of it in the past at the hands of Arab slave traders hunting pretty women for the harems of Arabia.

The Batonga had outwitted the slavers by drastic measures—they had deliberately knocked out the four upper incisors of their own women, and inserted porcupine quills through holes bored in their noses to lessen their attractiveness and their value in the slave marts.

Now they put up equally strong resistance to the new tyrants, the police who ordered them to abandon the river-shore villages that had been their home for centuries. More fertile land was promised them elsewhere. They refused to move.

They were backed up by zoot-suited agitators from the African National Congress who told them the government order was a plot to steal their land. These unprincipled trouble-makers exploited the villagers by selling them magic tickets which guaranteed that the white man would be foiled in his evil designs by the chief god of the Batonga, the great "Snake of the Zambezi," whose whiskers are the rising rain of Victoria Falls and whose tail stretches three hundred miles to Kariba.

So when the police arrived to evict them they stood fast, each clutching his ticket in one hand and spear in the other. An official advised them to throw away their tickets and lay down their arms. They would not. He told them the order came from the Queen.

"I asked them," he reported, "if they would refuse the Queen's words. They said they did refuse the Queen's words."

Five hundred young tribesmen charged the police, who retaliated with a volley of gunfire, killing eight and wounding twenty-two. The undaunted Batonga clung to their homes and the police retired.

What the authorities had failed to do, the rising waters accomplished. As the relentless river climbed the bank and crept into one house after another, the Batonga slowly retreated to higher ground, shivering in the unaccustomed cold of the uplands. Here newly built villages were ready to receive them.

"Operation Noah's Ark"

No such advance preparation had been made for the wildlife. Hills became islands, and on these islands thousands of animals were trapped. They quickly exhausted all food available on the islands and many starved to death.

"Operation Noah's Ark" was belatedly begun. Game wardens and rangers set out in small boats to rescue marooned animals. I begged a ride in such a boat. A hoarsely blowing elephant swam close. He was twice the size of the boat.

"What can you do for him?"

"Nothing," said the warden. "Luckily we don't need to. He can get to shore. So can the buffalo, lion, leopard and cheetah —they are all good swimmers. The bushbuck and waterbuck can make it provided the distance isn't more than a mile and a half. Zebras are limited to about six hundred yards. Baboons can do only four hundred, the monkeys two hundred, night apes and squirrels hardly ten yards. Impala and warthogs won't even step into the water. The ant bear too hates to get his feet wet."

A tiring sable bull made straight for the boat. He looked as big as an ox. If he came aboard would we have to go overboard?

The sable is one of the finest of the antelopes—and most dangerous. He is equipped with magnificent horns shaped like scimitars. He has a ten-mule kick—he can knock out a lion with one blow of a hind hoof.

He is as handsome as he is powerful. His coat is a brilliant blend of chocolate brown, pitch black and pure white.

And he is good meat. Altogether, an animal well worth saving.

The beast came alongside and tried to get a forefoot over the rail of the boat. The warden raised his gun, aimed at a point just back of the shoulder, and fired.

A Gun that Does not Kill

It was not a hysterical act of desperation against a deadly enemy. The gun was no killer. It fired a hypodermic dart that penetrated an inch deep through the tough hide. There it released not poison but a potent tranquilizer.

At the same instant the man at the tiller swung the boat so that the sable's foot slid off into the water and the animal found himself confronted by the high prow. His effort to scale this eminence failed.

He circled to the port side and again tried to clamber aboard. This time he made it with both forefeet and the men close to the brandishing horns tumbled out of the way. Again a sharp whirl of the boat loosened his hold.

Now both weariness and the drug were beginning to take effect. He made no further effort to climb in, but swam alongside, his fine head drooping until his nose was in the water.

At a signal from the warden, a noose was wangled over the animal's muzzle and another over the horns and the head was raised free of the surface.

I wondered what would come next. More nooses perhaps, snaring the feet—then the exhausted sable would be hauled aboard. But a sable is dangerous to the point of unconsciousness. One of his favorite fighting positions is on his back, with all four feet flailing and the sharp horns sweeping in a half circle.

The incident ended tamely enough. The boat simply towed the animal to the mainland, keeping his head raised so that he could breathe and snort and wheeze—which he did with less and less vigor until when the craft touched the beach he could barely stagger ashore. Then he collapsed.

"He'll be up and away in half an hour," the warden said, "good as new."

A question was troubling me.

"Suppose a snake tries to come aboard—what do you do?"

"If it's nonpoisonous," the warden said, "we let it come. If it's a black mamba or a cobra we have to shoot it—and *not* with a tranquilizer."

For animals unwilling or unable to take to the water, beaters must start at one end of an island and drive the game to the other end where nets have been erected to snare them. Impala or reedbuck or hartebeest or chimpanzee well tangled in a net can be loaded aboard and transferred safely to a new home.

The Camel Bird

Our most exciting passenger was a mere bird. It seemed strange to have to rescue a bird—for any winged thing should be able to fly to safety. But the ostrich is at home in neither air nor water. And it fails to appreciate succor.

Caught in a net, a magnificent eight-foot-tall male ostrich was bundled into the boat. Before it could recover from the shock, a shirt was hastily bound over its eyes. This, said the warden, was usually enough to subdue this greatest and strongest of living birds.

He seemed to be right. The ostrich lay quietly, a three-hundred-pound mass of muscle and rich black feathers, interspersed with gorgeous white plumes.

The "camel bird," the ancients used to call it, and with reason. Its long curved neck is like the camel's. Like the camel, it eats the coarsest of plants and swallows stones to help grind up the roughage. Its long strong bony legs are camel-like and can carry it across the desert at the thirty-m.p.h. speed of the racing camel (*mehari*). In high gear, it can cover twenty-five feet in a single stride. And it has a camel kick. Not only do the deadly hooves strike out to the rear in orthodox fashion, but forward or sideways with equal force. One blow may dispose of an animal or man.

Like the camel, it is usually speechless but can utter a surprisingly loud "boom-boom" in moments of stress. Of course it has a talent that the camel lacks. It can lay eggs, and what eggs! One weighs three pounds or more, equal to two or three dozen hen eggs.

I was roused from these reflections by a sudden show of life in the pile of feathers. With a twist of its neck and right leg so that head and claws were brought together, the bird tore off its blindfold.

It glared about at the other occupants of the boat. Not liking what it saw, it boomed loudly and struck out in all directions with its sharp-shod feet. One man got a silencer in the stomach. The net was torn into strings by the flailing weapons.

A sidekick striking below the waterline tore a hole in the hull and Lake Kariba poured in. Fortunately we were near shore and reached it with nothing worse than a wetting. The bird was out before we were and went booming away, trailing the remains of the net behind it.

Such rescue operations did not end with the completion of the dam and the filling of the lake. They still go on, for the 175-mile lake encompasses 150 islands, the remaining animals breed new generations, and the force of rangers available for rescue work is small.

This huge reservoir, wedged between Northern and Southern Rhodesia, its power lines reaching out to the Congo copperbelt and the new industries of all Central and South Africa, can produce more hydroelectric power than any other station in the world, and at the lowest cost. It has been called "the greatest single step ever taken toward the industrialization of Africa." Along with Victoria Falls, it places the Zambezi among the most dramatic and significant rivers of the planet.

5

Canoe on the Congo

"CAN YOU SWIM?"

I stared at the boatman. He had agreed to take me in a hollow log through the rapids of Stanley Falls. I had assumed it would be safe. No responsible guide, even in Africa, will take you anywhere if he does not expect to bring you back alive. The question was disconcerting.

"Yes," I said hesitantly. "A little. But I thought—"

"Good," he smiled. "I always ask. But it will be all right. Up there."

I stepped into the bouncing canoe and made my way up to the bow. He came close behind. I crouched to avoid being tossed out of the unsteady craft, but he stood as nonchalantly as an acrobat on a tightrope. He had been brought up in this wobbling world. He was a chief in the Wagenia tribe which enjoys the monopoly of fishing Stanley Falls.

He was followed by a tribesman with a snakeskin drum. Of what possible use would this be on a fishing expedition?

The men climbed in, twenty of them, and took up their sharp-pointed paddles. They all stood. It was embarrassing to be the only croucher. But I endured the indignity. Better embarrassed than drowned.

A coxswain took his place in the stern. The chief signaled to the drummer. He broke into a staccato rhythm, the paddles bit the water, and the dugout shot out from the bank like an arrow from a bow.

It seemed too clumsy a craft to be capable of such a burst of speed. It was simply a mahogany tree trunk, thirty feet long, hollowed out to a depth of two feet. It had no keel and would roll over as easily as the log it was. Every lurch of the standing figures as they paddled made it teeter to one side or the other, shipping a little water every time.

Well out from shore, the canoe turned abruptly and headed straight upstream toward the roaring falls. The water grew rougher and the paddling tougher. There was none of the long easy stroke of the Canadian paddle. The African stroke consists of a plunge and a jerk, flipping the passenger's head back and forth until the neck aches.

Dancing in a Dancing Boat

The drumbeat became faster, the paddles snapped like whips, the dugout edged its way against the boiling current. The faces of the men became ecstatic, fanatical. They began a wild chant. Their bodies writhed to the rhythm of the drum. They were not so much paddling as dancing.

Now I understood the drum. It was not just to keep time. It was to rouse excitement and energy to the highest pitch, charge the paddling with the thrill that comes to an African only when he dances.

It was contagious. The passenger felt it too. Everyone danced, in spirit, in the dancing boat. The waves danced, the black rocks closing in around us shook off their indifference and joined in the frenzy of the dance.

Savage currents sideswiped the boat, sending up showers of spray that drenched the clothes of anyone foolish enough to wear clothes.

Birth of the Congo

The thunder was deafening. We were now close to the falls. Stanley Falls are nothing like Niagara. They do not make a single plunge, but roar down in a series of seven cataracts. At the foot of the final dive, the Congo is born.

Born Grown-up

Here is something unique in rivers. The Congo as officially recognized does not begin with a spring or a dribble or a rivulet that you can span in one stride. It begins as a roaring torrent a quarter mile wide.

It is born like Athena, adult. You remember the Greek tale. Zeus had a headache. To cure him, Hermes split open his head with an ax. Out leaped Athena, full-grown and full-armed, and Zeus's headache was gone.

So it is here. The mighty Lualaba River, after the headache of the seven cataracts, is split by savage rocks at the base of the falls and from that point on the flood is known officially as the Congo.

It is fully adult from the moment of its birth. With this advantage, it does not go through the puling infancy of other rivers, but is able to expand almost at once to gigantic proportions, broadening in some places to a width of twenty-four miles, pouring into the Atlantic with twice the volume of the Mississippi, and continuing a hundred miles out to sea before it tires.

Fishing by Basket

Our heavy mahogany log was churned about like a leaf in the turmoil at the foot of the falls. It crashed repeatedly into boulders that would have crumpled a lighter craft. Water poured in and three gourd bailers were constantly at work.

Overhead stretched a fantastic framework of bamboo scaffolding that stretched from shore to shore. Suspended from it, great woven baskets, cornucopia-shaped, dragged in the current. They were fish traps and several canoes besides our own had arrived to harvest the catch. Trap after trap was hauled up and emptied into the canoes.

I was not prepared for the size of the monsters that haunt these troubled waters. Our first trap contained a threshing five-foot catfish. It was clubbed into insensibility while still in the basket, then dumped into the canoe. My amazement grew when I saw the occupant of the second trap, a giant which the chief identified as a *capitaine,* a form of Nile perch. Weighed later, it tipped the scale at 520 pounds. The record is 580.

But even the quarter-ton perch was dwarfed by the crocodiles, too wily to be caught in a trap. Only their bulbous eyes projected through the foam as they waited their chance to gobble down a fish dinner.

Some lay on rocks, open-jawed, allowing crocodile birds to walk in and pick their teeth.

One bold croc actually plunged into a trap and backed out again, holding a fish in his jaws. What might happen if our canoe should upset into this roaring maelstrom of currents, rocks and crocs was something I did not care to think about just then—but it disturbed my dreams that night in the Stanley-ville hotel.

World's Largest Private Garden

Of course both Stanley Falls and Stanleyville are named for the doughty explorer who found Livingstone on his first trip, and on his second discovered the Congo. He approached it by way of the Lualaba which, because it flowed north, he supposed to be the Nile. This assumption was rudely shaken when the river, after tumbling through the seven cataracts, turned abruptly westward and chose to make its way to the Atlantic instead of the Mediterranean.

Stanley emerged at the Congo's mouth after a transcontinental journey of 999 days that left him prematurely aged and cost him the loss of all of his white companions and two-thirds of his African porters.

He tried to persuade Great Britain to take over the newly discovered territory, but Britain was not interested. So he cast about for another sponsor and found one in Leopold II, a king of the Belgians. In 1882 Leopold accepted the "Congo Free State," not as a possession of Belgium, but as his own personal property. So this vast area, greater than France, Germany, Italy,

Greece, Spain and the British Isles combined, became the possession of one man—the largest private estate in history.

Unspeakable atrocities put the tyrannical Leopold in such bad repute that Belgium in 1907 took Congo sovereignty out of his hands and governed the country until the day of its independence, June 30, 1960.

Stanleyville is a bright, bustling modern city with a dozen hotels and residents of all races. Yet in spite of its cosmopolitan air it is buried in jungle. It has an airport but no railroad nor any good road except the river—and that none *too* good. It takes seven days for a riverboat to make the trip upstream from Léopoldville to Stanleyville, five days to return. It is a journey punctuated by mosquito bites, dubious food, sandbars and wild tribes who sometimes forget that cannibalism is no longer in fashion.

We preferred to make the journey by canoe, but with liberal interludes by riverboat since 1,068 miles in a small boat was hardly practicable in the time at our command.

We started out bravely enough in a 24-foot dugout with a dozen paddlers, plus drummer. Near the bow was a thatch arch under which we could when necessary escape the equatorial sun. If we must sleep in the boat, mosquito nets and curtains afforded a little privacy.

Our crew were only fair paddlers but excellent songsters; and one who spoke English assured us that the songs were made to order and all designed to praise the virtues of the two passengers.

It was just as well that we could not understand the lyrics— we might have been flattered into virtues we did not care to possess and generosities we could not afford. The African has remarkable powers of ingratiation. Our companions did everything possible to make us comfortable, and the fact that it was the most uncomfortable small-boat trip we ever made was not their fault.

Python Aboard

They were not responsible for the python that chose to fall into the boat from an overhead branch on the first day of the trip. It was far below the maximum of thirty feet that nature allows to this species. Yet in a 24-foot craft even an 18-foot snake is something of a problem.

Mary looked up from her book. She is not easily distracted from a good story, but she did trouble to remark to whomsoever it might concern, "Get that thing out of here."

We had met pythons before and were aware that they are not poisonous nor necessarily unfriendly—in fact they are used as pets in some African households to keep the place free of vermin.

But Mary was right—the thing ought to be got out of there. Bena, the man who spoke English and captained the crew, seized the portion he could reach, which happened to be the tail.

That may not have been the best choice. The snake, its composure disturbed, whirled back on itself and came for him, jaws agape. Several men grabbed it, but three preferred to dive overboard. For although the python has no fangs, it has a plentiful supply of sharp teeth, and they curve inward. Once it takes hold, it does not let go. Like the anaconda and other members of the boa family it can spread its jaws to receive an object far larger than a man's head. A full-size pig or a small forest deer is easily accepted.

But Bena hung onto the tail. He tried in vain to flip the creature out of the boat. His efforts were frustrated by the other men who gripped the snake, each with his own confused idea as to what was to be done with it—toss it out to starboard, or to port, or kill it. The net result was that it stayed where it was. The head plunged back toward Bena. The mouth, stretching wide, seemed as big as a crocodile's.

The sight was enough to paralyze an ordinary man, but Bena was not ordinary. In a flash decision he let go of the tail, met the oncoming head with both hands, locked his fingers back of the jaw, and dug both thumbs deep into the eyes.

Wrestling Match

The constrictor's next move would normally have been to whip its coils around its enemy and squeeze the breath out of him. But by this time the men knew what they must do. They tightened their hold on the writhing body.

The snake's convulsive muscles flung them back and forth,

hurling one man so violently against the gunwale that he struck with a loud snap. Whether it was his ribs that broke, or the boat's side, we didn't know until later when we had time to notice water seeping in through a crack seven inches long in the stout mahogany.

Now the men stopped to argue. It seemed a poor time for a discussion. But Africans, like American businessmen, hate to lose an opportunity to hold a board meeting. They are skilled, eloquent and long-winded debaters. After ten minutes of loud talk while the snake continued to thrash about, I cut in, "Bena, what's it all about?"

"The snake—" he said, "throw away, or keep for skin?"

"What would you do with the skin?"

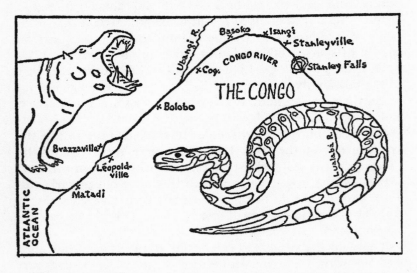

"You no want?"

I mentally scanned the inside walls of our California house. Where could one mount an 18-foot python skin? There seemed no place—except—there *was* a blank wall back of the kitchen stove.

I turned hopefully to Mary.

"Would you like it in the kitchen?"

"I would not," she replied decisively.

Of course her point of view was quite unreasonable—who in her right mind wouldn't want to share her kitchen with a python?—but there was nothing I could do but shrug my shoulders and tell Bena, "No want."

Far from closing the argument, this only started it again. After it had run on for a quarter hour I interrupted once more, "Bena! Let's get along."

This forced a decision. Upon orders from Bena, a man pulled out his bush knife and with a single strong slash cut off the head. It was tossed overboard and was promptly retrieved by a lurking crocodile.

The snake was now technically dead, but the muscles continued their spasmodic contractions even as the men slit the underside of the body and began to strip off the skin.

Python Hide Is Valuable

I thought Bena had misunderstood me.

"I no want skin," I reminded him.

"No, *bwana*," he replied. *"We* want."

"What for?"

"Sell."

Of course. It would net the crew a tidy sum. Python hide makes excellent leather. It is waterproof, dampproof, wear-resistant. It does not crack, chip or peel.

Coming from a creature that must drag its 200-pound body through thorny brush, it is necessarily far tougher than the skin of cow or goat or any animal whose hide, borne aloft on legs, is not subject to such severe friction.

Python skin can be turned into shoes, handbags, briefcases, luggage, upholstery, hats, belts, cigarette lighters—even cameras, fountain pens and tennis racket covers. It is in such demand that unscrupulous manufacturers emboss cowhide in python designs and pass it off as snake leather.

But to avoid putrefaction of the skin, it is essential that it be stripped off the dead snake without delay. So I understood the haste of the crew. But when the hide had been peeled free, I didn't understand why the still squirming body, now white as breast of chicken, should continue to share the canoe with us—particularly since several crocodiles, attracted by the scent, were quite ready to take it off our hands.

"You throw out?" I said to Bena, indicating the startlingly

naked body still twisting and jerking like a Tahitian hula
dancer.

"Oh no, bwana, please. Lunch."

"That? You eat?"

"Yes, bwana. Very good. Very good."

Lunch came early that day. All in the boat, including the
passengers, were eager to get ashore. In a small cleared area
beside a thatch village a fire was made and gargantuan python
steaks were broiled. When urged to partake, we did so with
some hesitation but found the meat more delicious than
chicken or fish.

It called to mind the predicament of missionary translators of
the Bible into Central African languages. They had difficulty
with the passage:

"Or what man is there of you, whom if his son ask bread, will
he give him a stone? Or if he ask a fish, will he give him a
serpent?"

The second question would make no sense to an African. If
it were a choice between fish and serpent, he would much prefer the serpent. So the translators, to convey the true meaning
of the passage, felt compelled to change the word "serpent" to
"centipede." Now it was clear to the African. He has no taste
for centipedes.

Snake Meat and the Gourmet

The African is not unique in his liking for snake meat. Some
tribes of American Indians appreciated this dish. It was once a
favorite article of diet in Europe, and there are French gour-
mets who still enjoy it—though for the benefit of persons who
find the idea revolting, the meat is apt to appear in the market
as "eel." The *Société Nationale d'Acclimatation* until recently
featured giant-snake meat as a special delicacy in its annual banquet.

Rattlesnakes contributed to the winning of the West. Califor-
nia-bound covered-wagon trains running short of provisions
paused beside rocky slopes to collect rattlers. Canning rattlesnake meat is still a minor industry in Florida; some fifteen
thousand cans of the meat are sold annually.

So the African, who lives in a land where snakes abound, is

hardly to be considered peculiar because he takes advantage of this source of supply.

To him, it is not only food, but a magical medicine. Bena explained, "Snake strong. Man eat snake—he get strong. Wear python backbone around stomach like belt—make stomach strong. Wear like necklace around throat—cure cold. Pray to big snake—he make you live long, be happy."

Such worship was once common enough. The Brazen Serpent was venerated by the Jews for five centuries. It was believed to have healing power. The Greeks agreed in principle. They adopted a serpent wound around a staff as the symbol of the healing art, and it remains so to this day.

In Mexico a Mayan medical student had to find a boa constrictor and persuade it to put its tongue in his mouth before he could qualify as a doctor. Snake medicine is still a standard remedy in a Chinese drug shop and is said to be good for colds, malaria, earache, eye trouble, rheumatism, convulsions, epilepsy, insanity—in fact, any ill that flesh is heir to. Wine containing pickled vipers was a panacea in Europe. Viper flesh remained in French pharmacopoeias until 1884. Rattlesnake oil has been widely sold in the United States.

The fifteen of us, eating our fill, made hardly a dent on the huge carcass. Villagers stood about and eyed us enviously. The meal over, the men began to drag the remainder of the carcass back to the boat. The tropical sun was already giving it a heady aroma.

"Eat tomorrow," Bena said happily.

"It will smell," I protested.

He smiled and nodded vigorously. "Yes, yes."

I wouldn't get far with that argument. I took another tack.

"These people—" indicating the village folk. "They are hungry. Let us give it to them."

A look of infinite sadness came over his face. I relented a little.

"Cut off enough for supper. Cook it now. Give them the rest."

It was so ordered. The villagers, informed of their good fortune, danced with joy and the headman made a long speech of thanks. Then they all fell to, cutting off great chunks and eating them at once, raw and dripping. They *were* hungry. With our own portion, well-cooked, we took off downriver.

Dramatic Congo

Spectacular is a mild word for this reach of the Congo. The river is strong and self-conscious. It knows its power and dares anything to get in its way. It picks up the canoe and hurls it forward as if it were a chip. It swallows incoming rivers with cannibal appetite.

We hear a roar that sounds like thunder, but continuous, as thunder would not be. Then we round a bend and see a precipice from the brink of which the Tshopo River plunges straight down several hundred feet to join the Congo in a frenzy of foam.

Congo shores, which we had expected to be flat and monotonous, twist and heave into hills and cliffs, sudden ravines choked with tropical growth offering ideal shelter for wildlife, black rocks the size of houses, and white sand beaches and jungle that really deserves the name.

Here is one of the last forests primeval. Most of it has never heard the snarl of the lumberjack's chain saw. Undisturbed giants tower two hundred feet, many of them togged out from head to foot in close-fitting robes of vine spangled with flowering orchids.

Beneath the trees is dark, silent mystery. But the forest roof where the leaves are young and fresh and the sun bright, is alive with the moving color of tropical birds and butterflies. Monkeys leap along the roof without visible means of support, following the course of the canoe as dogs chase an automobile.

The Congo is full of islands—there are said to be four thousand in all—and they take on every conceivable form according as they are filled in or gnawed away by the whimsical currents. Some are sandbars, as naked as the day they were born. Some are covered with scrubby growth marking them as juveniles a year or two old. Others are as ancient as the hills, rockbound, rising far out of the river's reach and crowned with venerable trees. They may be as old as the river or older, dating back to the age when the Congo was not a river but—like the Amazon—an inland sea, lapping restlessly against a mountain range for millions of years before it found its way through to the Atlantic.

Islands Aloft and Adrift

The islands play tricks. Those nearby rise out of the water, which is what any well-behaved island should do. But those at a distance have shaken off all earthly ties and float serenely in mid-air. Shimmering and quivering, they seem like ethereal Isles of the Blest, outposts of paradise. But as we come closer the mirage fades, the islands quit dancing and settle down stolidly upon the surface.

As strange as the sky-borne islands are the islands adrift. At any time we can count dozens of them, calmly proceeding downstream on the current. Some are as small as a living-room rug, others as big as a city block.

They are a brilliant almost unnatural green, flaunting heart-shaped leaves and lavender flowers as much as three feet high, undulating in green billows as the waves pass under them. They are thin and flexible but evidently very strong, for on one we see a bewildered boar rushing from edge to edge, and on another a worried chimp who must have weighed close to two hundred pounds.

We were privileged to watch the birth of such an island. Disturbed by the plunge of our twelve paddles, what looked like solid shore began to heave and hump as if troubled by an earthquake. Then it tore itself from its moorings and followed us downriver.

As we had brushed past it I had seized a flower. We recognized it as the water hyacinth, the pestiferous plant that chokes certain rivers of Florida and the bayous of the Mississippi delta. Back in 1884, a dozen water hyacinths were brought to the United States and a flower lover planted them in his water garden. He didn't know that in twelve months a dozen plants can propagate a million. The much-admired flowers escaped from the garden and beautified streams and bayous but, alas, soon plugged the waterways so tightly that navigation was impossible.

But how had the Brazilian beauty found its way to this remote corner of the world? We jotted down the question to be

put to the agronomists of the famous research center at Yangambi which we were supposed to reach before nightfall. There
we would find a European colony and a comfortable guest
house.

Four Skulls on a Shelf

We might have made good this schedule but for a sudden
strong upriver wind that practically held us in one spot despite
the best efforts of paddlers and currents. We barely made a
small trading post before night closed in.

It was a bleak, comfortless, hotelless place surrounded by neg-
lected rubber, coffee and palm plantations. The Belgian plantation bosses had prudently retreated to Belgium. The people, still flushed by the riots and bloodshed of the fight for
independence, did not welcome white visitors. A flying stone
barely missed us as we walked between the rows of mud-and-
thatch huts.

"This place no good," Bena said.

"Where is the chief?" I asked. "He'll take care of us."

"Chief no good," said the pessimistic Bena.

The chief's house was easy to find—it was the largest in the
village. The chief himself stood in the open doorway, a huge
black silhouette against the light of a cooking fire within. Bena
bowed respectfully and so did we. Bena and the chief talked
and the talk developed into a lengthy argument, as we stood
first on one foot and then the other, longing only to fling ourselves down on whatever beds the place might offer.

Then the chief went in and Bena signaled to us to follow.
The house was a disappointment. It was large enough, but one
room only, and already occupied by three wives and eight children. There were no beds. The floor was of dirt, and dirty.
Three wives were evidently not enough to keep it clean. It was
littered with bones among which ants, cockroaches and others
of the less popular of God's creations were searching restlessly
for scraps of food.

Then we found ourselves both staring at a gruesome spectacle on a shelf—a group of four skulls. Chimps or gorillas? No,
the jaws were not prognathous and the foreheads did not have
the simian slope. They were unmistakably human.

The chief was watching us. His face, lit by the fire, was not prepossessing—bulging eyes, flat nose, teeth bared in a savage grin.

Cannibalism Dies Hard

"We can't sleep here," Mary said.

"You can't refuse an invitation. They'd be offended."

"I didn't hear any invitation."

Neither had I, but had taken it for granted. I turned to Bena. "Does he want us to stay?"

"No."

"Then why did he let us in?"

"To see those," indicating the skulls. "He want make you 'fraid."

"Well, if he thinks we can be scared off by a few skulls . . ."

". . . he's right." Mary completed the sentence. I let it stand —with secret satisfaction.

More bows all around, and we let ourselves out. We returned to the canoe, wedged ourselves into the thatch cabin and let down the mosquito nets. The men had gone ashore and Bena followed but sent back one man to keep guard duty in the stern of the canoe.

Mary said, "I won't sleep a wink."

She was asleep in two winks. I lay awake thinking of the skulls on the shelf.

Of course cannibalism was a thing of the past—or so we had supposed before coming to Africa. Yet we had stumbled upon disquieting facts on the journey south from Morocco through the newborn nations of Senegal, Guinea, Ivory Coast, Ghana, Togo, Dahomey, Nigeria, Cameroon and Gabon, to the Congo.

A century of the civilizing process under French, British and Belgian colonialism had not completely wiped out practices many centuries old.

This was true not only in the vast and relatively backward Congo, but in the most modern and advanced countries as well. Even in what is probably the most enlightened black nation in the world, Nigeria, cases of cannibalism are still reported.

In the Nigerian back country the housewife who wishes to be sure that she is not buying human meat will select a piece with a bit of animal hide attached. On the other hand, many are not so finicky and will even pay a higher price for human flesh because they consider it a special delicacy.

Missionaries report the grinding of human skulls into powder to be devoured like sugar.

Persistent and unavailing efforts have been made to stamp out the Leopard Society, the members of which dress in leopard skins, leap upon the unwary and tear them apart with metal claws. Leopard murders rose to a peak in 1947, and seventy of the killers were caught and executed.

A postmaster opened a suspicious-looking package to find parts of a dismembered girl being sent to friends on the coast as a Christmas present.

An inland hospital employed an ex-cannibal as a medical assistant because he had learned from personal experience the nature of human organs and how to dissect the joints of the body.

Human meat is referred to as "intelligent meat." Animal meat is "non-intelligent meat." Intelligent meat is preferable because the one who dines upon it absorbs the intelligence of the deceased.

A Lagos newspaper published the story of a tribesman arrested on the train for carrying a human hand, a delicacy which he was taking to his sister's birthday party.

If such incidents were common in Central Africa's most advanced nation, how much more so in tradition-bound Togo, Dahomey, Ghana, Gabon, and particularly in the enormous and almost impenetrable jungles of the Congo.

However, I knew from our own experience that one might travel through all these lands, and indeed anywhere in Africa, with less danger than in a Chicago alley or New York's Central Park.

This was a comforting thought, and I grew drowsy, listening with only half of my mind to the sounds of the night—the croak of buffalo toads, the cries of night birds, the distant barking of a pack of wild dogs, the harrumph of a hippo in the river, the rasping, sawing roar of a leopard in the woods.

Then I sat bolt upright at the sound of a soft bump against the outside of the hull. Was somebody about to climb aboard?

Reaching for a flashlight, I crept out of my thatch cocoon and pressed the button. Two big beady eyes stared up at me. A crocodile's muzzle quietly sank below the surface.

I turned the light on our guard. He was fast asleep. My first thought was to rouse him; but he would only fall asleep again. After all, the crocodile was a better guard than he against any possible boarder.

The Flower that Devours Rivers

The next morning brought us to Yangambi, the largest agricultural research station in Africa. Belgian scientists, who absented themselves during the Congo's birth throes, had returned. They were busy with experimental plantings of palms, rubber, coffee, cocoa and food crops. They had developed a marvelous botanical garden of the greatest possible value to Congolese farmers.

One department was concerned with the water hyacinth which was well on the way to ruining the Congo's waterways. I asked the scientist in charge:

"How did this Brazilian pest get to the Congo?"

"It came from Brazil to the United States. From there it jumped to the Congo."

"But that's a long jump."

"Yes, but a Baptist missionary helped it make the jump. He was from the Congo on furlough in America. There he saw the water hyacinth and thought it would look pretty in his Congo garden. He brought five specimens and planted them in his reflecting pool. That was twenty years ago. Since that time the government has spent an average of sixty million dollars a year fighting the progeny of those five plants."

"Is it so serious? What does it do besides obstruct waterways?"

"It absorbs the oxygen from the water so that the fish die, and river people who used to depend upon fish as their main food supply starve. It roofs over the water so ducks and geese can't feed. Muskrats the world over have been prized for their fur—but they can't live under a hyacinth mat. There used to be a large export business in frogs' legs to Europe. Congo bullfrogs grow as big as footballs when they have a chance but they can't survive under hyacinths. River villages and even towns have had to be abandoned when the streams were turned into impenetrable hyacinth swamps."

"Good People, These"

It was too early in the day to take advantage of Yangambi's excellent guest house. We traveled on to Isangi, to spend the night there most comfortably in a Protestant mission. The Topekes of this region still file their front teeth to sharp points, profusely tattoo the entire body including even the lips, and don shirts and shorts only with the greatest reluctance. The women cannot understand why their bosoms are shameful and must be concealed. However, both the Protestant and Catholic missions are doing valuable work in their schools and hospitals.

"Good people, these," said a brisk young French priest, more advanced than some of his confreres. "Bright. They learn easily. Too easily sometimes. They pick up the ways of disreputable Europeans. Back in the bush where they haven't been touched by civilization, crime is rare."

"But *you* are touching them with civilization."

"Right. But, I hope, with the better things in civilization. Things that will cancel out the evils of civilization—drunkenness, syphilis, selfishness, money-grabbing, decay of family life. They're coming out of the old life into the new—you can't keep them back. They're bound to go ahead. All you can do is help them onto the right track."

What Is Freedom?

"Now that they have independence, how do they take to it?"

"They're only gradually learning what freedom is. A truckdriver was asked what freedom meant to him. He said, 'Before freedom, I had to drive on the right side of the road. Now I'll be able to drive where I please.' But they're learning that freedom carries responsibility with it."

"How about voting?"

"It came hard at first. They didn't understand what it was all about. One man was shown into a voting booth and stayed so long that the officials finally looked in to see what was the matter. They found that he had stripped completely naked. He thought he was to have a medical examination. Of course there are still millions back of beyond who haven't even heard of the vote. But in the towns, they vote, and like the feeling of power it gives them."

"Europeans are coming back. How are they being received?"

"With suspicion. That's natural. It will be a long time before old grudges are forgotten. And there are all sorts of misconceptions. For example, the idea is widespread that white people eat Africans. Yes, pack them in cans and eat them."

"How come?"

"They are convinced of it, because there is a brand of corned beef with the picture of a Negro's head on the label. Some irresponsible newspapers spread all sorts of wild notions."

"Do Congolese fear the Belgians will try to get back control of the country?"

"Many do. Others actually fear 'American imperialism,' exercised either direct or through the United Nations. The Congo is a land of fear. Only time and education and fair treatment will make the people sure of themselves and sure of us. I'm certain they'll come out of it a great people.

"The Africans have real character, you know. As a white timber trader said to Albert Schweitzer: 'What a good thing it is that the Negroes have better characters than we have.'"

First of the Slave Traders

And so on, every day revealing new wonders. At a bend of the river, an improbable cliff with the town of Elisabetha perched on its crest. At Basoko, a walled city with ramparts and towers, like Carcassonne, but quite unlike anything we had seen anywhere else in Africa. Why these lofty stone battlements in the midst of the jungle? The explanation is even more amazing than the walls.

They were a defence against the Arabs. It may salve our consciences a bit to know that we of America and Europe were not the first of the slave traders. Long before we got the idea, dhows

were sailing down from Arabia along Africa's east coast seeking
slaves to wait on the languid ladies of Arabian harems.

The search was not confined to the coast. The piratical Arab
chieftain, Tippo Tip, sent armed bands far into the continent,
even to this point, well on toward the shore of the Atlantic.

When Leopold objected to these intrusions into his private
park and the theft of black labor which he regarded as his own
property, Tippo Tip boldly launched an attempt to steal not
only men but the country itself. So a fort had to be built
against Arab raiders here, three thousand miles from Arabia!
With its help, the invaders were finally driven out of the Congo
basin.

Incidentally, illicit Arab slave traffic goes on to this day, but
the quest is confined to parts of Africa closer to the Arab home-
land.

Below Basoko, the fiercest faces we had seen yet looked out
from the jungled shore. It was here that Stanley, who only
wanted to pass peacefully across the continent, was forced into
twenty-eight battles with tribesmen. They doubtless supposed
that he and his company were slave hunters. Stanley wrote:

"The twenty-eighth engagement fought against the furious
fools of this savage country inspired us with fear of everything
resembling man."

Nothing lasts long on the Congo. As we travel on, the
"furious fools" give way to people of quite different customs
and another language, the troublesome and warlike Budjas.
They are succeeded by the Maniemas who, a missionary tells us,
used to have an unpleasant smell because before eating human
flesh they followed the crocodile's custom of placing the corpse
in water until it became putrid.

On the shore are the ruins of a well-built brick village
erected by a plantation company for its African workers. A
hundred people were comfortably housed here, but the village
was suddenly deserted when crocodiles took two children and
the place was supposed to be bewitched. It is only one example
in many of the ways the painfully progressing primitive is set
back on his heels by his own superstitions.

At Bumba, overlooking myriad islands, is a hotel, considered
quite modern for it actually affords its guests cold running water.

Comfort on the Equator

The great town of the middle Congo is Coquilhatville. Here there are no less than three hotels. One has three stars in your Congo handbook, but it still does not rise above cold running water. However, hot water may be obtained, and on the run too, by boy from the kitchen. A superb botanical garden graces this beautiful town.

The place was formerly called Equatorville since it practically straddles the line. Thanks to the cooling effect of the great river, the temperature is quite endurable. Moreover the altitude, though steadily decreasing as we have been coming downriver, still stands at 1,200 feet. In general it can be said that the heat of equatorial regions, whether along the Congo, the Amazon, or in the South Seas, has been greatly exaggerated. Certainly there are places that are hot, very hot, almost as hot as New York in July. But on the whole, life can be lived here in comfort.

Coquilhatville's population of thirty-five thousand is most cosmopolitan, including considerable numbers of Belgian, French, German, British and American residents. On the main shopping street, frequented by more or less fashionably dressed Europeans, it is startling to come face to face with primitive Bakutu, the men wearing little but a scarlet-beaded loincloth and necklace of leopard teeth, the women loaded with ten pounds of brass rings on each leg from ankle to knee. A blacksmith welds on these decorative shackles and they are never removed.

It is said that the Bakutu watch white folk with interest but no envy. They observe carefully and don't approve of all they observe. The phrase for "white man" in their language is *Lolema djola feka feka,* meaning "the bat that flies fast without knowing where it is going."

Canoe to Riverboat

Here as prearranged we dismissed the faithful Bena and crew and boarded a steamer. There is regular service between Stanleyville and Léopoldville. No farther up because of Stanley

Falls, no farther down because of impassable rapids. The riverboats were formerly woodburning stern-wheelers. Now they are
diesel powered. The cabins are comfortable, the decks are spacious, the food is not bad (but don't expect such delicacies as
python meat).

We expected the trip to be monotonous after the varied and
and sometimes exciting eleven-day journey of six hundred miles
down the swift-flowing river by canoe.

But the Congo makes monotony impossible. Submerged sandbars across which the canoe slipped easily were a real hazard
to the steamer. More than one riverboat had slid up on a sandbar and broken in two.

There was always a man at the steamer's bow probing the
bottom with a long pole and chanting back to the helmsman,
not "Mark twain," but *"Mai moki"* for little water, *"Mai
mingi"* for much water.

Several times we stuck fast and could not back off. On such
occasions the captain philosophically smoked his pipe for a few
hours or all day if necessary until a sudden downpour raised
the water level and he could pull free.

Most interesting were the ports of call. They were only small
villages backed by jungle. The leisurely boat stopped at such
places for long periods, affording time for strolls along forest
paths. The jungle growth was forever amazing—the gigantic
ceiba tree, a single specimen yielding more cotton (*kapok*)
than a three-acre cotton field; the copal resin whose oozing sap
makes varnishes, lacquers, linoleum and plastics; that vegetable
in the sky, the cabbage palm whose terminal bud is considered
a great delicacy; wild rubber trees, tapped, dripping latex into
gourds; tree ferns twenty feet high; bamboos that pop out of
the ground overnight and grow at the pell-mell rate of a foot a
day; and vines in serpentine tangles tying the treetops together
in an almost impenetrable mat.

Few animals liked the heavy shade except the dark and de-
vious leopard.

We paused one day in the gloom, uncertain about the path.
There was a thick, oppressive silence. Not a bird note, not a
rustle in the leaves. Suddenly Mary raised her hand in a gesture
that said, "Listen."

I listened.

"Don't you hear it?" she whispered. "Like somebody breathing."

"I'm breathing," I said helpfully.

"No—it's somewhere else—I can't tell where. Do you suppose we're being followed?"

Now I heard it too. "Not a man," I said, "unless he's been running." The breathing was fast, excited. I looked up. On a branch just above us I could dimly make out black spots on a yellow hide.

A cold breeze went through my ribs and down my spine.

Can a Leopard Smell Fear?

"Don't look up," I suggested. "Just move back. Very slowly. Quietly."

Safari men had told us that a leopard loves nothing better than a chase. Show fear, and he is after you. Show none, and the fear is his.

But how about the purported ability of animals, such as dogs, to *smell* fear? If fear could be smelt, I must be reeking, for I could fairly feel already the beast's claws in my shoulders.

Mary reeked too when I told her. "I guessed it was some kind of cat," she said. "I thought perhaps a wildcat or serval. But a leopard . . . ! Let's get out of this awful place."

Emerging from the wood into an open space, we were assailed with life and sound. Parrots screamed. A cloud of egrets sailed by, the water-ouzel and snakebird fished the backwaters of the river. The handsome colobus monkey posed in the young trees along the edge of the clearing. A party of baboons, out of sight but not out of earshot, were engaged in noisy conversation.

On other shore expeditions we saw elephants, particularly in the Ubangi River region where they are so numerous as to give their name to impressive Elephant Falls. And it was not necessary to leave the boat to see buffalo, rhino and antelope drinking at the river's edge or wading in the shallows in the cool of dawn or sunset. The dreaded seven-foot-tall gorilla we never saw but heard sending out his reverberating boom-boom as he slapped his huge drumlike chest with hands as big as hams.

Hippo Hunt

We took an inactive part in a hippo hunt. While the boat lay at Bolobo we paddled out in a hired canoe to see what was causing a chorus of human shouts and hippo thunder a short distance off shore.

Eight or ten canoes filled with men wielding crude harpoons had pulled in among a herd of hippos. We were just in time to see one canoe rise straight into the air as an angry hippo came up beneath it. Then the canoe tipped and the men spilled out into the river. The blood of speared hippos had attracted crocodiles. It was not the time or place for a swim and the men worked fast to right the canoe and scramble aboard. No sooner were they in and apparently safe than a frustrated crocodile struck the craft a terrific blow with his tail, splitting it open and precipitating the men once more into the river. The hippo hunters took all this as great fun. Roaring with laughter, they splashed furiously to scare off the crocs and clambered aboard the other canoes.

The Strange Habits of the Hippo

A hippo can stay down some ten minutes, walking on the bottom, grazing on river weeds. Then he must come up for air. Usually mild in disposition, these enormous beasts are most dangerous when wounded. They can readily crush a canoe between their three-foot-wide jaws. Another of their favorite tricks we were now to witness.

A big bull, instead of rising level-backed as usual, shot up out of the water fore-end first, and with very evident intent crashed down upon a canoe with at least half of his four-ton weight. The canoe was smashed, two men were badly hurt and were taken ashore.

But the game went on.

A fatally harpooned beast rolled feet up and sank. This ended the festivities. One carcass would supply enough meat to feed many families many days. No attempt was made to dive for the body and bring it ashore. The generation of gases in the carcass would finally bring it to the surface. How long this would take would depend upon the warmth of the water and the amount of food in the stomach. Warm water and a paunch full of fermentable material might raise the body within an hour. Cold water and an empty stomach might delay the process as much as forty-eight hours. There was only one certainty —the body would surface. Watch must be kept day and night lest the surfacing take place undetected and the prize float away.

The Fantastic Beast

A fantastic beast is the hippo. His voice is farther down the scale than that of any other member of the animal kingdom. It sounds like the deepest note of the tuba. He can stay underwater longer than any other mammal except the whale. When he submerges his nose automatically closes. His eyes are on top of his head and may be raised like periscopes above the surface, easily mistaken for bubbles. If he wishes to breathe without being seen he will project only his nose under the concealment of a lily pad.

With one scoop of his enormous jaws he can take up as many roots, stems and leaves as would fill a wheelbarrow. He can bite a crocodile in half—though usually he ignores the crocs since they give him no trouble; they fear him too much to tangle with him.

Attacked by a lion on shore, the hippo drags his enemy into deep water and drowns it, or crushes it into a pulp between his terrific teeth.

The teeth of a fullgrown hippo are unmatched in the kingdom of land animals. Besides two rows of huge grinders, he has four remarkable canines, two in the upper jaw, two in the lower. These are normally three or four feet long. They are sometimes called tusks, but the word is misleading. We think of tusks as projecting outside the mouth, like those of the elephant. But the hippo's "tusks" are inside, and some idea of the cavernous capacity of the mouth may be gained from the fact that it is vast enough to accommodate teeth more than a yard in length. The longest hippo canine on record, making room for itself by growing in a curve, measured five feet four inches.

Ivory curios are made from hippo teeth. Their oddest use

perhaps has been in the manufacture of false human teeth, and more than one hunter has gone gunning for hippos unaware that he is indebted to them for the dentures he carries in his own mouth.

The Two Congos

The great Ubangi joins the main river. From this point on, the Congo divides the Congo from the Congo!

On the north side of the river is the former French Congo, now independent as the Congo Republic. On the south side is the former Belgian Congo, now the Republic of the Congo.

Each of the Congolese nations eyes the other with a lustful eye. An attempt by one to take over the other is perhaps only a matter of time.

Cliffs eighty feet high look over the broad island-studded river from Lukolela. At Bolobo the river contracts to a width of only a mile. This is an ivory-carving center, some of the material coming from the elephant, much more from the hippo, not only because hippos are more numerous but their ivory is less brittle and more easily carved.

Nobody Works in Heaven

The mission station in Bolobo—I shall not name the denomination—won favor by shaping its doctrine to fit the African's predilections. This ritual was recited by minister and congregation.

Minister: *"N'Jambi koulouba nini?"* (What does the good Lord say?)

Congregation: *"N'Jambi koulouba: 'aoua n'toto mabi.'"* (The good Lord says: 'On earth nothing is good.')

"But in heaven?"

"Up there, in heaven, nobody works and everything is good. There is plenty of meat and manioc and lots of women."

Whatever one may think of this catechism, it should be said that the missions up and down the Congo, while their spiritual impact is limited, have done invaluable work in the fields of education and health.

Canyons and Cataracts

Now the river plunges into a gorge 125 miles long, ending in a rush around the Kallina Cliffs into the twenty-by-fifteen-mile expanse of Stanley Pool.

On the south side of the Pool is the Republic of the Congo's greatest city, Léopoldville, and on the north side, the chief city of the Congo Republic, Brazzaville.

This is the end of the steamer run. The river below for 215 miles is a roaring, seething riot of rapids leaping into waves ten to twenty feet high and proceeding at an average speed of fifty-five miles an hour. No boat could live here. But this part of the river is not potentially valueless. It has been estimated that its tremendous volume and its drop of eight hundred feet would make possible the generation of enough electric power to illuminate all tropical Africa.

Léopoldville and Brazzaville, though separated only by a brief ferry ride, are no more alike than a computer and an abacus. Léopoldville scorns Brazzaville as "dead." Brazzaville shrugs its shoulders and dubs Léopoldville "commercial."

Léopoldville *is* commercial, yet one of the most handsome cities in Africa. Its beauty is precise and patterned. Its palms stand in rows down the boulevards, its flowerbeds are formal, its grass is kept clipped, its buildings of glass and concrete suit each other and the surroundings. It has been a city of rich men who could afford the best. Since it has been the capital of the Belgian Congo, all the wealth of this fabulous African empire has poured into it. Its atmosphere is electric with ambition and change.

But Brazzaville is traditionally French, therefore easygoing. It is not dead, only tranquil. It has a quiet loveliness that touches the heart. Its palm trees grow where they please. Its magnificent old mango trees are untrimmed, and its gardens are a riot of flowering acacia, frangipani, poinsettia (grown to tree size), Bougainvillea, hibiscus and thousands of wild flowers that the citizens of Léopoldville would call weeds. The French homes are old and comfortable and the native quarters are full of song and laughter.

At Léopoldville, all cargo bound seaward must be transferred from boat to railway car. An exciting railroad, cut into cliffs and soaring over canyons, built at a cost of one life for every meter, skirts the rapids from Léopoldville to Matadi.

Here we took to the canoe once more for a thrilling ride through the violent whirlpools of "Hell's Cauldron." Then the river spreads and slows, and one feels the ocean tides. Grimy freighters take over the uranium, copper, tin, diamonds, gold, cobalt, zinc, coffee, cottonseed, rice, cocoa, palm oil, rubber, hippo ivory and elephant ivory to be transported to European and American ports.

This is the only sea outlet for the two Congos, and no other port in tropical Africa sends out treasure so precious. The major role in the collection and carrying of the treasure has been the Congo River, equatorial Africa's chief highway.

Now the river is resting, its job nearly done. It broadens into a great estuary. But its deep currents still have such force that they have carved a canyon nine hundred feet down into the floor of the estuary and this trench extends for a hundred miles into the open sea. From a plane as we leave the Congo, we can plainly mark its course by the black of its depth outlined sharply in the shallower blue.

And so goodbye to a great river, majestic and unforgettable.

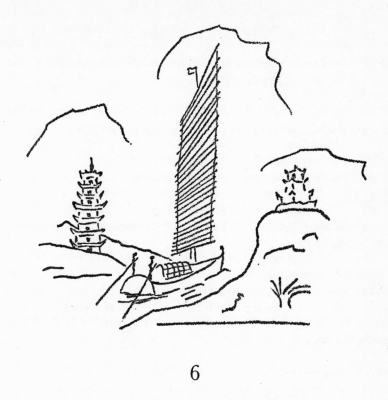

6

Bandits of the Grand Canal

WE DIP BACK a bit into history for this one. It was in the days just before the Communist takeover of China.

Americans still traveled freely in China. But when I dropped in at a travel agency in Peking and asked about the Grand Canal, the clerk's forehead wrinkled.

"The Grand Canal?" he said. "That's in Venice."

I thought everyone knew about China's Grand Canal. In my earliest geography lesson on Asia an imaginative teacher pictured China as a vast yellow land crossed by the Grand Canal and girdled by the Great Wall. Thenceforth the mention of China always brought up the vision of majestic junks sailing along a magnificent waterway in the shadow of a mighty wall.

Then to be told that the travel agency could give me no information about the Grand Canal, that they never had an inquiry about it, that no one ever went there, roused in me a feeling of personal resentment. It was as if one of my own most precious treasures were scorned.

Friends in Peking had heard of cruises on the southern part of the Grand Canal between Soochow and Hangchow. But all the great northern stretch of the canal was, so far as sightseers were concerned, unvisited and unknown.

And what a sight they were missing! The railroad and motor road are like pneumatic tubes that shoot passengers through North China, often over monotonous stretches, seldom giving even a distant glimpse of one of the greatest achievements of the ancient world.

One might suppose that the Grand Canal no longer existed —or at least that it was no longer used.

Yet, after actually penetrating to it, I was to have the curious feeling that here was the real heart of China. Moderns might go by train or motor. But 4,000-year-old China still swarmed along the ancient waterway.

Don't Annoy the Bandits

These river dwellers bumped cargo boats, shouted "Lend me your light" (Make way to pass), lived down in the hold with a dozen children and the memorial tablets of ancestors, took down the great sail and mast to slip under ancient bridges, and cooked millet on the afterdeck.

They made regular visits to the prow to burn incense before the "Goddess-ever-listening-to-the-prayers of mortals who pass over-the-water," and tossed a sack of grain to the bandits who, if they were not given a little, would take all.

Hearing that the head of navigation of the Grand Canal was at Tungchow, a town twelve miles east of Peking, I took my wife, blankets, food, and a Flit-gun and sallied thence. There we found Professor James A. Hunter, scientist connected with an agricultural experiment station. He agreed to find a boat for us and to leave his researches in animal husbandry and voyage with us.

On the morning of departure we rose at dawn. At the breakfast table one of the ladies of the station admonished Mr. Hunter, "Now James, if you meet bandits, don't get angry with them. You did last time. You lost your temper! They might have shot you."

"But they didn't," Hunter reminded her.

"I know. But that's no way to handle bandits. They're not used to being treated that way. You must be polite—and patient."

Hunter gave her his sweetest smile.

We rickshaed through the waking streets of Tungchow. At a small store we paused to buy coolie hats. Centuries of Chinese experience had designed them to keep out glare and heat. Plain ones of straw only, with ribbons to tie under the chin or behind the head, may be had for three cents (U.S.).

We purchased the finest the store afforded, seven-cent hats, cloth-lined for coolness. The ribbons were patterned in blue, and had a coquettish flare when tied in a bowknot beneath a masculine chin.

Through the musty darkness of the East Gate we went, past the bayonets of the constabulary who guarded the city by day and closed the great iron-studded doors firmly against all comers by night, and arrived soon at the water's edge.

River of Romance

Here was the beginning of romance. Here was the northern terminus of what was, next to the Yangtze River, the chief highway of the Celestial Empire. Approximately one thousand miles long, it connected two civilizations, that of the big raw-boned millet-eaters of North China with that of the sleek, neat rice-eaters of South China.

Above this point barges could not go, although the river itself, the Pei, has its rise in the hills north of Peking.

Much of the Grand Canal consists of rivers. Insofar as was possible, the canal was sensibly routed to follow the beds of existing rivers and lakes. There are few places where there is not a considerable current.

The Chinese name for the Grand Canal is Yun Ho (*ho* meaning river). Our Chinese boatmen referred to the whole colloquially as the "Move-Goods River." Our own term, Grand

Canal, is of course unknown to the Chinese. The practical fact is that the entire thousand-mile stretch from Hangchow to Tungchow is used as one thoroughfare.

Its most honored use in pre-railway times was the transportation of tribute from the southern provinces to the Imperial Court at Peking. This tribute consisted mostly of bags of rice. They were unloaded here at Tungchow and laid out on the shore to dry, musty from long confinement in damp holds.

The trip decidedly affected the flavor of the rice. People got used to it. A taste for musty rice grew up among the epicures of North China, so that finally they could tolerate none that was fresh, a fact reminding us of the city boy who spent a day in the country and complained that the eggs had no taste.

Even today there are rice dealers in Tungchow who, by a special process, make their rice musty to satisfy this demand.

From a tangle of boats a tall, browned Chinese with an open face (so many Chinese faces are shut) and a pleasant smile came to greet us.

Green Mountain King

"This is our captain," said Hunter. "His name is Wang Yu Shan. It means Green Mountain King."

Green Mountain King grinned and led us to our boat. If we had been expecting a Cleopatra's barge, we should have been partially disappointed. This was a barge, but Cleopatra would have disowned it. There is no reason for passenger boats where there are no passengers. This plain craft was not sufficiently skilled in the arts of deceit to conceal the fact that it was just an honest fishing boat on a vacation.

The Chinese called it a "net boat," and Green Mountain King was a net fisherman of no small skill, as we were to find out. The boat was twenty-five feet long, seven wide, blunt at both ends, flat-bottomed, equipped with a coal-ball stove forward for cooking. The crew slept in a covered hold aft along with other forms of life which neither rested nor slept.

The suite deluxe was amidships. It consisted of an eight-foot stretch of floorboard canopied by straw matting on a bamboo frame. This formed a sort of cave. The roof was so low that one could not stand without making a deep and continuous Oriental bow, doubtless good discipline for Westerners, who respond so clumsily to the courtesies of the East.

We stowed our duffel, spread camp blankets on the floor, and reclined in regal indolence for our trip down the Chinese Nile. Our boat was no sooner free of its moorings than it tore downstream with the bit in its teeth. Our speed was increased by the poles of the crew.

On each side of the boat was a narrow deck, or runway, extending from bow to stern. Along each of these ran a stout lad with the haft of his fifteen-foot pole braced against his shoulder and the push-pull end, consisting of metal point and hook, planted in the mud bottom. Upon reaching the stern he jerked his pole free (unless it jerked him overboard), carried it back to the bow, then repeated the process.

The captain was perched on the prow watching for hidden trouble and shouted instructions to his small son at the rudder.

We darted to one side or the other of sandbars. Even the sixth sense of a boatman could not always penetrate the rich water—which, by the way, was not at all disagreeable in color, but looked exactly like delicious cocoa requiring only that you add sugar and serve—and we would come up with a sickening lurch upon a concealed mudbank.

Then there would be a sort of college yell from the entire crew and a mighty straining and heaving against the strong current to get the boat free.

Some mudflats were ingeniously negotiated by whirling the boat like a merry-go-round, spiralling ourselves downstream.

Frequently we shot down a boiling, swirling stretch of rapids. There the crew gave themselves up to unrestrained shouting and prancing, disproving all statements about the unemotional character of the Chinese.

Captain Overboard

Our captain was like a small boy—a most engaging personality. He was in high spirits. He enjoyed giving orders. Was he not for the first time responsible for passengers, just like the captain of an ocean liner?

His enthusiasm was dampened when he lost his footing while trying to hold the boat with his pole against the spiral course of

a violent whirlpool. Over he went and came up with a comi-
cally tragic countenance. He, the commander, had lost face, and
there was not a word from him for the next hour.

My boyhood notions concerning the Grand Canal were rapidly being modified. Here was no straight artificial trench
with high banks. As in many parts of its vast length, the canal
here followed the river windings and coiled dragonlike over the
plain. True, there were high banks, but they were a mile apart,
and summer rains would swell the stream until it became a
hurrying flood a mile wide.

But now peasants were harvesting wheat on the floodplain
beside the canal, which as yet confined itself to a channel only
one or two hundred feet wide. The farmers worked against
time to complete their task before the July downpour.

Meanwhile the ragged poor squatted in groups, waiting to
glean. After the harvest they would go over the field to pick up
stray heads. Neither farmers nor gleaners would get much.
There had been no rain for weeks and the crop was poor.

I had thought of the canal as stable and fixed; but it is fickle.

"Last year the channel was there," said Green Mountain
King, pointing to a cut in the plain a half-mile away.

Drowned Farms

An interesting question came to our minds. Who owns the
bottom of the Grand Canal?

Last year some farmer raised wheat or corn on the very
ground over which our boat was now gliding. This year he had
lost a good part of his small farm, perhaps all of it. He would
be supported by the community until next year when the bad
luck might turn to some neighbor—was already turning, as a
matter of fact, if we might judge by the way the current was
biting into the land at sharp bends, and good grain, under-
mined, was tumbling into the water.

Where the stream cut against one or the other of the high
dikes which flanked the floodplain, the villagers had strewn the
bank with bricks for the current to gnash its teeth upon, and
had planted trees to hold the soil together.

It was then necessary to delegate police to protect the trees.

For in this desperately fuel-less land unguarded trees disappear overnight and are next seen as smoke oozing out through the cracks and cicada holes of kitchen walls.

Charming scenes unfolded ahead of us. Stretches of golden wheat or jade-green corn. Great sails moving as if through the grain. The glint of dragonflies, the flight of larks, crows, and haughty hoopoes. The rich brown water, brown earth, and brown mud houses against a cornflower sky. Beautiful old pagodas. Old temple roofs shaded by sacred trees, ancient and gnarled. A deep quiet over all, as of old age with folded hands.

Every country is older than its cities. And so is this country more ancient than one of the world's most ancient of living cities which you could see from the top of yonder Tungchow Pagoda.

Peking's walls, gates, columns, temples, *pai-lous,* and palaces are old; yet they are young compared with this land of farm and village through which we sail. Here before cities existed life moved along probably much as it does today.

When You and I Lived in Caves

When Europe's cavemen dressed in skins, a wooden plow already had been invented and was furrowing these fields. Women were spinning silk in houses like these. A calendar, weights and measures, bronze dishes and ornaments were in use. Most remarkable of all, the art of writing and reading had been devised. And Chinese gentlemen were reciting lyric poetry a thousand years before the Golden Age of Greece.

That seems long ago. But it is only yesterday in the life of this land.

When we try to think of men moving and working here ten thousand years ago, one hundred thousand, perhaps even a million years ago, our imagination breaks down and we can only rely upon the facts unearthed by the scientists. Fossils of the so-called "Peking Man" were found at the little village of Chou Kou Tien in 1929. They bring him closer to the chimpanzee, so far as cranial contour is concerned, than any other remains yet found upon this planet. These excavations carry man's life back through the first stages of the Ice Age to a period variously estimated to have been from a half million to a million years ago. That, of course, is not all that there is of his history, but merely all that we know.

How enduring human life is! All man's works crumble, but he goes on. Even the earth changes beneath him; ice sweeps away mountains, climates change around him, but he muddles through. He may be stupid, but he is stubborn. Especially the man of China, as Lin Yutang has said, "has a sound instinct for life."

Punishing the Drought Dragon

The age-old hush of the countryside was shattered by the blare of bugles and the throb of drums. From a village on the dike came a strange procession. It was a crowd of villagers led by a boys' bugle corps. Red and blue banners waved. What sounded like machine-gun fire at a distance proved to be the crackling of strings of firecrackers dangled from the ends of poles.

"A rain procession, I do believe," said Hunter.

"How about photographing it?"

"Bad joss. They wouldn't let you."

"Let's land anyhow."

We leaped ashore and ran to intercept the parade before it should reach the canal. Coming near, we saw what looked like a kitchen table being borne in great state on the shoulders of four particularly solemn village elders. Upon the table was a board, and upon the board a savage, scaly dragon three feet long.

"What's the idea?" I called to Hunter, who ran beside me.

"To bring rain. The dragon is supposed to be the evil spirit that has kept rain away. They'll drown it in the canal—then rain can come."

The procession halted beside the canal. The table was set down. There was a sharp command. Men dropped to their knees about the hated dragon, kowtowed until their foreheads touched the ground, and begged the evil spirit not to be angry with them for what they must do to it. There were no priests. The leader in this ancient superstitious rite was, oddly enough, the only "modern" in the crowd, the young schoolmaster. Thus do old and new merge in China. We asked permission to take photographs. He demurred.

"I don't mind," he said. "But it's the farmers—if it doesn't rain they'll blame you. You may be followed and hurt. You see, it's a matter of life and death with them. So I wouldn't if I were you—unless you're sure it will rain."

Hunter looked at the sky.

"I think it's going to rain," he said, and we took photographs.

When the elders protested we promptly yielded and closed the camera, ostensibly out of regard for their feelings, really because the photography was finished. If we thought we were being adroit we were soon to have a lesson in the Oriental practice of this art.

The dragon was cleverly made of clay. The realistic "scales" were clam shells. The sculptor had shown no mean ability in designing the brutal head and the savage mouth bristling with ferocious teeth. One could easily share the feeling of the villagers that when so horrible a monster had been extinguished the world would be a better place.

Another sharp command. The band burst into pandemonium, firecrackers set up a terrific din, and the dragon was borne to the water's edge and slipped from the board into the stream. It sank at once. There were nervous shouts of joy. The procession reformed and goose-stepped away through the wet morning grass, the boys playing lustily, some of their elders glancing back now and then to the swirling current where their enemy had disappeared. The impression they left with the onlooker was one of pitiful, tragic earnestness. This meant so much to them.

Under Surveillance

A quarter-mile away they stopped and huddled into a conference. Then they went on. But one detached himself from the group and sauntered after us.

Green Mountain King looked at the bowl of brass above us and shook his head. He mourned our follies.

"Much trouble if rain does not come," he said.

After our boat had rounded a great loop in the canal we found our mentor on the towpath above us.

"Going to keep us company?" called Hunter.

The man stared blankly. "No, no, I'm just going to Shang P'u K'ou."

"Then you'd better ride," said Hunter, plotting to win our enemy with kindness.

We pushed to shore and he came aboard. He was a mild little man. His name, he said, was Li Yuan Kai. He sat on the fore-deck by the stove, where something was usually cooking, and ate incessantly. When the stove offered nothing, he opened tin after tin from the boat's stores. The exotic had no terrors for him. His most amazing performance was the simultaneous engulfing of jam and sardines.

He never looked at the sky. The others stole furtive glances at the relentless blue.

"But," I said, "one man could do nothing. Why do we worry?"

"We're not worrying," said Hunter. "But don't get the idea that Li is just one man. As a responsible elder, he has all the bandits of this region at his call. The bandits are a sort of volunteer force. In fact, the line between bandits and official police is rather vague. Bandits become police, and police become bandits, or they may even be police and bandits at the same time. In short, we have the law on board. But it doesn't matter— it's going to rain."

"Have you eaten?" came the customary greeting from passing ships. Some of the craft were of considerable size, topped with a great rectangular sail and drawn, when the wind was faint, by two ropes extending from the top of the mast to yokes across the chests of half-naked men trudging along the towpath.

A temple fair attracted us ashore, and we were soon engulfed in a swirling crowd which found us even more interesting than the stilt dancers.

"We have seen only one foreigner in a whole year," an old lady explained apologetically. "He came with pills."

One man, his face twitching, followed us steadily for an hour. Then he said: "So you're not selling medicine?"

It was easy to guess the sort of "medicine" he had in mind. It is an unhappy fact that the only outsiders visiting many villages remote from road and railroad are the sellers of heroin.

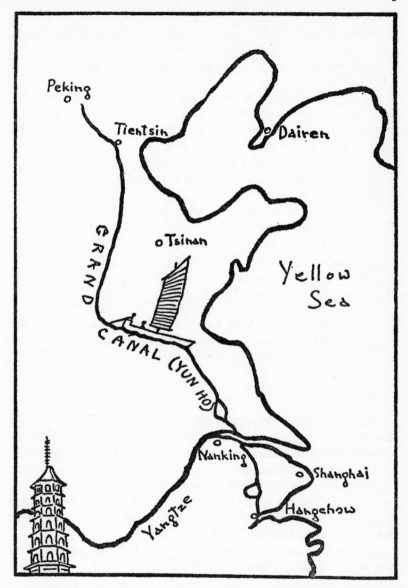

Sunset found us on a rather forlorn stretch of the canal with no village in sight.

"Where do you sleep?" asked Green Mountain King.

There was hardly room in the boat for all. "One of us on

board—two on shore," suggested Hunter. "Just roll up in our blankets."

Green Mountain King was worried.

"Too many bandits," he objected. "Better go on to the next watchman."

Dusk was deepening when we came to a small mud hut occupied by a lone watchman. This was a "loading station." Farmers might bring produce here to be placed on board the canal boats. But at present there were no boats and no farmers —only the frail little old watchman armed with a rattle.

"So, this is our staunch protector against a bandit foray," I commented.

"It's done with money, not with guns," Hunter explained. "This watchman represents all the farmers of the district. They make a bargain with the bandits to keep away from this loading station. So we are quite safe here, except. . . ."

He was studying the sky. The stars were shining brilliantly. There was not a cloud the size of a man's hand.

"I trust Li does not become impatient," he remarked.

Hunter slept in the boat amidships; Li and the crew in the hold aft; we two on our cots set up in a shed, mud-made, roofed with cornstalks, and half-filled with coal.

Night in a Coal-Hole

We lay listening to gentle chewing sounds in the walls and roof and clutched the Flit-gun. The shed was open to the night on one side. It was easy to imagine rain fanatics crouching yonder among the standing corn.

Toward midnight Mary gasped "The dragon!" and awoke with such a violent start that her cot collapsed, tossing her into the pile of coal. The watchman, alarmed, shook his rattle, and stayed discreetly indoors.

At dawn we awoke to the blessed sound of rain pattering on the cornstalks above our heads. Boarding the boat, we were met with the news that Li was no longer with us. We sailed away and luxuriated in the life-giving drops that trickled down our necks as we huddled over the preparation of bacon, eggs, and coffee on the galley stove.

But the rain proved abortive; by nine it was no longer even a drizzle. An hour later, there was Li smiling down upon us from the towpath. With spurious pleasure we took him on board. He sat down beside the stove and began to eat.

Tired of close quarters, we walked along the towpath and viewed the pageant of Chinese life. Farmers lighted incense before a small brick Temple of the Fields in gratitude for the drizzle and in petition for a real rain.

A housewife was making slippers. To give bulk to the sole, she had inserted between the two thin layers of cloth a copy of an old American newspaper.

One man was cleaning a rifle but hastily concealed it when he saw strangers coming. The atmosphere of impending trouble hung heavy over North China. Everywhere there were preparations for no one knew what—certainly those who were preparing did not know.

Our boat sailed through a gorgeous canary-and-purple sunset into a flea-bitten settlement bearing the proud name of Great Wang Town. It was chiefly the village of the family Wang. There are thousands of cases in China of an entire village inhabited by a single family. And so complicated are relationships, early and late intermarriages, and adoptions that the truth, "The boy is father to the man," is here carried a step further, and a lad may actually be grandfather to a patriarch of seventy.

Again, the problem of sleep. The ramshackle houses, howling curs, and piratical aspect of the inhabitants did not suggest a good night's rest on shore. The Wangs flocked to see us and streamed out upon the flat deck of a ferry barge moored to the bank. We drew up alongside the ferry. For a few moments, gaping silence. It was an evil-looking crowd. Some peered down into our boat, seeming to scan our possessions with covetous eyes.

"Trust we haven't dropped into a nest of canal pirates," remarked Hunter. "We'd better try to drum up a little friendship. Where's that magazine with the pictures in it?"

He took a *National Geographic* and clambered up on the barge deck. Instantly he was mobbed. Everyone wanted to see at once. With a football rush, a brawny fellow pushed his way through to Hunter.

"I'm the headman," he said. "Who are you?"

Hunter explained and beguiled the big fellow with pictures.
The headman peered at the unfamiliar English type.

Hunter indicated me.

"He wrote this."

The headman, misunderstanding, supposed the exhibit to be
a sample of my calligraphy. He inspected the page again.

"He writes very well," he said. "It looks almost like print."

We Drink White Boiled Water

He pointed to a mud house half hidden behind compost
heaps.

"That is my house. Come and drink white boiled water."

We went up, sat on the headman's *k'ang*, and drank white
boiled water. In many poor Chinese villages tea is rare. The
water is called white to distinguish it from tea.

The villagers crowded into the room. Some of the old men
still clung to the queue. We noticed that not only every woman
but every girl in the room stalked about on bound feet. The
custom was happily disappearing in the cities but not in the
country. A country swain would not marry a girl with natural
feet—they were considered huge, flat and ugly.

Li circulated through the crowd, dropping remarks, quite
evidently defaming us. He even took the headman aside for a
moment—but that worthy persisted in his hospitality.

"Stay the night," he said. "Sleep here."

Since this was the only room of the house, it was evident that
the entire family would sleep with us. And it was more than
probable that half the village would stay to watch us sleep.
These considerations, and Li's suspicious performance, caused
Hunter to decline courteously. He explained that we had full
equipment in the boat.

We went back to the shore. The lady was made comfortable
in the boat; two cots for the men were perched on the high flat
deck of the ferry barge. Both craft were then pushed off and
anchored in midstream. One of the crew was placed on watch.
We lay gazing up at the stars. Vega was straight overhead. Gradually a blanket of river mist covered us—an additional sign that
no rain was at hand. I resolved to supplement the official watch
with my volunteer efforts. Just a little nap first. But I had not

counted upon the soporific effect of a long day of wind and sun and did not wake until daylight.

A Night in Jail

The headman had come down to the shore to see us off. He was arguing with Li. When we pulled ashore, he expressed his appreciation that his village had entertained a great scholar and a great calligrapher. Perhaps it was this reputation that had protected us. He took Hunter to one side.

"Be careful tonight," he suggested.

The canal was now deeper, wider, and alive with traffic.

Green Mountain King flung his net and drew in some toothsome fish that added zest to the menu for both crew and passengers. With less success he tried to snare turtles which lay on the mud along the water's edge. He politely referred to them as round fish. The word turtle is considered improper since it is used only in curses; and to call a man "son of a turtle" is the worst of insults.

Cables across the canal served as guidelines for ferry barges. Traffic must either push the cable up and crawl under, or call to the ferryman to sink his cable so that boats could pass over.

Li grew weary of sitting on deck; said he must hurry on. With many expressions of enduring friendship and regard he thanked us for our kindness and took to the towpath. There he developed a speed quite uncommon for him, and was soon lost to sight.

Night fell as we came to the considerable village of Shang P'u K'ou. We determined to pass on; for the place was, in Chinese parlance, "hot and noisy."

A garrulous crowd thronged the landing place. When we passed by there was great commotion; evidently we had broken a well-laid plan. A policeman appeared and brandished his arms. When we disregarded him, he ran up into the town, calling.

We had not gone half a mile farther before a launch bearing six uniformed police armed with rifles pulled up alongside. The chief came aboard. He was a huge fellow for a Chinese and had the air of one who is accustomed to have people step smartly out of his way or be stepped on. Without that uniform, we should have set him down as a bandit chief or petty warlord.

"Where do you intend to spend the night?" He made a show of politeness but he had not been bred to it.

"Probably in the boat."

"We cannot allow you to do that. We should have to be responsible for your safety. Conditions are dangerous. Kidnapping a few miles north of here this afternoon!"

"Then where do you wish us to stay?"

"Better sleep in town."

"Is there a hotel?"

"It is full. But we will give you a place to sleep."

"Where?"

"It will be a good place. You will be safe there."

We turned about, perforce, and went back to the "hot and noisy" spot. In the heavy dusk, by the light of torches, crowds stood in circles about jugglers, strong men and acrobats. But they suddenly deserted those entertainers when they saw us and came to the water's edge, jostling and jeering.

Hunter said to us: "Just to prepare you so that it won't be a shock—I believe we are to spend the night in the police station."

We were escorted through dark alleys, where black dogs leaped snarling from doorways, to a great gate set in a high wall. The gate opened, we went in, the gate ponderously closed. We stood in a black courtyard before a dimly lit altar-room. Rifles lay on the altar before an unsurprised Buddha. An old temple had been converted into a police station and prison. The wall about the compound was twenty feet high.

We were led into an adjoining room, high, bleak, the cracks in its white plaster walls promising that we should be devoured by sand flies. The portrait of Sun Yat-sen looked down from under the crossed flags of the Kuomintang and the Chinese Republic. The windows were barred. There were a few canvas cots about. Well, this was not too bad. As sleeping quarters it was quite as good as anything we should ordinarily have had.

The only hitch was that we were not to be allowed to sleep—at least not for four endless hours. Sheet after sheet was filled in with our answers to all manner of irrelevant questions. Age, nationality, father, grandfather, marital relationships, travel details, whence, whither, why—the queries gradually narrowed down to our trip on the Grand Canal and interference with the rain rites. Finally, the suggestion was gently proffered that we might care to pay an indemnity to the suffering village. Possibly one thousand dollars gold would do. The chief bent his great fierce smile upon us.

Hunter smiled back. "I can ask our consul at Tientsin if he thinks that would be a good arrangement. Is there a telephone here?"

"No telephone," grunted the chief. He plainly disliked the mention of the consul.

"Then I think there is nothing we can do tonight." Hunter rose. "We shall not keep you longer since it is time for you to rest."

None too promptly, the chief and his men withdrew, taking the only light with them. A rusty key turned in the lock. We stretched out on the cots. The sand flies began their work.

Detained or Entertained?

During the tormented shufflings and shiftings between naps we talked. Would the inquisition continue the next day? How long were we to be detained?

"Not detained," corrected Hunter. "Entertained. Outward appearances are important in China; we are supposed to be guests. We'll be out in the morning. There's no charge they can hold us on."

We were out in the morning. The chief was all smiles, slightly crooked smiles, and seemed eager for us to be on our way. There was no further mention of the indemnity, not one more question. We were bustled away breakfastless to the land-ing stage. There we expressed our undying gratitude to the chief for his abounding hospitality and took off. We sat stiff and smiling on deck until we were around the first bend—then dived into the larder.

Hunter was not properly elated over our freedom.

"Too easy," he commented. "We're due for trouble yet—un-less it rains."

But there was considerable encouragement aloft. A solid

black pall stretched from one horizon to the other. It might not spill rain at all; but, if it did, it would be a real rain, no passing cloudburst or drizzle.

About three miles beyond the town we came to a ferry cable stretched across the canal two feet above the surface. Green Mountain King called to the ferryman to sink his cable so that we might slip over. Nothing was done. As the boat nosed the cable the crew tried to hoist it and pass under. The cable was taut; cries to slack away were not heeded on shore.

"No use making a scene," Hunter counseled the captain. "Better push over to shore and we'll have a talk."

As we touched the bank a score of unkempt men, armed with rifles, swarmed out of the doorways of the mud shacks of the small village. They wore cast-off army uniforms, but we clearly recognized two who had worn police uniforms the night before. The administration of justice had been shifted—from the police, who had no charge against us, to the bandits, who needed no charge.

Their leader, a tight-knotted little man, came on ahead. Hunter exchanged cordial greetings with the thug and invited him on board to have a cup of tea. Sipping his tea, the leader said: "The village of Shang Ma Tou wishes an indemnity of one thousand dollars."

"For what reason?"

"They say that your magic angered the Rain God."

"Now listen, my friend," said Hunter seriously. "You are intelligent, you have traveled widely, seen many white men. You know that white men have no magic to stop rain. If we had magic to stop it we would have magic to start it. I might try to put you off by telling you that I would bring rain. But you would only laugh at me. I couldn't fool *you*. No, we have no magic to bring rain or to prevent it. But there is one thing we do have—science—you have heard of science." He pulled up one of his books and opened it to bewildering and impressive diagrams. "Well, I am a student of science, and I can tell you that it is going to rain before night."

The bandit pondered.

Hunter added, "Of course you, being a wise man, know how dangerous it is to interfere with foreigners in this country. As your friend, I should advise you to wait until tonight."

He waited. We also waited, for there was no move to let down the barrier. Fortunately Hunter's time allowance was well on the safe side. By three in the afternoon the misty air had begun to sift. Feathery drippings became positive drops, and presently a reliable rain was falling.

The men sought the shelter of the village inn. We huddled under our straw roof, through which water began to seep. But we had nothing but the most kindly feelings toward the storm.

When the downpour had continued for two hours and showed every sign of persisting indefinitely, the head of the bandit chief blocked the forward opening of our straw cabin.

From Prison to Banquet

"We are at the inn," he said. "Come. We shall hold a feast in your honor."

It would be a sad feast, we thought, in a remote village hostelry. But the band had evidently prospered of late, and at their command the hotelkeeper had imported the day before a bargeload of eatables from Tientsin. In the dark smoky inn, which fairly rocked with loud talk, the long tables were loaded to the edge. The chief stilled the noise. He honored the foreign guests with a rough speech of welcome.

Then followed an amazing and almost endless meal. Fifty courses came and went. *Hors d'oeuvres* of jellied eggs and melon seeds. Duck. Fish. Hot wines. Liqueurs, one flavored with rose leaves, one with almonds, one with apricots. Bears' paws. Fish cones. Sugared apple blossoms. A procession of soups made from seaweed, pigeons' eggs, silver fungus, birds' nests. Then a new relay of entrées—sharks' fins, honey-cured ham, lotus leaves, pheasant, fish bellies, ducks' feet, pigs' elbows, sweet and sour pork, shrimps and eels, and much more. Near the end came other soups, and last of all, rice.

This mighty meal had taken six hours. It was now nearly midnight. The downpour persisted. The innkeeper made room for us to stretch out with our fellow-gourmands on the k'ang.

The band was up and away at dawn, but we lay late. Then we loitered over tea, for the unremitting deluge made our boat seem unattractive. We discussed the bounty of the bandit.

"We got off easily," we said. "Here we were in his hands—

he might have taken us and held us for ransom. Instead, he gave us a feast."

Hunter was knitting his brows over a slip of paper the innkeeper had handed him.

"Yes," he said resignedly. "I suppose we are getting off easily —even with this."

It was the bill for the feast.

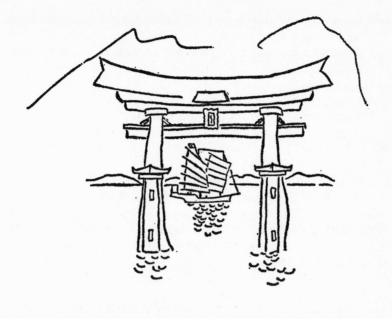

7

The Sea River by Junk

"I THINK . . . small boat . . . Inland Sea . . . very danger."

Captain Hikeda's English was not perfect, but his meaning was clear. He did not approve of our plan to sail a small boat from end to end of the Inland Sea. He knew its labyrinth of islands, reefs, shoals, hidden rocks, savage tide rips, and whirlpools.

What had we let ourselves in for? When we first conceived the idea of a small-boat expedition the length of the Inland Sea, we knew its reputation as the loveliest of the world's waterways, but were not aware that it was considered by sailors to be dangerous for small craft.

On previous visits to Japan, we had seen the Inland Sea from the decks of large steamers. These brief glimpses were tantalizing. We wanted to loiter around its ravishingly beautiful islands, probe its bays, land on its warm beaches, walk through its villages tucked in snug coves between blue sea and pine-clad mountains, and learn what sort of folk live in this secluded island world. The way to do it was in a small boat.

A Sea that Is a River

"Don't forget," went on Captain Hikeda, "Inland Sea . . . it is a river . . . strong currents, rapids, like other rivers—but worse."

"Why do you call it a river?"

"Much fresh water—because it carries water of many rivers to ocean. I call it Sea River. Look on your map."

It was true. The map showed no fewer than seventeen rivers contributing to the Inland Sea.* Besides, it drains Biwa, by far the largest of all Japanese lakes. The combined floods sweep down the "Sea River" for 250 miles between banks ten to thirty miles apart to empty finally into the ocean through two outlets, the straits of Bungo and Shimonoseki.

On the way the current encounters three thousand rocky islands. These obstructions, as we were soon to learn, throw the stream into wild confusion, a confusion compounded by raging tides that twice a day rush in through the straits, funneling furiously between islands, rocks and reefs.

The Lure of the Islands

But those islands—three thousand of them—Captain Hikeda admitted that to see them was worth almost any risk. But how to find a boat?

In Osaka a new friend, Kunitsuna Sasaki of the Kansai Steamship Company, came to our aid.

He took us to the fishing village of Sumoto, and there we found a craft suited to our purpose. The owner agreed to rent it and entered into a verbal contract on the spot. We returned to Osaka, drew up a written contract, and sent it to Sumoto for the boatman's signature.

But he had had time to think it over. The Cassandras of

---

* The rivers: Yedo, Muko, Kako, Ichi, Ibo, Chigusa, Hoshii, Asahi, Takahashi, Ashida, Ota, Wakuni, Saba, Hiji, Ono, Oita, Yamakuni.

Sumoto had filled his ears with stories of wrecks in the far parts of the Inland Sea. His boat might be smashed on the reefs or pulled down by the *kappa*, water goblins that haunt the whirl-pools. Instead of signing the contract, he suggested that we *buy* the boat; then any disaster would be on our shoulders, not his.

Hardly prepared to acquire a Japanese fishing junk, we looked elsewhere. Sasaki had another idea. He sent two newspaper friends to see us at our Japanese hotel. One of them snapped photographs, the other took our story.

He ran it in an Osaka paper under the title, "I Want to See the Real Japan," with the subtitle, "I Wish to Borrow a Boat to Sail the Inland Sea." Boatowners were invited to write.

This brought a handful of offers. But when they were traced back to their sources and the boatmen learned how far we wished to go, the offers were withdrawn.

All except one. The letter came from Kanonji, an Inland Sea port which has played a part in Japanese history as a pirates' nest. It was founded well over a thousand years ago by Indonesian buccaneers who then terrorized the Inland Sea, looting ships and taking their crews captive.

Their descendants are no longer pirates, but they furnish some of the Inland Sea's most venturesome sailors. Kanonji's ships are all of a pattern—low, swift, piratical-looking, not much changed since buccaneer days.

Captain Wide-Margin-of-Safety

We journeyed to Kanonji and met the young man who had written the letter. His name, freely translated, meant "Wide-Margin-of-Safety." That was reassuring. How could anything go wrong under a captain with a name so auspicious?

He took us to the waterfront, off which some of the Kanonji fleet lay at anchor. Draped with brown nets drying, the vessels looked like enormous bats.

He pointed out one lying about a hundred yards from shore. That was his. It could be ours for six weeks if we wished.

Yes, he would take us anywhere. He had not been to other parts of the Inland Sea, but he was not afraid. His two uncles would go along as crew. He regretted that neither he nor his uncles could speak English. That was a handicap, though not too serious; we had a modest knowledge of Japanese gained through five years' residence in Japan before the war.

The boat took our fancy at once. Riding the waves, head in the wind, it looked as if it could hardly wait to be off in quest of adventure. It was a seven-ton boat, forty-five feet long, with ten-foot beam. It carried two sails and a twelve-horsepower auxiliary engine. It looked more like a schooner than any other Western vessel, but it was of the junk type with a moderately high poop, overhanging stem, shallow draft, and lugsails.

But I wanted to see it close up.

"May I go aboard?"

A high sea was rolling into the roadstead, urged on by a smart wind. The captain grinned doubtfully, but went for a dinghy.

When I saw it, I was tempted to change my mind. It was a cockleshell not more than eight feet long. It rolled and tossed and skipped. Beside it a Canadian canoe would look as steady as Gibraltar. Wide-Margin-of-Safety, standing in the stern manipulating the sweep, brought the boat within jumping distance of the stone steps of the mole. Spray showered into the boat. That would not be good for a camera, so I handed my Rolleiflex to my wife to keep until my return. My color camera was in my pocket where it should be safe from spray. I watched my chance to go down the steps which were buried in water one instant, bare the next. I leaped into the boat and crouched.

The captain waggled the sweep and we zigzagged out into the roadstead. It is impossible to pursue a straight course by use of the sweep. The great blade is not removed from the water but, projecting behind the boat, presses back and forth, now to starboard, now to port. The bow, responding to this pressure, also swings from side to side. Only for a split second in each swing is the bow pointed straight for its objective. It behaves like a small dog being wagged by an oversized tail.

But that is not the worst of it. If the oarman is vigorous, the boat light, the sweep heavy—and all these conditions applied in our case—the action of the sweep violently rocks the boat. You must brace your feet and grip the gunwales firmly to avoid being tossed out. If you have been brought up in the anti-

quated doctrine that a boat should be held in steady equilib-
rium at all times, you unlearn your lessons fast in a dinghy.
There, the admired boatman is he who can tip his craft farthest
without filling it with water or spilling its passengers.

And so, rocking and weaving, not more than a cupful of water slapping my trousers each time the gunwale sank, we
squirmed through the high waves. Coming at last alongside the
ship we did not exactly scramble onto it, but allowed a wave to
throw us aboard.

The drying fish nets suspended from the masts were weighted
with flat stones four inches across and these tossed back and
forth, giving me several decisive konks on the head before I
learned to skulk beneath them.

Two towering masts marked the ship off roughly into thirds.
Aft of the mainmast was the engine and crew's quarters. Beyond the foremast were the big rusty anchors and coils of line.
Between the masts was a good expanse of deck that we would
have to ourselves. The captain explained that an awning would
be erected to keep off the sun. There was a covered tub of fresh
water and we could cook on a charcoal brazier.

"But where do we sleep?"

Fishbin Becomes Stateroom

The captain cheerfully removed a hatch and I looked down
through the hole. If I had expected to see a roomy cabin I
would have been sadly disappointed. What I saw was a compartment of the hold ordinarily used as a fishbin. It did not smell
fishy—it had been scrubbed perfectly clean—but it was very
shallow, not more than eighteen inches deep.

I looked at the captain unbelievingly.

He promptly undertook to convince me that a human being
actually could squeeze himself into this sandwich of a space. He
slipped through the hole, extended his legs under the deck in
one direction and his head and shoulders in the other and lay
still, leaving me to contemplate his stomach, the only part of
him still visible. With the hatch on, as it would be in stormy
weather, the place would be as dark as a pocket, and airless.

Wide-Margin emerged grinning, expecting my approval. I

nodded. After all, what quarters could one expect on a fishing junk? If the weather were not too cold or wet, we could sleep on deck.

"When the sea is rough, does it wash over the deck?" I asked.

The captain laughed and nodded vigorously.

Oh well, we would see what we would see. Travel problems, if you don't worry about them, often have a way of solving themselves.

But there was one other thing. I looked about, hoping my eye would light on it, then I wouldn't have to ask. The captain followed my gaze.

"Ah, you wish to see the engine."

Well, that wasn't it. But we went aft to see the engine. The captain lifted a hatch and there it was—a clean, well-kept little oil burner.

I looked around again. "What's down there?"

"We sleep there," and Yasuhiro lifted a hatch to reveal a cell as snug as our own.

"Yes, but . . . *where's the benjo?*"

"Ah, the benjo, the benjo. Very sorry, no benjo." He looked over the side.

"The lady . . ." I objected.

"Ah, *so desu*. The lady." Then he brightened. "But we will make a benjo, oh yes. Right back here, over the water." He took me back and indicated a point in space, just beyond the stern. "A little room. Will that be good?"

"That will be fine."

In general the boat was just what we wanted, picturesque and piratical, with the glamor of a sailing ship backed up by the efficiency of a motor, a craft small enough to fit the budget, but large enough to brave the dangerous tidal rips and whirlpools of the Inland Sea.

Accident Number One

We took off in the dinghy for the mole where my wife had now been joined by several hundred citizens of Kanonji. The sea was more choppy than ever. Halfway to shore Wide-Margin-of-Safety lost control of the treacherous little craft, a wave filled it, the boat turned turtle, and we were in for a swim.

The overturned boat, tossed about by the waves, struck me a blow that nearly bereft me of my senses. I thought confusedly that I must not drown because in that case I would lose my camera just as I had, in a similiar upset, lost a three-hundred-dollar Contax in the waters of the Nile.

I struck something else—it was the rudder of an anchored junk. Clinging to it, I took the camera from my pocket, reached up, and placed it safely on the deck. Then I climbed up and joined it. After a short wait another dinghy, a larger and more seaworthy one this time, put out from the mole, picked up the captain and myself and took us to shore.

The captain was all apologies. He assumed that our deal was off.

A kindly fishwife insisted that we come into her house, remove our wet clothes and don *yukatas*, summer kimonos. She washed the salt out of my clothes and ironed them—and refused to take a penny for her pains. I was touched by her kindness to a stranger and an American, the more so when I learned that her son, an aviator in the war, had been killed by our troops in New Guinea.

In an upper room looking out on the fishing fleet, we sat on the matted floor by a low table and sipped hot tea. The captain was crestfallen. I assured him that all was not lost. I quoted the proverb: "A bad beginning makes a good ending." Calling for paper and pencil, we drafted a contract for a six-week voyage with Wide-Margin-of-Safety.

His demands were reasonable enough. For the boat and the services of three men we were to pay 2,500 yen a day ($7) with an additional charge for fuel, depending upon the amount used. The men would buy their own food, and we would buy ours.

For us this was eminently satisfactory—and for the crew as well, since it meant that they would earn more for six weeks of pleasurable cruising than for a year of toilsome fishing.

We returned to Osaka in high spirits. It would take four days for the men to construct the awning, build the convenience overhanging the stern, and put a floor in the fishbin bedroom. Then the boat would be brought to Osaka and our voyage would begin from there.

In the meantime we bought necessary equipment—heavy *fu-*

ton or comfortables for sleeping on deck, pots and pans, a few dishes, a little cutlery—and a Shinto shrine!

Fishermen, because they always face the unpredictable, are usually superstitious. The captain had, half in jest, remarked that my dunking in the sea on the first day was a bad omen. The shrine seemed to be the answer. We would place it on deck and dedicate it to Kompira, the Japanese sea god who is supposed to protect sailors. His sanctuary at Kotohira overlooking the Inland Sea attracts thousands of pilgrims, especially seafarers. We would go further—we would honor Kompira by naming our boat after him. Surely he would then feel bound to give it special protection.

The Mysterious Box

On a lovely September morning the little craft arrived at Osaka, took on her passengers, was duly photographed by newsmen—some of whom had come all the way from Tokyo for the event—and sailed away to the west with flags flying. We placed the shrine at the foot of the foremast. It delighted the crew, who made offerings of fish and rice before it throughout the voyage.

Now we met for the first time the uncles of Wide-Margin-of-Safety. One was "Good-Fortune-in-Autumn." Would his name prove as inauspicious as the captain's? The other was "Literature-Pursuing-Sixth-Son." It was true that he was a sixth son, but as for literature, he pursued it at a respectful distance.

Both men wore towels around their heads, brigand fashion. With their brown faces twisted out of shape by a lifetime of squinting out to sea, and their mouths studded with teeth like those of a killer whale, they looked as if they could rob a galleon or slit a throat with equal ease.

We were to learn that they were as gentle as lambs.

The wind was fair, and we sped toward Kobe without benefit of engine. The two big lugsails towered above us, the larger reaching to a height of thirty feet. In the best junk tradition, bamboo slats or battens kept them stretched to the wind, and other bamboo strips held them to the masts.

Pegged with wooden dowels, built without nails, bolts or

screws, weatherbeaten until its flanks were as gray as the whiskers of Confucius, the entire ship breathed of the long-gone past.

Well, not the *entire* ship. There was one thing that was brashly, painfully new. It was a large box built of fresh unpainted wood contrasting sharply with the old gray stern on the edge of which it perched. It projected backwards into space over the water. It looked like a piece of cargo that had been thrown aboard just as the ship was leaving and had only just made it.

I went aft to examine it. What could it contain? Observing a small door in the front of the box, I opened it, stooped down, and peered inside. The box was empty. I stood up to find the captain beside me, grinning his satisfaction.

"*Suki desu ka?* It pleases you?"

Then the light broke. This was the benjo. I stooped again to look in. Through a large opening in the floor I gazed down into the blue waters of the Inland Sea. The floor aperture was similar in size and shape to that to be found in any Japanese toilet. But being men of the world, the captain and his uncles knew that foreigners are not content with a hole in the floor— they require a seat. So one had been constructed above the large opening. But the opening in the seat was so small that it might have been designed for a two-year-old.

The master builder had now been joined by his two fellow craftsmen. Their pleasure and pride were touching.

"Enter, please enter."

I crawled into the box and tried it for size. Seated, I was curved like Cupid's bow, my head forced down to my chest by the low roof.

"Ah, we fix." The captain seized an iron spike and pried off the middle board of the roof. My head emerged through the hole. It did not seem to occur to my companions that this would affect the privacy of the contrivance in any way.

Being taller than the rest of the ship's company, I was fortunately the only one to be thus embarrassed. But even the shortest could not stand up in the business without emerging chest-high. This proved to be a convenience since the latch had been so cunningly devised that it sometimes locked the occupant in and it was necessary to reach down on the outside to open the door. If this did not work, one could always call for help.

Sometimes the temperamental latch relaxed too easily due to the violent vibration of the box when the engine was in use. On such occasions a roll of the ship would swing the door wide open to a point where it could not be reached from the inside, and only another roll could close it.

When the rains descended the seat was soaked, and the occupant too, unless an umbrella were held over the hole in the roof—then the umbrella handle was very much in the way. This difficulty was solved one day by a stiff gale that carried away the umbrella.

It would all have been more simple without the seat. We would have had it removed, but the men were so pleased with themselves for having thought of it and exhibited it with such pride to all visitors that we hadn't the heart.

The cleanly Japanese never fail to wash on emerging from retirement. This nicety of polite society was not forgotten even on a pirate junk and the captain was always waiting with a dipper of fresh water to pour over our hands.

But though the situation had its ludicrous aspects, the enduring impression we brought away from these experiences was of the everlasting solicitude for our comfort, the unfailing tact, frankness and genuine delicacy of our shipmates.

Japan's Main Street

Much of the Inland Sea is remote and mysterious, but this part is like Main Street. It vies with Tokyo as the industrial and commercial heart of Japan.

Cities stretch continuously along the shore from Osaka, second largest metropolis in the nation, with three million people, to the great port of Kobe, twenty miles away, with a million. We knew that beyond the hills only twenty-eight miles away was million-big Kyoto, for a thousand years the capital.

What a triumvirate are these cities—Osaka building industrial machines, Kyoto fashioning art objects, and Kobe helping to ship these products to all parts of the world. Osaka and Kobe were flattened by war; Kyoto was spared because of its temples and art. Now it would be hard to find in any of them the scars of conflict, except perhaps in the minds of men.

The chimneys of large shipbuilding yards belched a smoky welcome as we entered Kobe harbor and tied up at the American Pier. We were surprised and pleased to find waiting for us a group of officials who drove us around town, took us to the beautiful Mansion Kobe (formerly a luxurious private home, now a hotel) for tea, and to the Hotel Seigaso for an elaborate *sukiyaki* dinner.

From such luxury we returned to the boat to sleep in the fishbin. Exploring the place with a flashlight, I killed a spider and one of those bugs that frequent wet, dark places. However, we counted ourselves fortunate to find no rats or mice.

When my head was on the pillow, my nose was just six inches from the deck above. If I happened to get under a beam, there was only three inches of leeway. We tried to disregard a feeling of claustrophobia and went to sleep. I dreamed I was crawling through places that became smaller and smaller, until I was finally trapped. I came to with a start and raised my head, only to hit the hard deck.

"If you're leaving, you'd better use the hatch," Mary advised sleepily.

"It's hot as Tophet here," I complained.

The captain had said it would be too cold on deck; the Japanese habitually sleep between smotheringly thick quilts in a tightly closed room. Accustomed as most Westerners are to open windows, we found the sea breeze on deck more to our liking.

Blind Leading the Blind

We sailed at sunrise. Kobe's food stores were not yet open, so we would buy something for breakfast at our first landing, the fishing village of Iwaya on Awaji. We had brought along some canned goods for emergencies, but we intended to live off the country for the most part.

But where was Iwaya? A heavy blanket of fog covered the sea. No land was visible except the hills of Kobe behind us.

The captain and Good-Fortune were having an argument, pointing in quite different directions. Presently a fishing boat hove in sight, and we altered our course to come alongside. The captain asked the way, and the fisherman pointed.

We proceeded, but, having failed to bring the pointing finger along with us we were soon lost again. The captain began to look for another fishing boat.

Our boat carried no chart or compass. I had assumed that these hardy seafarers would know their way by a sort of sixth sense. But, after all, they were fishermen, not voyagers. I had to admire the nerve of a captain who would embark so nonchalantly on a hazardous voyage, but I doubted more than ever the suitability of his name, Wide-Margin-of-Safety.

Fortunately, Captain Harada of Kansai Steamship Company had persuaded me to take along a score of detailed charts, each covering a small area of the Sea. I dipped into the hold and brought up a mighty roll of them. Each was some three feet by four feet, and altogether there were enough to carpet most of the deck. I found the chart for this immediate area and called the captain. He tried to understand it, but gave up and looked for another fishing boat.

I rooted out of a suitcase a pocket compass I had thrown in at the last minute, never dreaming that we would actually need it. With charts and compass I took over as navigator. The navigation was far from perfect; destinations seldom appeared where they should have been, and islands often bobbed up without the approval of compass or chart. But at least we did not have to zigzag from boat to boat asking the way.

Thus we innocents abroad blundered our way through the Inland Sea, while Kompira chuckled in his shrine at the foot of the foremast but benevolently diverted our stem whenever we might have struck something.

The morning mist burned away before we reached Iwaya village. The sea was dotted with small boats in which the tentacles of octopuses waved, for this is a famous octopus fishing ground.

The method of catching these eight-armed frights is curious. An earthenware pot is let down at the end of a cord, the other end being made fast to a small buoy. The octopus loves nothing so much as a dark hole and crawls into the pot. If the pot is drawn up gently, the tenant does not realize what is happening until it is too late.

Along the beach of Iwaya, octopuses stretched out by bamboo sticks to dry in the sun looked like kites. We passed them by, asking for food, and were referred back to the octopuses, the only breakfast the village could offer us.

Octopus for Breakfast

We boiled sun-dried octopus over our charcoal brazier on the deck. The tentacles were not bad, once you forgot their similarity to snakes. The suction cups were as crunchy as nuts, but the body was as tough as rubber.

The eyes are supposed to be a great delicacy. They look much like human eyes, and after you swallow them you have the guilty feeling that they are continuing to look at you from the inside.

We sailed a glassy blue sea along the mountainous shore of Awaji to the sizable town of Sumoto. Here welcoming officials took us to see their most notable citizen, an eye-ear-nose-and-throat physician who in his spare time pursues one of Japan's most famous arts. Dr. Tatsuzo Matsutani was introduced as the father of Japanese puppetry. From bamboo and brocade, plaster and paper, he contrived puppets two-thirds life-size. Made mobile by multiple controls, they did almost everything but talk. The remarkable Bunraku theater puppet shows in

Osaka and other great cities have their inspiration in this island port.

So many things move in a complicated Matsutani puppet that one operator is not enough; it takes three or four. They are in full view on the stage, but their black clothing, covering face and body, is supposed to make them invisible. From the point of view of the Japanese spectator, they just aren't there.

Dr. Matsutani insisted that we stay to dinner, lodged us for the night in a room in his hospital, and sent us on our way with a good breakfast, all because "We are grateful for what Americans have done for us. Makasa was a *kamisama* to the Japanese."

"Makasa" is as close as the Japanese tongue can come to MacArthur, and "kamisama" means Mr. God, or Honorable Deity. MacArthur seemed more firmly enshrined in the hearts of Japanese than he was when actually in Japan. When he left, a town official said, "We have lost our basement." He evidently meant foundation.

We stopped at the atoll-like harbor of Yura and also at primitive Nu Island where, in accordance with old custom, a crier was passing through the streets of the fishing village ringing a bell to announce a death. Then we sailed to the city of Tokushima on Shikoku. There three newspaper reporters, one of them a young woman, met us.

Newspaperwomen are rare in Japan, and the kimono this one wore made her seem still more out-of-place. She looked on shyly as the men conducted their interview and, when urged to come forward, retreated so abruptly that she stumbled over an anchor and sat down hard on the deck. Now she was all blushing confusion and would have run away in utter disgrace. Mary gently detained her until she controlled her fit of tears, then gave her an exclusive story "from the woman's angle."

And so to bed on the deck, but not to sleep. A phonograph in a seamen's bar split the welkin with a badly scratched American record of "Silent Night, Holy Night." Whistles blew and stevedores shouted as steamers docked or put to sea. Back and forth along the mole above our ship paraded the policeman delegated to guard us. Not content with patrol duty, he came aboard periodically to wake us up and tell us what good care he was taking of us.

The Whirlpools of Naruto

At Naruto Strait we had the first taste of the perils of the Sea River. Through this bottleneck the current rushes like a mountain torrent. When it meets a tidal rip coming from the opposite direction, the conflicting waters make giant whirlpools that sometimes suck down large ships.

We were advised to circle Naruto Strait by the Ko Naruto (Child Naruto or Little Naruto), a safer passage. But what a pity it would be to miss one of the most dramatic phenomena of the Inland Sea!

At least we could have a look at it from the steamer which takes Japanese tourists to view the spectacle. But when we went aboard, her captain explained at length why he could not go near the whirlpools that day: the sea was too rough, the waves too big.

The ship did roll violently, and a Japan Travel Bureau man who went with us spent the trip on the salon floor. But when we reached the strait the waves miraculously disappeared, the captain changed both his mind and his course, and we steamed into the channel.

It was an eerie sight. For a time the surface about us remained as smooth as glass. Then in a perfectly quiet spot a peculiar boiling began. The water humped itself up into a dome and started to whirl. Faster and faster it spun, a deep pit forming in the center. Then the updraft of a moment ago was replaced by a strong downdraft.

It was easy to imagine the fate of a small boat caught in the centripetal whirl. Some of the pools were fifty feet across, some much larger. Where the outer edge of the whirlpool encountered still water, waves rose sometimes as high as thirty feet.

When a whirlpool began to form dead ahead, our steamer promptly changed course. The edges of the whirling disks caught our bow, and at such moments the ship would not answer her helm but staggered to one side or the other at the mercy of the merry-go-rounds. We did not go through the strait but only skirted it, then returned to Naruto town.

Wide Margin of Risk

A debate took place on the dock. Could *Kompira* sail the strait? Captain Wide-Margin-of-Safety, being an adventurous soul, was inclined to accept a wide margin of risk. Old tars on the waterfront were unanimous in warning him not to challenge the deadly Naruto.

It wasn't just a matter of whirlpools, they said; there were devils under the channel. One of the most persistent of Japanese superstitions is the belief in *kappa*, evil mermen or water goblins who delight in drawing humans down to a watery grave.

The prophets of doom won. It was decided that next morning we would sail the safe passage. Much disappointed, we put up at an inn for the night.

There we met our good angel. Mr. Takehisa, owner of the hotel, is also a civil engineer engaged in the salvage of sunken ships. Having operated often in the turbulent waters of Naruto Strait, he knows the channel as few men do. Of course we could go through Naruto. He himself would pilot us.

Even with an able guide it was a dizzying experience. The current tears through the mile-wide passage at from eight to ten knots, a speed greater than that of many river rapids. The pilot selected a time when the outcoming tide should have nearly spent itself. However, as we entered the strait, we seemed to be looking up a staircase. Mr. Takehisa told us that the water is often five feet higher at one end of the strait than at the other.

Powered only by the engine, we began to weave among the whirlpools. We were surrounded by holes and water hills. Carefully we avoided the pits, but allowed the hills to crash against the prow and drench us with spray. The surface rose before us in different levels like great steps. Some plateaus of water were higher than our deck.

The boat staggered like a drunken man as the whirling currents caught her, now on one bow, now on the other. Crosscurrents rushed in from unexpected angles. She heeled so far to port that everything on deck began to slide, and I, taking pictures, had to embrace a mast. Then as suddenly she lurched far over to starboard.

With all this frenzied movement it was odd to hear the pilot say, "We're not moving." Taking a sight across trees on shore, I could see that we were making no progress. The top speed of the engine was six miles an hour. Evidently a six-mile-an-hour current was holding us stationary.

Narrow Escape

Uncle Good-Fortune ran up a sail. This was nearly our undoing. A whirl of water swung the ship broadside. With the current pressing one way against the hull, and the wind the opposite way against the sail, our lee rail sank deep under water. A few inches more, and the shallow-draft, keelless ship would certainly have capsized.

Uncle hastily pulled down the sail. We turned and fled ignominiously with the tide.

When the tide changed, we tried again and got through. Once when our craft seemed certain to be hauled down by the kappa, I had the distressing thought that our pilot earned his living by salvaging sunken ships. Had he diabolically plotted to sink *Kompira* so he could raise her? If so, I thought, he calculated without our sea god, for we came through safe and drew in to a cove to put the pilot ashore. Then he proved his good intentions by refusing payment for his services.

"Any time you want to do it again," he said cheerfully, "let me know."

"Thank you," I said. "Once is enough."

Joys of a Japanese Inn

We sailed across stormy open water to another large island, Shodo. Here at the town of Tonosho officials set a valuable precedent. Ignoring our protestations that the deck of *Kompira* made a comfortable bed, they insisted we spend the night at the town's expense in a delightful seashore inn.

Thereafter our captain, upon arrival at a new port, would fill officials' ears with the story of the wonderful treatment we had been accorded in the last port. The eyes of the officials would grow round, and one could see the determination forming in their minds that they were not going to be outdone.

The mayor's car would be requisitioned to take us about, and often the mayor along with it, and we would be lodged at the best inn, entertained at an official dinner lasting as long as three hours, and tucked in for the night.

The captain's motives in instigating these plots were not altogether altruistic. He always managed to get himself invited as well. In some ways the Japanese are undemocratic; yet there is a camaraderie between high and low that would seem strange in America. This young fisherman's best shirt was always soiled, and he was usually coatless and always tieless; yet he was readily included in the dinner parties, expressed himself freely to high officials, and was treated as an equal by them.

One expects to find excellent inns in the large cities, of which there are many along both shores of the Inland Sea. But nearly every town, too, has a well-appointed inn.

We would remove our shoes in the vestibule, put on soft slippers, and be led through shining corridors to an artistic room carpeted with straw mats. The chief feature of the room was always the *tokonoma*, or sacred alcove, occupied by a beautifully designed hanging scroll and a flower arrangement. Sometimes there were chairs, but usually one sat on the floor. This was no hardship, except at a three-hour dinner. Meals were served in the room on an ankle-high table. There is no public dining room in a Japanese inn.

At bedtime the maid spreads out soft, thick quilts—eight inches too short for a tall Westerner—and supplies guests with a sack of oats as a pillow.

The crowning joy of the day is the hot bath in water three feet deep. The tub is sometimes as big as a swimming pool. A Japanese bath is the most nearly perfect bathing device on this planet since the baths of Caracalla of ancient Rome.

Charm of the Japanese Garden

The gardens of these inns are often places of great charm and beauty, and nearly every town has its public park, quite unlike anything of the sort in Western lands. The Japanese garden depends much upon irregular outlines, rocks, stone lanterns, arched bridges.

It tries to achieve an effect of cultivated wildness, or careful naturalness. A woodland glade may be so naturally covered with moss that one never dreams that every bit of it was planted by hand. Hillocks look natural, though in many cases they are manmade. There is usually no straight path in a Japanese garden.

Nor are there beds of flowers in the Western sense. In fact, flowers are seldom seen, except where they grow in seeming naturalness in the woods or on the edge of a stream.

One rarely finds a garden in Japan without water. It may be a large lake; it may be a small pool; it may be only a waterfall or brook; but water there should be to satisfy the Japanese love of beauty. About the water there are always rocks, for Japanese garden designers believe in them. Many rocks in the old gardens were donated by feudal lords.

Enchanted Islands

The myriad islands of the Sea River were of all shapes and sizes, but alike in one particular—they were all up and down. We did not see one flat island in our entire voyage. Some rise to a height of several thousand feet. Everywhere our hosts were determined to take us to the highest peak in the vicinity. We did more climbing in six weeks in Japan than in six years in California.

Japan crowds a population of 96,000,000 into a land the size of Montana, which has 675,000. So even the islands of the Inland Sea have a considerable population, and the island mountainsides are often cultivated to the very top.

We think of rice as Japan's staff of life. So it is on the mainland, but on the islands sweet potatoes and fish are the staples. Here sweet potato vines will cling to any slope.

Many an island is too abrupt and rugged to do anything with except perhaps crown with a temple. Many are just gaunt, towering rocks. Although several hundred thousand people live on the islands of the Inland Sea, scores of charming islets are uninhabited, enchanted spots with beaches and gnarled aged pines, ideal places to step ashore, broil fish over a campfire, have a picnic, and spend a night.

The blueness of this enchanted world amazed us. The sky was a porcelain blue, the sea was an exquisite blue-green so clear that one could look down into it to great depths, and the boat seemed at times to be floating in air. The islands, especially in the morning, were wrapped in a soft blue haze.

The people of this dream world are not greatly affected by changes taking place on the mainland. Nevertheless, some major reforms have reached them.

The Occupation's land reform broke up large holdings and enabled tenant serfs to buy land for the first time. However, they choose to ignore the new law which requires that a man's land, upon his death, shall be divided equally among his children. Even on the mainland the average farm is only about two and a half acres; on the islands it is much smaller. To divide it into several still smaller farms would mean that each heir would get only "a cat's forehead," to use the Japanese phrase. So the islanders stick to inheritance by the eldest son. The other sons must leave home and make a new life for themselves.

To the islanders, fishing is of top importance. It is equally important to Japan as a whole. Eighty-five percent of Japan's animal proteins come from fish. Japan leads the world in fisheries production. In a representative postwar year, Japan produced almost three million metric tons of fish, the United States 2.5 million, the U.S.S.R. two million, and the United Kingdom and Norway 1.1 million each.

The motorized fishing boat is common, and yet the age of sail has not vanished on the Inland Sea. Near Tomo we counted twenty-eight sails within view at one time.

But the Inland Sea has many other industries besides fishing. The city of Marugame makes fans. Imabari makes towels. Niihama mines and refines copper.

Skyscraper Upside Down

I was taken by tunnel two miles inside the mountain of the Besshi mine. It is like a skyscraper standing on its head; the floor at the top is called the first, while the newest and lowest level deep in the heart of the mountain is the twentieth. The mine contains many miles of tunnels, and they are being extended at the rate of four miles a year.

In an island world of fishing villages with humble houses it was astonishing to come upon a sample of architecture that out-

Nikkos the great shrine of Nikko in color and splendor. It is the magnificent temple of Kojoji on the island of Ikuchi. The many sanctuaries are gay, almost giddy, brilliantly decked out in red, blue, white, silver and gold. The temple is so modern that it was recently upset by a strike of its priests.

Roosters with Twenty-foot Tails

To see a curious art of Shikoku, we journeyed overland to Kochi. Here is the place for raising *onagadori*, or so-called "long-tailed fowls." I call it an art rather than an industry because a bird with tail coverts twenty feet long is not of great utilitarian value, nor is it intended to be. The breeders of such birds are artists. I found that the price of a fowl depends upon the length of the feathers, which are valued at about two dollars a foot.

In olden times the feathers adorned tops of samurai lances in the processions of the feudal chiefs.

Only the cocks have long tail coverts; the hens are quite ordinary. The average growth of the tail is two and a half feet a year, and the longest tail on record measured twenty-four feet. The bird is kept in a tall, narrow box, its tail draped over a hanger, though on Honshu Island it is sometimes coiled up and wrapped in cloth. Once in three days it is taken out for a ten-minute walk. Someone must walk behind it, carrying the "train."

Some of the most famous of Japan's legends have to do with the islands and bays of the Inland Sea. There is the story of Momotaro that every Japanese child knows. An elderly couple who longed to have a child one day opened a peach and out stepped a baby boy. They called him Momotaro, Peach Boy. We remembered his story when we landed on Megi Island (Oniga Shima), the Isle of Devils, for when Momotaro grew up to be a mighty warrior he came to this island and conquered all the devils.

We were told of an island called Contrary because legend has it that disobedient children were sent there. Even today mothers warn their children, "Be good, or I'll send you to Contrary Island." During our stay in Japan the newspapers reported that two families had gone to court, each claiming to own Contrary Island because an ancestor had been sent there for being a bad boy. Another island in the Inland Sea goes by the name of All-the-Saints-Got-Drunk (Sensui).

Japanese Rip Van Winkle

In one of the deepest spots of the Inland Sea we looked down to what legend glamorizes as the sea king's palace. It looks like a palace, although it is nothing but an immense rock with many openings through which swim colored fish. It plays a part in the famous story of Urashima, the Japanese Rip Van Winkle.

Urashima, a fisher boy, was borne on the back of a friendly tortoise down to the palace of the sea king. There he met the king's daughter, married her, and lived with her for three dreamlike years. Then he longed to visit his native village. His princess gave him a jewel case as a remembrance of their love, but told him not to open it.

Returning to his village, he found everything changed. The houses were different, the people were strangers. Perplexed, he thought of his jewel case, the only friendly thing he had. He opened it, and a cloud of purple smoke came out. His black hair turned white, his youthful limbs withered, and he crumbled to dust on the beach—for three years in the sea king's palace were equal to three hundred on land!

Competing for honors with the king of the sea bottom was our sea god, Kompira, to whose shrine we climbed by eight hundred exhausting steps up the mount of Kotohira on Shikoku. Thousands of pilgrims, mostly grateful seamen, come here every year. One of the buildings of the temple is filled with models of ships supposed to have been saved from disaster by the friendly intervention of this god. Also there were numerous ships' shrines, and after our trip was finished Wide-Margin-of-Safety made a special pilgrimage to place our *Kompira* shrine among them.

Day by day and week after week we plied back and forth through fairyland, crossing and recrossing from one mainland shore to the other and circumnavigating the islands. We wished it would never end, except that at times a diet of raw fish,

seaweed, bean curd, squid, tea and rice becomes a little tire-
some. After Naruto we touched at many places and passed
through the strait of many wrecks, Kurushima. Its whirlpools
reminded us dramatically of Edgar Allan Poe's description of
the Maelstrom. Now the islands grew immense, a single bay of
one of them looking as large as New York Harbor.

Kompira *Cracks a Mast*

In Hiroshima the mayor showed us the Industrial Exhibition
Hall that is being preserved in its wrecked state as a memorial
of the world's first atom bomb attack; then he took us to the
roof of the City Hall to see how remarkably his city has been
rebuilt. Even its ancient castle has been restored, although the
new one is a temporary wood-and-plaster replica erected as a
feature of a sports fair in 1951. From a distance it looks very
much like the real thing.

Incidentally, there are many real castles left about the Inland
Sea dating from feudal times. Fortunately they came through
the war unscathed. Among the most picturesque are those of
Osaka, Himeji, Sumoto, Marugame and Matsuyama. They contrast with their modern settings, in which the only visible reminder of former times is an occasional kimono.

Though in westernized Tokyo the kimono has almost disappeared, it persists in and about the Inland Sea. There the
women scarcely know that they have been "emancipated,"
though they are aware of woman suffrage and turn out in numbers at the polls.

But in the home women continue their traditional role and
wear the kimono, although they object to its growing expense.
The eleven-foot *obi*, or sash, that goes round and round and
ties in a gorgeous bow behind is often superbly embroidered
and may cost more than an American woman's entire outfit.
Most stunning and expensive of all is the wedding costume—so
expensive, in fact, that most brides rent it, unless they use their
mother's or grandmother's.

We sailed on to the island of Itsuku (popularly Miyajima),
which the Japanese count as one of the most beautiful spots in
Japan. Here the well-known *torii*, Shinto sacred gate, stands in

the sea some five hundred feet from shore. Every fifty years or
so it must be reconditioned; we were lucky enough to arrive
just after it had been repainted.

A priest of the temple told us the torii was so high that *Kompira* could sail under it. Wide-Margin-of-Safety, in a narrow
moment, decided to try it.

The foremast struck the lower beam, and a shower of vermilion splinters fell on the deck. The mast bent and cracked omi-
nously and seemed about to break in two. The steel stay from
the peak of the mast to the bowsprit broke and whipped about,
lashing everyone who came within reach. The engine was
hastily reversed, and *Kompira* backed out.

The priest, to make amends for his poor advice, put on a
sacred performance of gorgeously costumed temple dancers for
our benefit.

Glory of the Maples

Even more impressive were the maples, for it was now October, the beginning of one of Japan's two most colorful
seasons, the other being the time of cherry blossoms. During
October and November schools throughout Japan organize expeditions to Itsuku, and as many as five thousand children a
day come to see the maples. They picnic under the trees, romp
about wildly, but rarely injure a tree or pick a leaf except from
the ground.

Japanese maple leaves, very small and deeply indented, look
much like stars. Their colors are breathtaking. Down Maple
Valley (Momiji-dani) flows a picturesque brook overhung with
hundreds of brilliant maples that are almost translucent as the
sun shines through them.

We could view them in peace and quiet on Itsuku, for no
wheeled vehicle of any kind is allowed lest its noise frighten the
sacred deer. Since the entire island is considered sacred, there
are many other restrictions. Formerly even birth and death
were not allowed, unless they happened without warning. Ex-
pectant mothers and dying folk were required to go to the mainland. Now people may be born or die there, but the dead must
be taken to the mainland for burial.

Typhoon Ruth

Japan suffers much from typhoons. "Typhoon Margie" had struck shortly before our junk sailed. Now "Typhoon Ruth" was reported on the way north from the Philippines.

Our captain did not take the report too seriously. About twenty typhoons a year scourge the western Pacific. They head toward Japan but most of them veer off before they reach it. Wide-Margin put an extra offering of fish and rice before the sea god and took a chance.

The typhoon caught us in the widest part of the Inland Sea, so wide that in two directions land could not be seen.

The first warning was a deathly calm. We floated on a surface as smooth as a pond. The air was oppressively hot. It lay against the face like a suffocating blanket. The sun was fogged and the blue sky disappeared behind a ghastly white pall, the typical "typhoon sky." A spiritless drizzle of rain began to fall. It was a sort of hot steam rather than rain.

The captain stuck his oil-spotted face up out of the engine hole. He looked at sea and sky and then at me. His manner was apologetic as if this were all his fault.

"Typhoon Ruth!" he said unhappily.

"Do you think we can make Beppu?"

He peered ahead and shrugged. He might well shrug for there was nothing to be seen ahead. Even the horizon had been blotted out. Every moment the sky was growing darker. One could have believed that the time was twilight instead of mid-morning.

I studied the chart and the poor little compass. We could rely only on the motor. The sails were useless without wind. With wind we might be even worse off for it would not be the sort of wind a sailor would choose.

"Better put back," I suggested.

Good-Fortune-in-Autumn pushed the tiller hard over and we turned toward the shore we had left. It was some two miles away. We could not hope to get back to the port where we had spent the night. No other ports were indicated on the chart. We should simply have to take a chance of finding a protecting bay in the savage precipitous coast.

Still we were smothered in the breathless calm disturbed only by our own motion. The darkness thickened.

"There it comes!" cried Literature-Pursuing-Sixth-Son, staring to starboard.

A smooth, rounded wave was coming our way. There was no crest on it. Not a ripple disturbed its surface. Not a breath of wind accompanied it. It swept under the *Kompira* and the ship rolled heavily.

Then came another wave, as smooth and windless as the first, but larger. Then another, still larger. Three, the usual number. They are the silent heralds of the storm. They roll from the scene of commotion into the region of ominous calm. Nature had given us fair warning; now she allowed us a moment for silent prayer before the first blast.

We were ready, or hoped we were. The sails were tight furled and the mainmast down. The dinghy had been double lashed to the deck and so had the oil barrels. A protective loop of rope had even been thrown over the benjo.

We could dimly make out a dent in the shoreline, a small bay backed by rocky precipices. A schooner was already huddled within its protecting arms. A few minutes more, and we would make it.

Vain hope. We were still half a mile out when Ruth struck. She came aboard all in a rush, spitting, shrieking, ripping up the calm surface into steep waves as if the sea had been dynamited. The wind fell upon us like a stone wall. We flattened ourselves upon the deck and clung to the ringbolts. It seemed that all the joints in the ship were rattling loose. Our jaws rattled, our brains rattled.

Good-Fortune stuck to the tiller, his cap blown away, his hair standing out stiffly, his eyes slitted down against the wind.

Suddenly the gale dropped to a breeze. This was not because the typhoon was diminishing, but we were getting into the shelter of the mountain range. The deck leveled out and we made better time.

Dangerous Haven

We slid into the bay and were relieved and disappointed. Relieved, because it was a haven of rest, free of waves and wind.

The mountain range towering beside us cut off the storm, which screamed across the peaks far above and out to the sea we had just left.

But we were disappointed because the bay had no curving horns to serve as breakwaters. It was wide open to the sea. This did not matter in the least so long as the wind was offshore.

But the one thing that was predictable about unpredictable Ruth was that she would change. I had been in typhoons before and of course they were an old story to our crew. I understood their concern as they studied our exposed position and the savage rocks along the shore.

Yasuhiro gazed at me sadly. *"Ikemasen!"* (It won't do!)

The captain of the schooner hailed us. The merits of the anchorage were argued between ships. There was a sharp difference of opinion. The schooner's crew was afraid of the sea, Yasuhiro was afraid of the bay. (I was afraid of both.)

"They don't understand how a typhoon works," our captain said bitterly when he had failed to convince them of the danger of staying in the bay.

A typhoon is a revolving storm. It is like a whirlpool, but a gigantic one, often a hundred miles in diameter. The wind circles counterclockwise in the northern hemisphere, clockwise below the equator. This wind may have a velocity of 150 miles an hour. The entire whirl moves forward, but slowly, at the rate of about twelve miles an hour.

The wind over our bay was from the south. But since it was a circling wind and the circle was moving forward, we were quite likely later to get the same wind from the north. Then it would mean great waves in our unprotected bay and almost certain destruction on the rocks.

As the schooner captain saw us preparing to depart he summed up his opinion of our captain in one roaring word.

"Baka!" (Fool!)

It is the strongest expletive in Japanese, the nearest thing to a curse that this polite language knows.

With it ringing in our ears and in our consciences—for he might be right at that!—we powered out of the bay. As we left the shelter of the range the wind began to reach down to us, first in gentle puffs, then more and more violently. Soon these spasms became terrific and we were whipped by the wind, deafened by its roar, drenched with spray, thinking regretfully of the peace we had just left.

The crew came forward with lines and proceeded to lash Mary to the foremast. I tied up to the lowered mainmast, Literature looped himself to the deck, Good-Fortune to the tiller, while the captain went below to coax every ounce of power from the engine.

The pressure of the air squeezed the breath out of us. It was necessary to turn one's face away from the wind to breathe and even then it was difficult, for the air currents moving past the head on both sides made a vacuum about the nose. The spray was blown back in the form of flying needles that cut into exposed flesh. The birds and insects were gone. The sun was gone and we were wrapped in dark blankets.

I had never known such a wind. It was later reported to have varied between one hundred and two hundred miles an hour. On the Beaufort scale it registered a reading of twelve. The force of the average strong gale is six. Now one could understand the derivation of the word typhoon—from the Chinese *taifung*, Great Wind.

The engine and rudder kept the ship's nose in the wind, but we were being relentlessly pushed back toward the shore we had left. If this continued we might just as well have stayed in the bay and gone to the devil all at once rather than by degrees.

Back, back we went. Now I could see the bay. Where was the schooner? For a time I could not make her out. Then when the wrack lifted momentarily she stood out clearly.

Wreck of the Schooner

She was upside down on the rocks with her two masts stuck out akimbo and tons upon tons of water thundering over her hull. Already half the strakes were torn off her counter. With good luck, the crew should have escaped to shore, but their ship would never ride again.

It gave us no satisfaction to see the wreck, for were we not hellbent to the same fate? Ruthless Ruth, have pity! Remember that typhoons are never consistent. Sea god, come out and command your unruly waters! The shrine at the foot of the foremast was half blown away. Had Kompira gone too?

Now, to add to our woes, came rain. Not rain, but a sea from the sky. It came down in solid masses, unbelievable weights of water pounding like pile drivers upon our shoulders. Typhoon Ruth delivered more rain in a day than Japan had received all the rest of the year.

The rain cut off all view of the shore. We were completely shut in. Our only guide was the wind and Uncle kept the ship's nose pointed into it.

When the wrack cleared for a moment Good-Fortune shouted with joy. I opened my wind-sealed eyes and looked for the shore. It was not where it had been. Instead of lying behind us it was now on our port beam.

The shore had not changed but the wind had. The typhoon had crazily altered its path. Now the gale was coming to us straight out of the great bay of Beppu, our destination. If the wind pushed us backward it did not matter too much—there was plenty of sea room behind us.

But the heavy rain seemed to have shaken the wind's confidence. It still blew fiercely but we managed for an hour to hold our own against it, and then to make some headway. As we neared Beppu the mountains behind the city gradually cut the force of the wind. Five more toilsome hours, and we pulled into the harbor lined by the hotels of this famous hot spring resort.

The two uncles stayed aboard to baby the ship through a bad night, the captain went to a Japanese inn, and we repaired to the home of the Shavers, American missionaires, in the nearby town of Oita. The storm again changed its course, descended with full fury upon Oita and Beppu, shook the big two-story frame house and gave the anxious missionaries not one wink of sleep all night. I am ashamed to say that we slept solidly through to late morning.

In bright sunshine we rode back to Beppu. The shore road, a magnificent stretch of cement highway and stone seawall, had been ripped up in a hundred or more places by the force of the waves. Power poles were at all angles. Many houses had been battered to bits by the waves or carried away by the wind.

In Beppu the streets near the waterfront were full of debris. Even whole roofs barred the way. About the ruins the indefatigable Japanese were as busy as ants, already rebuilding. By afternoon the streets were cleared so that traffic could get through. The process of reconstructing hundreds of ruined homes was already underway.

A Paradise of Hells

Beppu attracts visitors because of its delectable climate and its dramatic hells. The infernal regions lie directly beneath. Geysers of steam spout from volcanic fires under the city.

Every house has boiling hot water every minute of the day and night without the cost of a penny for heating, taps may be left running continually without waste, bathtubs overflow twelve hours a day and meals are cooked without fuel.

The boiling, grumbling, ever-flowing *solfataras* of Japan's greatest hot spring resort cover twenty square miles. Hot springs even bubble up through the floor of the bay and have a unique effect upon the fish population. The Black Current which washes the eastern shore of Japan comes from the equator loaded with tropical fish, but most of them soon die in the chilly northern waters. The fortunate ones that happen to be carried into Beppu Bay make themselves quite at home and the waters here are filled with brilliantly colored immigrants from the South Seas.

All Beppu sputters with hot springs. Growling, rumbling, hissing or screaming, these outbursts from the jaws of the earth are well called *jigoku*, hells. They have such picturesque names as Bloody Pond Hell, White Pond Hell, Gold Dragon Hell, Green Hell, Thunder Hell, Devil's Mountain Hell.

Hot water irrigates the rice fields. In greenhouses it maintains a perpetual summer and makes possible swiftly matured muskmelons, watermelons, green peas, cucumbers and tomatoes in midwinter. Here muskmelons ripen in thirty or forty days. A system of pipes carries hot water through twenty greenhouses. The temperature of the water as it enters the system is 180° F. After circulating through the twenty conservatories it still has a temperature of 150° F.

Experiments of engineers in using volcanic steam to generate electricity have led to ambitious plans financed by the government to make use, here and elsewhere in Japan, of the volcanic boiler upon which Japan rests. When the program is fully worked out it is expected that the total output of electricity from volcano-powered turbines will be four billion kilowatts per year. To generate this amount of electricity it is now necessary to burn four million tons of coal.

The Sea River Finds the Ocean

Another long jump across the sea, and we slept on deck in the harbor of Mitajiri. Then next morning the captain came forward, all excited, saying, "The end of the Inland Sea!" Ahead the main islands of Kyushu and Honshu faced each other across the Strait of Shimonoseki. Through this and the broad Bungo Strait, the Inland Sea delivers the waters of seventeen rivers to the Pacific.

We passed through the boiling tide rips of the strait, too busy packing to remember that the U.S. Hydrographic Office's *Sailing Directions for Japan* lists numerous wrecks in this vicinity and describes it as "the most difficult place to navigate in the Inland Sea." We fairly flew through with the tide to come to anchor in Moji's little harbor.

By force of habit we climbed a mountain to enjoy a final view of the Inland Sea. Its blue islands gradually turned melancholy as the sun neared the horizon. Its many capes and bays, its far reaches and white clouds, took on the appearance of an oil painting as the sun sank.

We came down to stand on the deck of *Kompira* one last time to enjoy the afterglow. Tomorrow we would take the train, while our companions sailed back to Kanonji.

Before Kompira's shrine we shared with them a last meal of rice and fish, a rather sad and silent meal, for in these six weeks we had come to have respect and affection for Wide-Margin-of-Safety, Good-Fortune-in-Autumn and Literature-Pursuing-Sixth-Son.

8

The Vale of Kashmir

FABULOUS. Unreal. A dream. We'll wake up and laugh tomorrow morning.

What a fantasy—a floating palace of seven rooms plus foredeck, afterdeck and sundeck, all fresh and new, built only three months ago, furnished as beautifully as any motel suite in Florida, paneled in unpainted deodar as fragrant as sandalwood, ceilinged with superb marquetry in Kashmir designs, anchored in a field of lotus with lush blooms a foot wide, on a mirror lake bound in by Himalayan ranges stretching up to the greatest heights ever scaled by man.

On a nearer peak, a storybook castle, on another the maharajah's palace, on another a dome-topped Hindu temple illuminated at night.

Luxury Afloat

But that's not the half of it. Along with the hundred-foot, two-hundred-ton houseboat go a *shikara* which is a canopied, cushioned craft some twenty-five feet long manned by a crew of three with heart-shaped paddles—this for making journeys down the lakes and rivers, and always at the door of the houseboat ready for service day or night—also a small *shallop* or dugout canoe for self-paddling when we need exercise or for play while swimming—also a kitchen boat where our delicious meals are prepared and the men sleep.

There are five men on duty, Ramzan Goroo who owns this and four other houseboats, his father Haji Karima Goroo who, as his title indicates, has been to Mecca and serves here as cook, Rasool who is Ramzan's cousin and does the housekeeping, waits on table, and names the trees and birds on shikara trips, and two paddlers.

And it doesn't take a maharajah's fortune to pay for all this. The houseboat along with kitchen boat and shallop and staff of three and all meals for two persons costs forty-eight rupees ($10) a day. The shikara and two boatmen add six rupees a day ($1.25).

And this is for a "Special Class" houseboat. The prices for First Class, Second, Third and Fourth are progressively lower.

As a matter of course there are electric lights (one in a camel's tummy!), electric fans (air conditioning is furnished by the altitude, 5,200 feet), complete bath with running water, a well-stocked library, hand-carved furniture, and oil paintings on the walls.

The name of the houseboat is *Lone Star*. Ramzan's other houseboats are the *California*, the *Vanessa*, *Tahiti*, and *Snowbird*.

But more intriguing than any of these is the name of the Cleopatra barge, the cushioned shikara. The inscription on its prow reads, "ABODE OF PEACE, Spring Seats, Fast Speed."

The Original Shangri-La

The emperors began it. More than a thousand years ago Kashmir became the summer capital of India. Royalty and nobility fled the steaming monsoons of the low country to this mile-high haven of coolness and crystal air refrigerated by eternal snows. It inspired the Emperor Jahangir to write a poem with the refrain:

"If there is heaven upon earth, it is this, it is this, it is this."

The mighty Akbar called it lovingly, "my private garden." As another Mogul emperor lay dying he was asked, "Is there anything Your Majesty desires?"

With a plaintive sigh, he replied, "Only Kashmir."

The British occupying India two centuries ago were not slow to appreciate Kashmir. Every summer they migrated en masse to the "Rooftop of the World." They really had little choice, for as a health resort Kashmir has no rival in India or, for that matter, in all of Southeast Asia.

It was they who developed the delightful custom of houseboat living. Their enthusiasm equaled that of the Moguls. Irish poet, Thomas Moore, sang the praises of Kashmir and British author, James Hilton, describing his imaginary Shangri-La hidden away from the world among Himalayan peaks, was dreaming of this secluded vale.

When the British pulled out of India, three hundred plush houseboats lay idle. But not for long. In the general affluence following World War II some British returned, supplemented by many Continentals. Now Americans in growing numbers are discovering Kashmir.

The Shutaway Land

It is not too easy of access. There is no railroad. A road exists but it must clamber over nine-thousand-foot Banihal Pass and the journey takes days.

The easiest way to reach Kashmir is by plane from Delhi. Even this is none too certain. Time and again the plane approaches Banihal only to find the pass blocked with cloud, whereupon it turns about and flies back to Delhi. And you get no refund.

But luck and fair weather favored us and we soared over the pass to get our first view of one of the most ravishing scenes a tired old earth can offer.

The gaunt, gray Himalayas crowned with snow and gleaming with glaciers completely encircled a valley so incredibly green that it must surely have been painted just that morning.

The green was embroidered with the silver threads of dozens of streams, canals and sinuous lakes, turning the whole into a sort of Himalayan Venice. As substitute for the Grand Canal, the broad Jhelum River coursed down the center of the valley, through the templed city of Srinagar, through farmland and woodland and lovely lake after lake on its way to join the mighty Indus.

The Jhelum is the presiding genius of the valley. Without it there would be no Vale of Kashmir. The river and its snow-fed tributaries turn what normally would have been a desolate waste of rocks and gravel into a smiling paradise twenty-five miles wide, eighty-five long. The girdle of mountains is complete except for a narrow canyon to allow the escape of the Jhelum.

The mountains to the north are particularly impressive—and should be since they are the world's highest. Nothing in the range to the north stands at less than eighteen thousand feet. Nanga Parbat climbs to 26,660 feet, Godwin Austin to 28,-500, while Everest tops the entire planet with 29,141. Just over the wall is Tibet.

Hard Life of the Explorer

Our houseboat was moored on Dal Lake whose waters, bubbling up from a thousand springs in the lake bed, flow out into the Jhelum.

We lost no time in commandeering the shikara for an exploration of the lake. We sat in maharajic comfort in our floating palanquin, legs stretched out before us on divan-length cushions, with more cushions behind us, more on each side, thatch canopy above, and curtains to be drawn at will against sun or wind. And a guilty feeling in our hearts for this unearned ease.

Behind us two men paddled while a third sang softly to the accompaniment of a stringed instrument called a *sarangi*.

In front of us, perched in the bow, was our English-maltreating guide, Rasool, who made up for any language deficiency with a charming personality and no end of information.

We plowed through beds of lotus with their magnificent foot-wide pink-and-white flowers and three-foot leaves, through squat contented water lilies and tall swaying reeds as graceful as young girls, under a sky so clear it seemed no sky at all, and over open stretches of water so smooth that they consisted merely of snow-capped mountains upside down.

Objects at a distance were carved out in finest detail. It was as if a magnifying glass were held up to Nature. The air had a tingling, tonic quality. The tourist folder had called the weather of Kashmir "ecstatic" and this time the brochure writer did not exaggerate. No wonder many Kashmiri live to be a hundred.

Other shikaras drifted by, their names neatly displayed: *Dancing Girl, Spring Rose, Kashmir Glory, Rock 'n' Roll,* and one with the rather mystifying moniker, *Doings on Full Spring Seats.*

When the sarangist finishes his song there is no sound but the dip of paddles and the swooping swoosh of orange-breasted, blue-backed kingfishers.

No roar of motors. In a far corner of the lake there are said to be two motorboats to tow water skiers but they are strictly confined to that area. With this exception, the tranquillity of the lake is not violated. We never see or hear a motor. A lake without speedboats—what a blessing! Truly an "abode of peace."

Floating Gardens

Now an odd sight—a floating garden evidently strong enough to support the man and woman who are poling it across the lake. We turn to Rasool for an explanation.

"They'll tie it up to the shore near their house," he says (I edit his English a bit), "and grow vegetables on it—tomatoes, pumpkins, melons. Many farmers around the lake do this. A good way to make their little farms larger—just add some floating gardens."

"But where do they get them?"

"In any bay or canal. Some water weeds grow without rooting to the bottom. They tangle together and make a solid mass floating on the water. Dirt blows in on them, grass takes root in the dirt, and there you have it. It's generally attached to the bank. All a man need do is to cut it free of the bank and take it away. When he gets it to his own place he stakes it to the bottom with poles and plants on it."

"Does it last?"

"Only for about ten years. Then it rots and sinks. Or a storm may blow it away. If the farmer doesn't want this to happen he can keep piling dirt on it each year until it rests on the bottom and becomes a permanent part of his farm. That's what we did."

"You? Where?"

"The strip of land your houseboat is moored to. It runs from the shore about two hundred feet out into the lake. It was just a floating garden we cut loose in one of these canals. We anchored it to our own land, piled lake weed on it until it sank to the bottom, then piled earth on the weeds, then planted willows so their roots would bind the whole thing together. Now it's solid land and makes a good mooring place for the boat."

Shalimar

We round a point and come suddenly upon paradise—a magnificent garden stretching back from the lake to the foot of towering cliffs.

"Shalimar," says Rasool.

The first lines of Laurence Hope's *Kashmiri Song* run through the mind:

> *Pale hands I loved beside the Shalimar,*
> *Where are you now who lies beneath your spell?*

And as our shikara brushes through waterborne flowers to reach the shore, we can appreciate those other two beautiful lines:

> *Pale hands, pink-tipped, like lotus buds that float*
> *On those cool waters where we used to dwell . . .*

The gardens of Shalimar were laid out by the Emperor Jahangir in 1619, as an "abode of love" for his queen, Nur Jahan. Our "Abode of Peace" pauses at the "abode of love" long enough for us to walk up through the garden which is still maintained in perfection after three and a half centuries.

A small river pours down the precipice and leaps and laughs its way through the garden, dropping from terrace to terrace and bursting now and then into dozens of iridescent fountains. The stream plunges into a beautiful structure with pillars of polished black marble and comes out the other side. More than three centuries before Californian water-lovers conceived of the idea of using pools, fountains and cascades within the house, Shalimar presented the spectacle of a waterfall pouring from a palace.

A gardener adorns the waterfall with lotus blossoms cunningly inserted in cracks of the rock behind the fall.

Flowers abound. There are orchards, some in bloom, some in fruit. Dozens of gorgeous hoopoes stalk over the close-clipped grass. Men evidently engaged for their raucous voices shout the birds away from the fruit trees.

Over all stand the majestic chinar trees, like sycamores but on a far grander scale, their leaves as big as parasols and their trunks from twenty feet to sixty feet in circumference. Their foliage is now a brilliant green and in autumn will turn to a blazing vermilion.

The Saint Nur-ud-din when invited to visit Shalimar refused, saying, "If I look upon Shalimar, I shall not relish Paradise hereafter."

We paddle on to visit other glorious gardens, "The Garden of the Breeze," laid out by the Emperor Akbar, the "Garden of Pleasure" with its fountains falling over ten terraces and the "Royal Spring" designed by that master architect the Emperor Shah Jahan, the same who erected what is perhaps the most beautiful structure on earth, the Taj Mahal.

Watery Main Street

Quite a different Kashmir comes to view as we make a journey of a few days down the Jhelum. This time our shikara carries six boatmen because although the trip down is easy enough it will be stiff work coming back against the current.

The river is the main street of Srinagar. Fantastic six-story houses abounding in lattices, balconies, turrets, towers perched on other towers, lean precariously over the flowing avenue.

The buildings are wedged too close together to allow for flower gardens, but the Kashmiri must have flowers, so they grow them on the roof. The roofs must be steep-angled because of winter snows, but despite this difficulty they have been laboriously bedded down with good soil, painstakingly planted, and now they blaze with flowers of all colors.

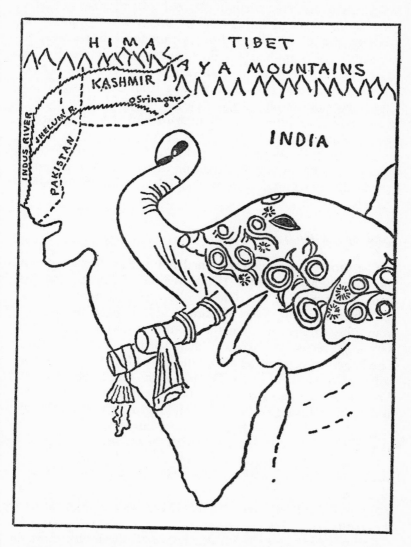

Flights of stone steps lead from these apartment houses down to the water's edge for those who want to wash clothes or babies, or board the water taxis.

Twenty thousand residents of Srinagar prefer to live afloat rather than ashore. The river and ramifying canals are lined with *doongas*, like our houseboat but plain, usually dingy.

These are far from airtight, Rasool tells us, and the wind goes in one side and comes out the other. This supplies adequate ventilation in summer but a bit too much in winter. The standard heating appliance in doongas as well as houses is a fire basket, called *kangri*, an earthenware pot covered with wicker, filled with glowing charcoal, and hung from the ceiling. When anyone goes out, he takes a fire basket under his very voluminous clothing and carries it about with him at peril of fire to the clothing. The portable heat is necessary since the winter temperature goes down sometimes to 40° below zero Fahrenheit. The water turns to ice, freezing in the doongas, and snow may be three or four feet deep. People get about on snowshoes and skis.

Land of the Gods

The procession of flower-topped houses is interrupted now and then by a picturesque Hindu temple or Moslem mosque. Some are incredibly old. On a hilltop stands a temple to the god Shiva built by King Sandiman who reigned in Kashmir from 2664 to 2629 B.C. On the mountain spur is a School of Astrology erected by the son of Shah Jahan of Taj Mahal fame. The largest mosque is the elaborate Jama Masjid built by Shah Jahan. Farther afield is the Temple of the Sun founded nearly three thousand years B.C. and notable for its beautifully carved stones. High among the snows is Amarnath Cave where female pilgrims who desire children worship a *lingam* or phallus of ice which, it is said, waxes and wanes with the moon every month.

The mosque of Hazrat Bal boasts a hair from the head of Mohammed. Once each year it has been shown to the faithful. In December, 1963, it was stolen. Hindus were blamed for the sacrilege and bloody riots between Moslems and Hindus were the result.

Kashmir is peppered with shrines, to all the Hindu gods, to Allah, and even to Christ since he is included by Moslems among their major prophets. It is a Kashmir legend that when

Christ rose on the third day he came to Kashmir and stayed here until it was time for him to ascend to Heaven.

It is not surprising that this land of the sky should think so much about Heaven. But it does seem strange that a land so shut away from the main currents of world progress should be regarded as one of Asia's chief seats of learning. Scholars came here to study Sanskrit. Great respect was paid to the graduate of Kashmir University.

Today, of course, the major Indian universities are in India proper. But an old ritual still persists: a student after graduation may take seven steps toward Kashmir and seven steps back. This is taken to mean that he has completed his education in Kashmir and is therefore a fully qualified scholar. Kashmir is still called Sharda Pit—the seat of learning.

Suffering Moses and Friends

Whether Kashmir lives up to this reputation is doubtful. Schools are too few and poor. But in one branch of learning Kashmir excels. Handicrafts.

Nowhere in Asia is more skill and taste shown than one may see in the shops that overhang this water street. We disembark frequently and climb a few steps to watch the woodcarvers, the silversmiths, the embroiderers, the carpet-makers, the papier-mâché-painters, the furriers, the silk-weavers, the jewelers, the Kashmir (cashmere) shawls prized even in the time of Julius Caesar, made from the soft underwool or *pashmina* of the shawl goat of Tibet and so delicately woven that one may be drawn through a finger ring.

You may buy these treasures in the shops where they are made or from the many merchants who give themselves fantastic names to attract trade—Cheap John, Suffering Moses, Cheerful Charlie, Marvelous, Wonderful, Superior Sam. A number proclaim themselves as The Best.

One goes to the other extreme. He is Subhana the Worst.

It seems that an Englishman, fed up with the exaggerated claims of Srinagar merchants, advised one, Subhana, to advertise himself as the worst. He does, and it brings him good business.

The River People

We emerge from the city into open country carpeted by beds of yellow flowers, fields of corn, rice paddies, and sprinkled with mulberry trees grown to feed the hungry worms that make possible Kashmir's silk industry.

Back of all the lush color is the saw-toothed Himalayan wall, each peak topped with a towering hat of white cloud.

Every quarter mile or so is a home but seldom on shore. Women lean out of the windows of doongas to wash the dinner dishes in the milk-chocolate Jhelum.

These floating homes favor the shade of the giant chinars. It is almost dark under a full-fledged chinar because the leaves, shaped rather like the leaves of the soft maple but four times as broad, are thick set. A heavy rain takes half an hour to penetrate a full-grown chinar—but the drops caught by the leaves keep raining half an hour after the rain has stopped.

Large rafts loaded with giant deodar logs are being hauled upstream by men at the ends of ropes walking at a forty-five-degree angle on the towpath. No horses, mules, oxen or other animals are used for towing, but manpower alone.

There is not a motor on the river. Everything is so quiet that we can plainly hear the chirp of the crickets on shore, distant bird songs, shouts of children in out-of-sight villages.

The Hubble-Bubble

And is it a bird making that bubbling sound close behind us? We turn to look. No, it is just the *hookah* being smoked by one of the men. The "hubble-bubble" is standard equipment. Almost every boat has its water pipe.

Few Kashmiris smoke cigars or cigarettes or short pipes—the smoke must pass through water to be truly satisfying. They claim that this makes the best filter and a stronger flavor.

The first and only village actually on the riverbank is Shadipur. Here the Senveli River, light green, cold, straight from glaciers, joins the Jhelum. We go up the Senveli a short distance and disembark in a grove of a hundred or more huge chinar trees.

Rasool spreads a Kashmir carpet under a tree, places two cushions, produces out of a large wicker hamper great servings of roast duck, roast potatoes, vegetable salad, bread and butter, hard boiled eggs, apple compote, fresh peaches, apples and plums, and makes coffee on the spot in a large charcoal-burning silver samovar.

The Gulf of Corpses

We return to the Jhelum and drift rapidly downriver on the tawny current. By night we have covered the twenty-four miles to Wular Lake and sleep aboard the shikara in the Gulf of Corpses.

It is a more beautiful place than its name would suggest. Apharwat nearly three miles high looms beside it, grand and ghostly in the light of the full moon. Water chestnut plants and fragrant lotus blooms adorn the surface and assure food for the farmers if their crops fail.

The chestnuts are large and delicious. The root of the lotus is eaten, also the kernels of the fruit—making this gastronomically as well as poetically the Land of the Lotus Eaters.

The Gulf of Corpses is so named because, they say, the current carries all dead bodies into it. Some claim there are evil spirits below always hungry for victims.

"If you dive in here you never come up," Rasool assures us.

The next day we follow the river out of the lake eighteen miles to the Baramula Gorge. The country grows ever wilder, the mountains closer. We see fewer men, more animals.

Otter, Bear, Snow Leopard

An otter emerges from the water, his wet smooth coat gleaming as if it had just been painted with black enamel.

Small antelopes bound through the woods. An ibex stands alone on the point of a rocky foothill.

We pause to watch the maneuvers of a Himalayan black bear. He lies on a branch extending from the bank and now and then scoops the water with his paw. After a few tries he is successful—he flips a fish onto the bank and scrambles ashore to devour it. He is not in the least disturbed by our presence.

More timid is the big stag of which we catch only a glimpse as he moves off into the brush.

"A barasingha," says Rasool. "Found only in Kashmir. Its name means twelve horns. Wonderful antlers—they branch twelve times. A very shy animal—he's been shot at so much. Hunters spend weeks trying to get one. This is one of the best hunting places in all the mountains. All kinds of game— gazelle, chital, musk deer, barking deer, brown bear, leopard, fox, jackal, wolf, wildcat. . . ."

"What's that?" I interrupt. A large white animal looks up from his drinking at the river's edge, bounds back into the brush and disappears. There was time to notice only that it was incredibly white, incredibly graceful and, strangest of all, its tail was a huge beautiful brush half again as long as its body.

"Snow leopard," Rasool says. "Lives up there in the snow— that's why he's white. Just comes down to drink."

"But what a tail!"

"That's to protect him against the wind. It's cold up there. He stands with his rear to the wind, with his tail spread out. If he lies down he covers himself with his tail. It's as good as a heavy blanket."

I remember that the yak also stands stern on to the wind, barricaded by his immense bushy tail.

I look up to the snows. "Are there yaks up there?"

"Certainly. Especially over on the Tibet side."

The Abominable Snowman

What other mysteries do those eternal snows hide?

"How about the Abominable Snowman? Have you ever seen one?"

Rasool looks at me sharply to see if I am kidding him. "He is a real thing. I have not seen him. But I have seen his tracks in the snow. He is a giant—we know that from his footprint. It is twice as big, three times as big, as the mark of an ordinary man."

I nod soberly. It is not prudent to try to argue a man out of a tradition that has almost the force of a religious conviction. It would do no good to explain that scientists now believe the tracks to be made by a foxlike creature progressing in leaps that bring down all four feet close together, the melting of the four marks into each other under the noon sun leaving what appears to be the footprint of a giant.

The shores become more abrupt. They rise into cliffs. The Jhelum quickens its pace. We can hear the roar of rapids ahead.

Late in the afternoon we reach Baramula Gorge and pull into a quiet cove just before the point where the Jhelum ceases to be a river and becomes a plunging torrent. The gorge marks the end of navigation and the end of the Vale of Kashmir.

Without the gorge to allow the escape of the river, the Jhelum would soon turn the Vale into a lake eighty-five miles long and twenty wide. That has almost happened at times in the past when the gorge became blocked with debris. The first such incident of which we have record occurred in the reign of Avantivarman eleven hundred years ago. The king's engineer ordered workmen to leap into the boiling waters and remove the obstructions. Since such a proceeding was highly dangerous, the men went on strike. That was before the day of labor-management negotiations. The strikers were given fifty lashes apiece. Even this failed to persuade them.

The engineer hit upon a quite different plan. In full view of his men assembled at the water's edge, he threw a thousand gold coins into the dam. They sank through the tangle of branches and logs to the bottom.

"They are yours, if you go get them."

They could not be reached without first clearing the channel. The temptation was too great. With one accord the men dived in and worked furiously to break up the barricade and set its component parts afloat so they could reach the river bottom. Five men were lost but the rest came up with their fists full of gold and the Vale of Kashmir was saved.

A Smiling Land

We had come down in two days. It took us three to get back. There was no hubble-bubbling now, no songs to the sarangi except in camp after hours.

While Rasool manipulated the steering sweep, the five boatmen at the end of a towrope plodded along the shore path bent so far forward that their noses brushed the high grass. It was backbreaking work, but the men kept up a cheerful chatter.

We grew to hate the soft cushions under us, but not quite enough to make us join in the labor. However, to lighten the boat, we frequently walked the towpath but were sharply reprimanded if we laid a hand on the line.

We had noticed it everywhere—the Kashmiri's independence of spirit, his willingness and even eagerness to work hard, his radiant smile even while he wipes the sweat out of his eyes. The smile appears to be Kashmir's trademark. Children on shore and on doongas were forever calling to Mary:

"Memsahib salaam!"

"They are very happy to see you," said Rasool. "A friendly people."

Down below on the plains of India, he went on, the people are sad. Here they are cheerful. Why the difference? According to Rasool the climate is responsible. It is invigorating. There is no malaria, no sleeping sickness, no bilharziasis. No monsoon with its horrible pall of depression. It's a happy land. Even the willows don't weep.

Not Perfect Bliss

Of course there are flies in the ointment, as everywhere else on this imperfect planet. The most bothersome fly is Red China.

The Chinese, after subduing Tibet, took advantage of the fact that the border between Tibet and Kashmir through the high Himalayas has never been sharply defined nor even surveyed. They pressed in to occupy twelve thousand square miles of territory claimed by India as part of Kashmir. Now (in 1965) an uneasy cease-fire line separates inactive Chinese and Indian troops.

That is in the northeast corner of Kashmir. On the southwest there is another cold war, practically a frozen war between India and Pakistan. Both claim Kashmir. Since 1949 they have been content to sit still and fling epithets at each other across a cease-fire line policed by the United Nations.

These matters disturb the average Kashmiri not one whit. He is non-political and happy-go-lucky. Even the literate, enterprising and politically-conscious Ramzan, owner of houseboats, says placidly, "It is better to leave things as they are than to go to war."

And the unsophisticated grower of melons and cucumbers, gatherer of water chestnuts and lotus roots, in this climate so germicidal that even a headache is rare, asks only for hard work and a hookah at the end of the day.

9

Small Boat on the Thames

THERE WAS no path through the woods. Stumbling and clambering a distance that seemed many times what it should be, we were about to turn back when we emerged into a meadow shadowed by only one big ash tree.

Under the ash was a stony spring three feet deep. It seemed perfectly dry. I knelt beside it, brushed away the pebbles at the bottom, and pressed my finger against the earth.

There was a thin film of water on the tip of my finger.

"That," I said solemnly to my wife, "is the Thames."

Here was the source of Britain's chief river. On the trunk of the old ash someone long ago had cut the initials TH for Thames Head. At this point on the government ordnance map appeared the words, "Source of the River Thames."

I wiped the Thames off on my slacks.

There is nothing in the upper reaches to suggest that this is one of the most important rivers in the world. It rises in a buttercup-spangled meadow in the dreaming Cotswold Hills. The place is not even as busy as it was nineteen centuries ago. Then the legionaries of a nearby Roman castle drilled in this meadow and brought their ewers to the spring for water. In those days it was never dry. Old prints of Thames Head show a spouting fountain and a lake.

Even now in wet periods the spring fills to the brim; in fact the entire meadow spurts thousands of tiny fountains whose streams join to form a crystal-clear brook starting on its 210-mile journey to the North Sea. On the way it is joined by other spring-fed streams so clear that the Upper Thames is called "the sweetest of rivers" and is London's chief supply of drinking water.

Down the Thames, Afoot

Celebrating the beginning of our Thames journey, we had a gypsy breakfast under the great ash. Then we took off on our voyage down the Thames—afoot!

There was as yet no water and not even a channel, but the meadow sloped gently toward the center. Following the low places, we came to a bridge, a culvert some four feet in diameter arched with stone under an ancient Roman road. What a contrast between this first Thames bridge and the last one, the mighty Tower Bridge at London, 142 feet high, affording passage for ocean liners.

From under the four-foot bridge we crawled out into another quiet pasture. The path of the stream was now more or less clearly marked and we walked down the dry bed of it. High above a skylark circled, spilling a cascade of melody. There was no other sound and no one to be seen. The lovely hills stretched away to the horizon without a single house. Only a distant church tower rising from a clump of trees marked the position of the village of Kemble.

And yet all this region once hummed with activity. Only three miles to the north behind those woods was the second greatest city in Roman Britain, Corinium, now called Cirencester. It is interesting that Britain's two largest cities were in the Thames Valley, one at each end.

But the Thames has always been the backbone of England. It was in the lush lands along the river that prehistoric man found the most favorable conditions, abundant water, fertile soil, plenty of game. And the Thames was the highway for Roman invaders. It was a ready-made road to the heart of England.

The Romans stayed four hundred years. When they left, the countryside went to sleep. It still basks in a sort of perpetual Indian summer of charm and contentment, the loveliest sample of Old England still to exist. It may have been the unique peace and beauty of the land that gave rise to the tradition that the county of Gloucestershire is more favored by the divine presence than any other, an idea expressed in the proverb, "As sure as God's in Gloucestershire."

With such thoughts in mind we walked down the dry Thames through a meadow that showed signs of being a marsh in wet weather. There was still nothing to indicate that humans lived anywhere near or had ever lived here. Then we rounded a hillock and came suddenly upon a windmill. Why a windmill where there was no farm or farmhouse? It stood over a well, evidently very old. There was an air of mystery over all this and we resolved to ask about it if we should ever again meet a human being.

The Thames channel which served as our path was now a good ten feet wide and a lush garden from bank to bank. And now, the first surface water of the Thames—two stagnant pools fringed with a green mat of algae. Soon, more pools, closer together, and presently we were walking beside a continuous ribbon of standing water.

Owner of the Infant Thames

We deviated into the village of Kemble which we had heard was the home of the man who owns most of this countryside including Thames Head and lives in a mansion called Kemble House.

He was not at home but his attractive sister received us cordially, told us we were just in time for morning coffee, and welcomed us into the cool, restful beauty of the great house. We told her of our interest in Thames Head.

"You did well to find it," she said. "I'm afraid we don't make it too accessible. People have suggested that we turn it into a tourist attraction, put up signs, build a road in to the spring, charge admission and all that. But we feel it would spoil the place. Don't you agree?"

We did agree. We asked about the windmill.

"Yes," she said. "You noticed that the well is deep and full of water. There is always plenty of water, no matter how dry the season. The underground Thames never dries up. When the surface channel goes dry it's a hardship to farmers along the river, so it became the custom, during periods of drought, to pump water from that well up into the bed of the river to keep it flowing. So when Thames Head is dry the real source of the river is the windmill well. The Thames is the only river in the world, so far as I know, that is started with a pump. However, it isn't necessary now—you'll find plenty of water in the stream below this point. Would you like to see the house?"

We were indeed interested to see the home of a typical country squire of old England. The great house was a beautiful old structure, much of it dating from the sixteenth century. But we soon found that, like many others of the stately homes of old England, it had suffered a great change, yet without humiliation. It still had vast dignity in spite of the fact that all the stables and the barn had been converted by the squire into houses and the main building had been remodeled to make two apartments upstairs and a home for the Philips family below. But on both floors the windows were still magnificent bow windows of leaded glass looking out on a front yard a mile wide —a lovely park with flower gardens, lawns and great trees.

These splendid surroundings now give pleasure to some twenty families instead of one as in the old times. Who shall say that this is not better?

Refreshed and informed, we returned to follow the strip of swamp that was soon, we hoped, to become a river. Three horses came to taste the water, disapproved of it, tossed their heads and went off to find something fresher in a watering trough.

People emerged from a thatch-roofed farmhouse and looked at us curiously as we waded through the high grass beside the water. If this was their property, they raised no objection to our crossing it. This is a delightful characteristic of English country

folk. So long as visitors behave themselves they are welcome
and property owners may even provide paths and stiles for the
use of the public.

Here, however, there was no path, for what stranger in his
senses would want to walk beside a strip of swamp? At the
fences there were no stiles and we had to crawl scratchily
through barbed wire.

Another small bridge, and another. Then an exclamation
from Mary.

"Look! It's moving!"

The grasses in the stream bed were bending toward London.
The stripling Thames was actually on its way.

After the stream took to flowing, the water seemed to wash
its face and become bright and sparkling, minnows appeared in
it, then three fish, then many fish, a mole swam across to his
apartment in the bank, a snake slid out of the grass, chaffinches,
crows and swallows obeyed the lure of running water.

Going was easier now. With shoes removed, we simply waded
down the shallow stream.

Nature's Own Pharmacy

The banks were a botanist's delight. The teasel lifted its bristling head; this wiry tuft was once used to raise a nap on
woolen cloth. The purple loosestrife and purple fritillary
showed how different two purples can be. There was water-lov-
ing comfrey, gathered by country folk to make cough medicine
and used to congeal wounds. There was water betony with purplish flowers like small helmets. The juice crushed from the
leaves is good to cleanse ulcers and relieve sunburn. Having
encountered some nettles, we rubbed the irritated skin with
leaves of the tall coarse water dock, a popular antidote. It did
seem to relieve the itch. The Thames shore is a natural phar-
macy, as well as a source of many wild foods.

And dyes of superior quality for those who have the patience
to extract them. The yellow iris yields a blue, the teasel a yellow, the water lily a brown, the meadowsweet a black, the devil's-bit scabious a blue, centaury and agrimony a yellow, and
from the roots of the lady's bedstraw one may get a brilliant
Turkey red.

We had to leave the river briefly to see the village of Somerford Keynes—for there are no villages directly on the river. While searching for the church we stumbled into the grounds of the manor house. The door opened and a lady with an inquiring and slightly querulous expression on her face came out. After our battle with brush, weeds and river, we looked like two tramps.

"Oh-oh," said Mary. "I think we're going to be thrown out."

Explanations followed. Half an hour later we were sitting at lunch with Mrs. Foyle Fawcett, lady of the manor and widow, who told us that her husband's ancestors had bought this place in 1556.

Four centuries. I thought of the remark of a neighbor of ours in California. "This house is very old," he said. "I built it twenty years ago."

Continuing through the village, we paused before a beautiful garden. A lady in her Sunday best, wearing a hat and carrying an umbrella, evidently on her way home from church, stopped beside us.

"Would you like to see the garden?"

She took us in and, after seeing the flowers, we were invited into the house for a glass of Madeira.

A favorite American misconception is that the British are cold, aloof, do not readily receive strangers. One wonders if those who pass such judgments have ever been in England.

Only after the Madeira did anyone trouble with introductions. Upon hearing our name, Mrs. Macmillan recalled that she had read a book by an author of that name and had a pleasant word to say about my British publisher, Heinemann: "Any book of theirs is good." Copies of *National Geographic* lay on her reading table. Warmed by these evidences of fellow feeling, of which one is so much more sensible in England than in non-English-speaking countries, we returned to the Thames and took off our shoes.

Fish were so numerous that they bumped against our feet as we waded. But a farmer told us, "Not many fish here now. Men came with nets and scooped them up and took them away to fishponds. Afraid the river would dry up. When we get some wet weather and the river fills again, they'll bring them back."

The Motorized Cowhand

The seventh bridge over the Thames led only into a barn-yard. Here the farmer showed us his old mill, run by Thames water. It used to serve all the countryside but now it only grinds "corn grain" for the family.

"It was here when I was a boy," said the farmer. "Must be well over a hundred years old."

I looked about for some sign of the corn but could see only some wheat straw. Then it occurred to me that the English use the word corn in the Biblical sense, not the American. Corn means any cereal crop such as wheat, barley, rye or oats. What Americans think of as corn the English call maize or Indian corn, and they know little about it for it grows poorly in England.

The farmer had a big place, 350 acres, two thirds of it in pasture, the rest in "corn grain." He had two hundred head of cattle. His two boys, both in their twenties, run the place now.

"They're full of modern ideas," he said. "Look in this shed."

The shed was full of complicated farm machinery. We were to find the same sort of thing throughout England. The farms of England are among the most highly mechanized in the world.

Motorcycle Cowboy

One of the boys came rumbling up on a motorcycle.

"Where are you going?" asked his father.

"To get the cows."

I remembered my own cow-getting days. I didn't go on a motorcycle. I went afoot, and barefoot at that. I stared unbelievingly at the motorcycle cowboy.

"I've been wondering," I said, "how you keep the cows from getting out of the pasture. We used to have rail fences and they would sometimes even break through those. But you have only hedges. Any determined cow could wriggle her way through a hedge."

The young farmer smiled. "Come down and I'll show you."

We followed him down the Thamesside path to the eighth bridge, which was the simplest yet, only a single plank with a guide rail. Beside it was a shallow ford leading to a pasture gate. He rode through the ford while we walked the plank. He opened the gate and showed us an electrically charged wire half concealed in the hedge.

"It runs around the whole pasture," he said. "The cattle soon learn to keep away from it."

It was an immense pasture with the cattle at the far end of it and it would have been a slow job for a barefoot boy to get them out. But in an amazingly short time the motorized cow-hand had them splashing through the ford while he rolled through after them.

"Do you milk them yourself?" I asked as he chugged by.

"Automatic," he called back. "No more of that hand stuff."

The Thames plunged into a picturesque forest that arched over the river, admitting only long arrows of sunlight. The stream was two or three inches deep and the bottom was a level spread of small pebbles. The water was as transparent as air and looked like a coat of clear varnish over a tessellated pavement.

But the tessellated pavement did not feel as romantic as it looked, therefore we dried and shod our weary feet and walked along the right bank.

The pebbles gave way to weeds which threatened to choke the stream. Presently we came upon a gang of Thames Conservancy men who were clearing them out.

"If we don't," said the foreman, "we'll have all these farms flooded the next time the river rises. It looks harmless enough now but during the spring rains it can be a real menace. Back in 1947 we had it pretty bad. The river below Chertsey was three miles wide. People all down this valley love their river, but they're afraid of it too."

So that was evidently why villages were seldom built close to the river.

We left the stream to walk through the pleasant and peaceful village of Ashton Keynes. We were pretty tired and ready to quit for the day but there was no inn to be found at Ashton Keynes. We returned to the river, a little disturbed about heavy cumulus clouds that were rolling up from the east.

Storm and Hospitality

A peal of thunder ripped the sky just above us. Where the sky had been torn apart, a lake fell out. Traveling light, we had not encumbered ourselves with umbrellas or raincoats. In two minutes we were soaked.

That would not have been so bad if a cold wind had not whipped up. We tried to keep warm by putting on speed, but it was no use.

We deserted the Thames and took shelter under a hay shed near a farmhouse. It was warm there, and dry. We stretched out comfortably on the hay and had about resigned ourselves to the idea of spending the night here when a gruff "Good evening" roused us. A farmer stood by us with a murderous-looking pitchfork in his hand. I made haste to explain matters before he might be tempted to use it.

"Of course," he said. "We saw you come in. But you are wet. Come along to the house."

The house was made of the famous honey-colored Cotswold stone. It was covered with climbing roses and roofed with rough-hewn stone shingles colorfully mellowed by moss and lichens.

The interior belonged to Queen Victoria, but Queen Elizabeth II evidently felt quite at home here for she smiled at us pleasantly from above the fireplace.

The farmer's wife was most solicitous. "First you must get those things off. Come into the bedroom. I think we can find something for you to put on. May not fit very well, but. . . ."

We protested that we would just sit by the fire for a while and warm up, then walk on to Cricklade.

"Indeed, you won't do anything of the sort. This is a real storm. It won't let up. You had best stay the night here. Now, this is the bathroom, and there are towels, and there's plenty of hot water. I'll get some clothes for you and when you're ready we'll have some tea."

There was no resisting such hearty hospitality. We stayed the night.

The farmer, typical of the well-to-do and well-informed Eng-

lish countryman, knew his Thames. He was an amateur naturalist and something of an archeologist as well.

"We've dug up many interesting things hereabouts. I like to
think of the Thames as it was long ago. Of course you know
that England wasn't always an island. Winston Churchill reminded us of that recently but the scientists knew it long before. England was part of the Continent. The North Sea was
not a sea but a great plain. The Thames ran out into this plain
and joined the Rhine—hard to imagine, isn't it—and together
they flowed into the Arctic Ocean. I have a book here somewhere that tells about it."

He fished out an old copy of *Scenery of England* by Lord
Avebury, opened it and handed it to me. I read:

> We must therefore picture to ourselves a state of things when
> England formed part of the continent of Europe . . . when the
> North Sea was a great plain and the Thames, after joining the
> Rhine and subsequently the Humber, ran northwards into the
> Arctic Ocean. It was along the banks of this great river, and over
> the surrounding plains, that the bears and lions, bisons and elks,
> rhinoceroses, hippopotamuses and elephants lived whose remains
> are so abundant on the bed of the North Sea as well as in many of
> our river valleys.

"They've found remains of the giant mammoth," said the
farmer, "and the musk ox, and the grizzly bear—the huge one
—and the hyena, and the great elk, and the lion. Look at this."
He turned up a page in his copy of *Treasure in the Thames* by
archeologist Ivor Noel Hume.

> The reader who believes that the only lions that ever sat in
> Trafalgar Square were put there by Sir Edwin Landseer would be
> wrong. Bones of the lion have been found in terrace gravel both
> there and in Fleet Street, while a rhinoceros lay down and died
> in Pall Mall. Bones of another were found under the Old Bailey,
> and remains of a hippopotamus were uncovered in Waterloo
> Place.

The thunder growled and roared and it was easy to believe
that prehistoric beasts were besieging the farmhouse.

But the morning was clear and bright and we met nothing
more fearsome than a weasel as we walked on to Cricklade.

Canoe through Fairyland

Here we picked up a canoe that had been delivered by lorry from a boathouse downriver. We slipped the canoe into the two-inch-deep Thames. When we got aboard, it sat placidly on the bottom. This seemed to amuse an ancient Crickladian who chortled, "You'll have to carry that dem thing more than it'll carry you."

It wasn't quite that bad. But frequently we did have to go overboard to walk it through shallows, haul it through weeds, or let it down gently through stony riffles. There was just enough exercise to relieve canoe-cramp. Fast water only finger-deep alternated with quiet stretches several feet deep. The sun was bright, the air warm, the countryside a paradise of perfume and song.

The riverbanks were a continuous delight. Wild roses climbed up into the willow trees to escape the competition on the ground where Queen Anne's lace, blue forget-me-nots, yellow charlock, elderberry, wild iris, buttercups, blackthorn and poppies fought for space. Yellow water lilies floated on the quiet pools. Over them hovered blue-black dragonflies.

The silence of the gliding canoe allowed us to hear the wind in the grass, the "peek, peek" of the moorhen, the dart of a startled fish, the paddling of a stoat in pursuit of a water rat. We found ourselves speaking in whispers.

The incredibly green and pleasant land stretched away without a house to a wooded skyline. It was good to think that here was something unchanged in a changing world. "In such a landscape," John Buchan has written, "you can cheat the centuries, for all that is presented to your ear and eye is what medieval England heard and saw."

We pulled out on the shore to have lunch—vegetable soup heated on Tommy's Cooker (the British counterpart of Sterno), cheese, biscuits, apples, oranges and milk chocolate—mixed with warm sunshine, solitude and comfort.

We shot some brisk rapids, then paddled down a long, lovely and solitary stretch to one of the most interesting spots on the Thames. A round tower like a castle keep marked the point where the Thames, the Coln, and the Thames-Severn Canal join. Near the tower was a house. And in the garden by the shore a Vandyked gentleman was taking his ease in a long chair.

He turned out to be Eric Edmunds, proprietor of twelve hundred acres of Thames and Coln country. The roundhouse and house adjoining are his home and he has transformed this confluence of three waterways into a charming estate with connecting bridges. On a point of land between the two rivers he has his studio—for in his spare time after managing large family interests including the farming of twelve hundred acres and running a chain of drapery stores, he paints. And the little studio is ingeniously contrived to turn on its base as the position of the sun changes.

He took us through the house and the quaint two-story roundhouse, his daughter served tea, and we heard the story of the famous and ill-starred Thames-Severn Canal.

It was opened in 1789. As implied by its name, its purpose was to connect the Thames and Severn rivers, thus providing a navigable waterway clear across England from sea to sea. There were many locks on the canal, the last one located at this point, and the lockkeeper lived in the round stone tower.

Barges to the number of 150 a day, each barge of from thirty to seventy tons burden, passed through the canal carrying grain, cheese, groceries and metals to London; merchandise, timber, hides and gunpowder to Bristol, Worcester and Liverpool.

Then came the railways to provide swifter and more efficient transportation and the canal fell into disuse. Now it is a dry moat overgrown with hawthorn bushes and wild flowers.

From this point the Thames is deeper and wider as befits a thoroughfare for barges. But the barges are gone. With the closing of the canal, they disappeared. While the world grows steadily busier, the Upper Thames has relapsed into medieval peace. Once a highway for trade, it is now a river of pleasure and history. Not until well down toward London does the Thames begin to think of buying and selling.

The Temperamental Punt

At Lechlade we turned in our canoe and the next day hired a punt.

It is only in recent centuries that this fantastic craft has become the favorite on the upper river. The ancient Britons used a still more extraordinary vessel, the coracle. We were later to ride a Welsh river in coracles and admire the genius of the ancients who invented them. It is possibly the lightest craft man has ever used on the water. A full-blown coracle weighs twenty-five pounds, half the weight of a small canoe. It is nothing more nor less than a roundish basket covered with tarred canvas. It floats on the water as lightly as a leaf and can easily be picked up and carried on the back from one lake to another or around rapids.

But the coracle is antisocial since it will accommodate only one person. On the Thames it gave way to the punt which will take a whole family and the dog. They can flop about in it without peril, eat in it, sleep in it, play games in it. It is dangerous only to the person who poles it.

We had sailed the world's waters in almost every sort of craft but this was our first experience with an English punt. Before starting out, we asked the boathouse attendant for a few points on punts. Most important—the pole—how should it be used?

"If you've never used a pole," he said grimly, "my advice to you is to leave it severely alone."

"But there always has to be a first time."

"Yes, but aren't you beginning rather late?"

I ducked that one and examined the pole. It was as long as four men placed end to end and seemed about as heavy. It terminated in a metal prong.

"You stand in the stern," the man said. "If you try to work it from the bow, the afterpart of the boat will wag back and forth like the tail of a dog—or go around in circles."

"Do you operate it over the middle of the stern or at the side?"

"At the side."

"Changing sides when necessary?"

"If you swing the pole across the boat from one side to the other you are quite likely to knock your passenger's head off. You keep it on one side and press in or out on it to steer the boat."

That was reassuring, for it was just what you did with a paddle. This was probably even easier than paddling. I comforted myself with the reflection that poling was a primitive art practiced by untaught savages for thousands of years before the use of the paddle was learned.

"Let's get along," I said, and we got along, but used only the paddle until we were through the bridge and out of sight of the boathouse man. Then I laid down that light, lithe and beloved implement and took up the twenty-foot, ten-ton pole.

The upper end of it promptly snagged a willow tree and the punt all but passed on without us before it was extricated. By this time the punt had turned about and was headed back through the bridge.

"This tub has no keel," I complained. "It spins like a top."

"Quick, do something," my wife advised me. "He'll see you with that pole."

Since this was something that obviously must not happen I pronged a pier of the bridge and swung the boat back under the willow.

Then I tried to reach bottom with the pole. The bottom was only some ten feet down and the pole was twenty feet long, so this should have been easy. However, when the pole was thrust into the water at an angle its wooden buoyancy promptly lifted it to the surface and no amount of pressure could get it to the bottom. It was necessary to thrust it straight down.

This I did with a mighty thrust—with the result that it went deep into the muddy bottom and stuck there. I heaved and strained to get it out. In the meantime, the punt was going on. There was a grave decision to be made. Should I stay with the punt or with the pole? The stretch between them was getting dangerously long. I decided on the boat and let the pole go, then paddled the boat back to retrieve it.

"Better stick to the paddle," my wife suggested. But my blood was up now. The pole and I were going to fight this out if it took all summer.

For a while it was simple. The wind was accommodating and pushed us along rapidly in the right direction. I had only to go through the motions of manipulating the pole, which actually never touched bottom. It was very easy and perhaps even graceful. A girl walking along the towpath with her man stopped and gripped his arm.

"You see, Henry," she said, "that's the way it's done."

Fortunately some of the Frisian cattle that graze on Thames

banks came between the couple and us before a bend of the river brought us into the wind and I was forced to give up the pole for the paddle. But at least I still had the glow of having thrilled a feminine heart and inspired deep envy and even resentment in a male one.

With either pole or paddle, the keellessness of the boat was trying. It would turn readily, but never knew when to stop turning. And it was peculiarly sensitive to the wind—a good point while sailing with the wind, but it slid backwards or sideways as easily as forwards. Sudden gusts of wind did different things to the bow and stern—the boat was so long that the two ends were in different weather zones. Both ends were blunt and wide and stood clear out of the water. The craft really had two back ends, so it could hardly be blamed for not knowing which way to go.

Now paddling, now poling, now walking the towpath and dragging the boat into the teeth of the wind while Mary fended it offshore with the paddle, we were grateful that Lechlade is not built directly on the riverbank. A broad field and screening willows separated us from the village. We approached St. John's Lock where a green flag labeled *Wreck* floated over a sunken motorboat. Since we were only a lone punt, the lockkeeper made us wait plenty long before he filled the lock and opened one of the upper gates.

Entering a lock when winds and currents are contrary can be like threading a needle in a cyclone. Under the critical scrutiny of the lockkeeper, his wife and his daughter, I took up the pole. Noticing that everyone including my wife wore a strained expression, I tried to set them at ease with an air of complete nonchalance. This was shaken slightly when we collided with the flagpole of the wreck. At that moment my guardian angel gripped the pole with me, and together we propelled the craft into the lock with a flourish so highly professional as to bring a smile to every face.

Dismissing my angel, and quite ready to take all the credit to myself, I tied the painter to a ringbolt and settled down in the boat with my copy of Jerome's *Three Men in a Boat,* for the scene of that tale was this very Thames. I turned to see what Jerome had to say about locks.

I am fond of locks. They pleasantly break the monotony of the pull. I like sitting in the boat and slowly rising out of the cool depths up into new reaches and fresh views; or sinking down, as it were, out of the world, and then waiting, while the gloomy gates creak, and the narrow strip of daylight between them widens till the fair smiling river lies full before you, and you push your little boat out from its brief prison onto the welcoming waters once again. They are picturesque little spots, these locks. The stout old lockkeeper, or his cheerful-looking wife, or bright-eyed daughter, are pleasant folk to have a passing chat with. You meet other boats there and river gossip is exchanged. The Thames would not be the fairyland it is without its flower-decked locks.

I was aroused by a scream from Mary. She was clutching the gunwales to keep herself from tobogganing down the punt into the swirling waters of the lock. The bow was high in the air and the punt was tilted like the roof of a house. At every moment the tilt grew worse.

I saw the reason. The painter snubbed tight to the ringbolt held the bow of the punt up while the stern went down as the water level in the lock fell.

"The rope!" I shouted. "Untie it."

But my wife had all she could do to hang on. If I tried to climb the boat from my place in the stern the result would certainly be an upset. The inside wall of the lock was wet and slippery and there was no way to climb it. The lockkeeper and his wife and daughter had all disappeared.

Then the rope parted under the strain and the punt slapped down into the water. The lockkeeper came running from his house with a scone in his hand. He had evidently been enjoying tea with his family while the lock emptied. He looked down into the dark abyss where we lay and said, "Anything wrong? I thought I heard you call."

I looked up from my book. "No," I said mildly. "Nothing wrong." My wife spoiled it by telling all.

The lower gates opened and we slid out into the sunshine. This was the first of the forty-eight locks of the Thames. We were to witness many misadventures in the locks, but the memory of our own in the first one gave us the proper attitude of sympathy and understanding.

Five-Room Flat Afloat

The river now being deep enough for motorboats we had arranged with a boathouse downriver for delivery of such a vessel at St. John's Lock.

And there it was—a sleek, trim cabin cruiser some thirty feet long, crisply painted blue and yellow and carrying the British flag at her stern.

The tip of the flag divided her name, leaving "Gosh" on one side and "awk" on the other. The first part suggested profanity and the second part seasickness. It seemed an unfortunate name for a boat.

Then the wind blew aside the flag and we realized that the name was not Gosh-awk but Gos-hawk, an excellent name for a boat, for the goshawk (originally goose-hawk) was that famous bird much used in falconry to bring down geese, hares, rabbits, pheasants, partridges, and celebrated for its power, speed and courage.

Just as puzzling as the name had at first been was the black mop that now projected itself from the wheelhouse. Coils of black hair shot off in all directions, some standing up like cobras, others drooping over the face and all but obscuring the eyes but stopping just short of an ear-to-ear grin. The owner of that magnificent tousle of serpents must have Harpo Marx as his father and Medusa as his mother. From under this ferocious snake nest came a remarkably gentle voice.

"You are Mr. and Mrs. Price? I'm Herbert."

Herbert, eighteen-year-old-about-to-turn-nineteen boat builder's apprentice, had brought the boat upriver and would accompany us down. In ten minutes we were aboard and examining our floating home.

It was actually a five-room flat with sundeck and back porch. Reading from the front: the head, crew's cabin with two berths, the wheelhouse, main cabin with two berths, galley, cockpit. And all within thirty-one and a half feet fore-and-aft and nine feet of beam.

We had not finished the first day's run before we realized what a prize we had in Herbert. He could take the wheel when there were pictures to be made or notes to be written—and that was much of the time. Every bend in the river revealed something picturable and memorable. He did most of the hopping about that was necessary to get the boat safely through the locks. He pumped the water from the bilges, swept the floors, swabbed the decks, filled the gas and water tanks, emptied the pails, dug holes to bury the garbage. No waste could be thrown into the river, since the Upper Thames is London's chief water supply.

He was hard to roust up in the morning. That, however, was not an individual peculiarity but a national one. The Englishman is not aware that there is any daylight before 10 A.M. We were usually awake at six or seven and fretting to be off since the sun, the photographer's best friend, generally shone during the early hours, then hid itself behind banks of clouds for the rest of the day. However, Herbert's schedule was really the more sensible, because the lockkeepers were Englishmen too. There was no point in starting early only to wait at the first lock.

The river meandered through lush meadows to Buscot Lock. This has no keeper of its own but the keeper of St. John's Lock occasionally rides over on his bicycle to Buscot to see if anyone wishes to go through!

In due season we were in and out again and sailing sweetly through the Vale of the White Horse, so called after the 374-foot figure of a horse cut into the flank of a hill at Uffington and believed to be either the work of the early Britons or a memorial of the victory of King Alfred over the Danes in 871. How deep in history is this lovely land! Dreaming back over the centuries one suddenly feels a thousand years old, and it's a good feeling.

All day the river was scarcely wider than our boat was long. Cattle grazed near the shore. All land along the river was pasture, the cultivated land being half a mile back and on higher ground so that crops would not suffer in case of flood.

Swallows dipped and twirled above us. Two big herons rose, trailing long legs. Ducks chattered past.

Queen of the Thames

The most distinguished birds were the swans, stately white caravels sailing without the least apparent effort. As the ibis is the bird of the Nile, so is the swan the bird of the Thames. From the point where the stream is so shallow that the birds' paddles scrape the bottom, all the way down to the Port of London, it is hard to go a mile without encountering some of these conspicuous beauties.

We came upon one sitting on her nest among the rushes at the water's edge. She had the air of a queen on her throne. She turned a haughty eye upon us as we nosed the boat close in and stopped within five feet of her so that I could get a picture.

"Go easy," Herbert advised. "When they get angry, they're bad."

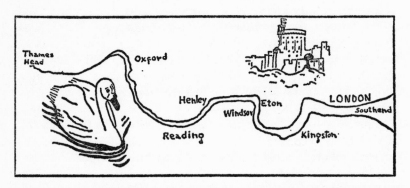

I went easy, but the click of the camera made her hiss and glare, and her mate came in a rush to the edge of the embankment to defend his home. Mary bribed him with a crust of bread held in her mouth. He boldly plucked it from between her teeth.*

The queen in the meantime had decided to ignore us. She ruffled her feathers, stretched herself, and rose, revealing seven eggs the size of giant hen eggs.

Then we saw a remarkable sight, and it was the only time we were to see it on our entire journey. Mother Swan placed her beak under an egg and deftly turned it upside down. She went on to do the same with all the other eggs. Then, with a disdainful look at us, she settled down to fry them on the other side.

After a five-lock day we tied up for the night in the shadow of New Bridge. Despite its name, it is quite possibly the most ancient bridge on the entire river.

* As sketched, page 166.

It was already more than two centuries old when Columbus discovered America. It is hard for an American mind to stretch back to the year 1250, when this beautiful stone bridge of five pointed and groined arches and projecting piers was built.

Let those who are aged and yet without achievement take heart; for this bridge was four hundred years old before it rose to fame. Then it played a part in one of the greatest social revolutions of all history, the extinction of the theory of the divine right of kings and the birth of democracy. It was here that Cromwell fought King Charles I and sent him packing northwards to final defeat.

The wind that has defied the wheel all day has died down. As darkness comes on, the river looks like a sheet of black glass reflecting the illuminated windows of an inn on the farther shore. The inn also is beautifully named. It was once The Old Rose, but after it burned down and was rebuilt it was quite appropriately renamed The Rose Revived.

Mary has an argument with the gas stove which grudgingly agrees to cooperate, the table is set up between the bunks, and Herbert joins us at dinner. The chill May air makes everything taste wonderful.

And the chill May air together with a dense river fog followed by heavy frost makes for a very uncomfortable night. The temperature drops to four degrees below freezing. The next morning we telephone a requisition for more blankets.

Ghosts Die Hard

At Northmoor Lock we left the boat with Herbert in charge and walked a mile over the fields to Appleton village in search of the home of Sir Basil Blackwell.

All Englishmen and tens of thousands of readers the world over know the four-story, block-deep bookstore in Oxford, one of the two or three greatest bookstores on earth. If any author wishes assurance that the public still reads books he has only to witness the surging crowd of book-hungry people who lose themselves in the labyrinthine mazes of Blackwell's. The house fills a dual role, not only selling books but publishing scholarly volumes by university dons. No less distinguished a pen than John Masefield's has honored this institution:

> *There, in the Broad, within whose booky house*
> *Half England's scholars nibble books or browse,*
> *Where'er they wander blessed fortune theirs:*
> *Books to the ceiling, other books upstairs;*
> *Books, doubtless, in the cellar, and behind*
> *Romantic bays, where iron ladders wind.*

In his letter inviting us to stop off from our river journey for Sunday dinner at his country home, Sir Basil had given us typically English directions: "My house, Osse Field, lies behind a tallish hedge three hundred yards from the village cross along the road to Netherton."

By ways as labyrinthine as the bookstore's we came at last upon a great house in large grounds radiant with daffodils and tulips. We were admitted to the library, a spacious and wonderful room richly walled with books from floor to ceiling and, through big leaded windows, overlooking acres of private parkland.

Sir Basil and Lady Blackwell had been joined for the day by their two married daughters and three teen-age grandchildren. Throughout the cigarette-and-Dubonnet period in the library and the lunch of roast mutton with currant jelly, fruit topped with custard sauce and whipped cream, cider, coffee, the conversation by some chance centered upon one fascinating subject, ghosts.

A daughter recounted how an American gentleman had actually laughed when told of English ghosts, and she had had a hard time convincing him that they actually exist.

I said, "Perhaps American houses are too new to be haunted. At any rate, we almost never hear of such a thing."

This caused much astonishment, and stories were told about the very active and numerous ghosts of England.

To American ears it was nothing short of amazing that highly intelligent people in this twentieth century should profess to believe in ghosts. And yet what could be more natural in this land of ancient mansions and castles, creaking floors, echoing corridors, unused rooms, gloomy dungeons, secret passages, all steeped in a long, romantic and bloody history? The American is like a cut flower, no roots. The Englishman has roots and sometimes longs fiercely to get away from them but cannot, and is a more interesting person because he cannot.

We started back to our boat, quite prepared to meet ghosts in the fields or find them under our bunks. We said something to this effect. Sir Basil smiled. "It's not their natural habitat," he said. "But during the war it might not have been safe to walk across those fields after dark, not because of ghosts, but thieves. For a while England became a nation of thieves."

A little apprehensively, we made our way back across the starlit moor to the sleeping river. We met neither ghosts nor thieves.

Winston Churchill and the Ferry Girl

We stopped in the morning to see the old-time ferry which is still, as in Matthew Arnold's day, "crossing the stripling Thames at Bablock Hythe."

Of course this is not the same vessel but is of the same type and worked in the same way, by sheer arm power. The ferryman stands amidships and grips a cable that runs from shore to shore. He simply pulls the boat back and forth across the stream, but this is some feat since the craft may be loaded with two or three automobiles and many passengers.

And yet a girl once operated the ferry, and thereby hangs a tale. She was Betty Rudge, the ferryman's daughter. The Rudges were of very humble and unpretentious stock and it was a great thrill to Betty when a viscount took an interest in her. He was young William Flower, second Viscount Ashbrook, a student at Christ Church College in Oxford, and he had come for a day's fishing. He forgot about his fishing when he saw Betty. It was love at first sight. He found her utterly enchanting, until she opened her mouth. Her speech was not precisely Oxonian. He realized what a gulf lay between them. Further meetings intensified his longing for her. He must have her, but not without an Oxford accent.

He solved the problem by placing her in a family of gentlefolk whose fortunes had declined but whose accent and manners remained intact. It is not recorded how long the tutoring continued, but finally Galatea passed all tests with honors and the two were married in Northmoor Church in 1766. Nor is it just a pretty story, for we found their names on the old register.

Contrary to the gloomy prophecies of friends, the marriage was a happy one. Her children and grandchildren carried the humble blood of the Thames ferryman into the veins of the aristocracy of England. One of the descendants of the inarticulate ferry girl was the highly articulate Winston Churchill.

Another Oxford student who frequented Bablock Hythe was Shelley, and it is said that a lark rising from its nest in the nearby meadow inspired the lines:

> *Hail to thee blithe Spirit!*
> *Bird thou never wert,*
> *That from heaven, or near it,*
> *Pourest thy full heart*
> *In profuse strains of unpremeditated art.*

Just poetic license? Doubtfully but hopefully, we walked through the meadow. Suddenly three skylarks rose like rockets of song.

Who Murdered Amy?

An unsolved murder mystery casts its shadow over the nearby village of Cumnor.

The chief figure in the mystery was the man who fell in love with Queen Elizabeth; or, at least, fell in love with the power she wielded and longed to share it.

The handsome Robert Dudley, Earl of Leicester, was much favored by the young queen. But he was already married to Amy Robsart. This awkward fact was all that stood in the way of a royal wedding.

Then Amy was found at the foot of a staircase with her neck broken. Her husband maintained that it was an accident. He himself had a perfect alibi. He was away from home when the "accident" occurred. The queen herself could testify to this, for he was with her.

But so widespread was the suspicion that he had contrived the death of his wife that the queen's marriage to him would have been a public scandal. Elizabeth's trusted adviser, Lord Burleigh, counseled her to abandon her plans for the marriage because Leicester was "infamed by the murder of his wife."

As the years passed, damning evidence leaked out. Two men,

believed to be the killers hired by Dudley, made deathbed confessions, but Dudley scorned them as publicity seekers.

One man who was convinced of Dudley's guilt was Sir Walter Scott, and millions of readers of *Kenilworth* have wept over the fate of Amy Robsart.

The Red Flag

We are brought suddenly back to today's world by a red flag waving in the middle of the river. Herbert, at the wheel, steers to port of it. At the eleventh moment a dredger by the shore blows its whistle and a workman calls to us to go to the right of the flag.

But it is too late to turn. To pass on the other side it will be necessary to back up first. Herbert throws the engines into reverse.

Nothing ever happens promptly when this is done, and doesn't happen at all now because the current is pulling us forward more powerfully than the engines can take us backward.

Again the call from the shore, "Go back." We don't go back. Thinking that the helmsman may not have heard, I call down from my camera perch above, "Go back if you can."

"I can't," Herbert answers. "One of the engines has gone off."

He tries a bit longer. But the current is too strong. We continue to slide forward.

"I'll have to try going ahead."

We strike with a jolt that dumps me from the wheelhouse roof onto the forward deck and sends all the pans tumbling in the galley.

The stern of the boat begins to swing around in the current. In a moment we are broadside in a most precarious position, listing far over and threatening to capsize under the powerful push of the current. Men from the dredger come running along the shore shouting unhelpfully.

Herbert stops the engine to save the propellers from grinding themselves to bits against the shoal. We all throw our weight on the upstream side to restore the boat's balance, but it does no good.

Then there is a grinding sound beneath. The stern of the boat passes over the obstruction and we are now pointed upstream. We deposit all our slight weight in the stern, the bow lifts, the current pushes us off, and we are free, floating downstream backwards. Herbert starts the engines and turns the boat about.

Our pulse beats slow down—but only for a moment. A big cruiser comes plowing upstream. Noting the side on which we have passed the flag, they assume that they should do likewise. Our shouts and those of the dancing men on the bank fail to register until they are stuck high on the shoal. The skipper calls, "Why didn't you warn us?"

He tries reverse but his boat does not budge. We throw him a line and, after an hour's wangling, get him off.

"What's the use of putting out a red flag," grumbles the dredge foreman, "if you fellows pay no attention to it?"

But Herbert will not argue.

"Got a line?" he says. Obtaining one, he ties one end on shore and the other to the flagpole. We wait to see how it works. The skipper of the next boat sees the line blocking the dangerous passage and steers his boat to the other side of the flag.

But we make no convert of the foreman. When we leave, he is still grumbling about people who can't see a red flag.

Do You Prefer Torture or Poison?

The pages of romance opened again as we looked at the tumbled walls of Godstow Nunnery where Fair Rosamond lived and sinned and now lies buried.

Sin was not a stranger in the nunneries, else why the proverbs, "Nuns wear their virginity easily" and "Clerks should not haunt nunneries neither early nor late"? However, there was still another proverb, "A king can do no wrong," and perhaps that was the excuse of Henry II when he seduced fifteen-year-old Rosamond in Godstow Nunnery, then carried her off to his palace at Woodstock.

He did not install her in the palace since that was already occupied by his queen, Eleanor of Aquitaine. In a faraway corner of the vast estate he hid Rosamond in a secret bower.

She bore her royal lover two sons before she was discovered by the queen who, being fair-minded, offered her a choice. She might die by torture or by poison. She chose poison.

She was taken back to the nunnery for burial and her king saw to it that she was provided with a magnificent tomb set about with lighted candles and drapes of silk. Possibly some of the more pious nuns did not approve of the burial of such a woman in a nunnery chapel. They may have been responsible for the rather dubious epitaph placed on her tomb:

> *Here lies beneath the earth without hope of coming*
> *up again, Rose of the World, not a pure Rose,*
> *Not smelling as a decent corpse should, but sweet as*
> *usual with cosmetics and perfume.*

There she lay until two years after Henry's death. In 1191 the Bishop of Lincoln, discovering the fine tomb and being told it was Rosamond's grave, cried, "Take this harlot from hence and bury her without the church."

It was done. But after the bishop had gone "the chaste sisters gathered her bones, and put them in a perfumed bag, enclosing them so in a lead and layde them againe in the church under a fayre large grave stone." And seven centuries later Peacock, on a river excursion to Godstow with his friend Shelley, wrote:

> *The windflower waves, in lonely bloom,*
> *On Godstow's desolated wall:*
> *There thin shades flit through twilight gloom,*
> *And murmured accents feebly fall.*
> *The aged hazel nurtures there*
> *Its hollow fruit, so seeming fair,*
> *And lightly throws its humble shade*
> *Where Rosamonda's form is laid.*

A Lock Is Not a Safe Bathtub

At Godstow Lock I took a ducking. Stepping on the gunwale with the intention of leaving the boat, I left it, but not as planned. A rope on the gunwale rolled under my foot and I found myself with one leg hip-deep in the lock. My other foot was still on the boat and my hands on shore, and the gap between was widening. In my hand was a Leica camera.

After one has lost a Contax in the Nile, a Leica in Nassau, and a Retina in the Inland Sea, one has acquired the habit of thinking of his camera before himself. When Herbert came running along the lockside to help me I said, "Take the camera." He took the camera and I dropped into the water.

A lock is not a good place to go bathing. The water rushing out from under the lower gates creates a dangerous undertow. The boat's deck was too high to reach and the lock wall was higher. I swam through the churning waters to the upper gates where the undertow was least and was ignominiously hauled up at the end of a rope. But the wetting seemed unimportant when Herbert handed back the camera, dry and safe.

Proud Oxford

The river was now, for the first time, smothered between grimy warehouses and factories. For thirty miles there had not been a town or village on the river. We had been passing through a green paradise that, except for the locks, had changed but little in long centuries.

Here, white swans were the only beautiful things. They refused to be daunted by the black cliffs, belching steam, growling machinery. Even the crowning horror, the gas works, did not lessen their majesty and pride.

So this was Oxford, called by some the most beautiful city in England. Where were the "dreaming spires?" All we could see were factory chimneys and coalyards.

But when we disembarked at Folly Bridge and walked up St. Aldate's the glory of Oxford unfolded before us, all the more amazing because of our first bad impression. Matthew Arnold was right after all about "that sweet city with her dreaming spires." They rose like a forest of fine architecture, each one different, but all beautiful.

We turned into High Street and soon found why it is called "the noblest old street in England." The colleges of Oxford are marvels in stone. One would be quite enough for a city. But Oxford University consists of twenty-eight colleges. That does not mean twenty-eight buildings. Each college comprises many fine buildings, and the visitor's astonishment grows when he realizes that this vast concourse of noble institutions is provided for the education of only a few students. In America such a plant might accommodate fifty thousand. Oxford University with its twenty-eight colleges has eight thousand undergraduates. For the objective of Oxford is not the education of the masses but the training of leaders.

Students come from many lands to Oxford—thirty-two of them each year from the United States, thanks to the Rhodes scholarships. These grants from the estate of South Africa's empire builder offer outstanding students two or three years at Balliol, Magdalen, Trinity, Jesus, Worcester, or the other men's colleges.

To see Winston Churchill's birthplace we journey north a few miles to Blenheim Palace. It proves to be as colossal as the man, as large as a dozen great hotels rolled into one. It is surrounded by a vast park with a lake a mile or more long, a river as broad as the Upper Thames, acres of formal pools, fountains and waterfalls, glorious flower gardens, wild woodlands and pasture, bronze and marble statues springing up at the most improbable places.

Returning a few days later to Oxford we bought in one of its delectable shops a huge white cake with red rosebuds and pink angels and nineteen candles and bore it to our waiting boat below Folly Bridge. Herbert could hardly believe his eyes when it was borne blazing into the cabin at dinner time to a chant of Happy Birthday.

Our sympathy for him because he could not spend his birthday with his family was perhaps misplaced. He had been having the time of his life in Oxford. The birthday dinner had to be curtailed a bit so he could make a seven o'clock cinema. He set off with a piece of birthday cake and an angel in his hand.

It Can Be Exciting

The lasher at Sandford Lock is a good place to drown yourself. A lasher, well-named, is the pool of thrashing, foaming water just after it has tumbled over a weir. The drop at Sandford is the greatest on the entire river, nearly nine feet. The tumbling tons of water create whirlpools and strong undercurrents. A monument stands on the bank as a reminder of the drowning of two Oxford students. The plinth of the monument is used as a diving board by young men who want to see if the pool really *is* dangerous.

Above the weir a large sign warns of danger. But that did not help the boating party whose engine had failed just at the critical moment. As we came up we saw their boat being sucked past the danger sign toward the weir.

The occupants of the boat seemed to be in a state of paralysis.

The man and two women were staring at the white edge of river where it disappeared over the weir.

Herbert flung them a line, but they did not seem to know what to do with it. It slipped off into the water. He threw it again, calling to them to hang on to it.

"Put it over a cleat," he called.

Quite evidently they didn't know what a cleat was. "Like this," we shouted, indicating a cleat on our boat. They were close to the weir before the line was fast and they could be pulled out of danger.

"How far are you going?" we called.

"We're going," said the man, "straight back to the boathouse. We've had enough."

Pale-faced Londoners pour out by the thousands to the Thames of a weekend and trust themselves to craft of every sort without previous experience. The Thames is fairly safe for such experimentation, yet every year it takes its toll of lives.

As distressing as the engine that won't start is the engine that won't stop. We came upon a motorboat wildly racing round and round, dodging other craft only by inches.

"The throttle's jammed," yelled the driver. "I can't stop her."

Everyone screamed advice, but no one advised him to stop his boat by crashing into a stone wall, which is what he did. The boat sank in a dozen feet of water.

Then there is the irresponsible skipper who sets his course down a wide empty stretch of the river and calmly leaves the wheel to step into the cabin for his pack of cigarettes or a box of matches.

His wife detains him for a moment, and in the meantime other boats have appeared or the river has curved and the driverless boat is headed straight for a cement pier and a salvage job.

Most English holidaymakers have a high regard for the rights of others, but there is the occasional Teddy Boy (English for hoodlum) who is looking for trouble. One such came charging down the river standing atop the wheelhouse and calling down to the boy at the wheel to go faster. He howled with delight as the wash of his cruiser nearly capsized punts and skiffs and he hurled back ribald taunts at anyone who dared to remonstrate. But the whole river had the satisfaction of seeing justice done when the cruiser's wash dashed against the hull of a steamer and recoiled upon the boat that had made it, and the wallow sent the man on the wheelhouse roof toppling into the Thames. He came up feet first to the delight of all observers.

The Monster

A sensation put the city of Reading in the news during February of 1956. A monster was photographed swimming up the river. The newspapers ran stories about it, speculating that it might be a *Dimetrodon,* a reptile that roamed the earth 190,-000,000 years ago. Then an inquisitive reporter discovered that the Thing was propelled by a young man in a rubber boat concealed behind a big dorsal fin. The "monster" had been fabricated by two Reading University students.

We timed our arrival at Henley on Thames to coincide with the beginning of the famous Royal Regatta. For four days we watched shells from all over England and abroad race a little more than a mile from Temple Island to the finish line near Henley Bridge. The three chief trophies went overseas, the Diamond Sculls to Australia, the Thames Challenge Cup to Princeton, and the Grand Challenge Cup to Cornell. The half million spectators, most of them of course British, were as warm in their applause of these winners as if they had been British too.

We had seen Windsor Castle before but had never been so thrilled by it as when, rounding a turn in the river, we saw its fabulous walls and towers mirrored in the still surface of the Thames. Set on a hill with the river forming a natural moat, the castle sends up rank on rank of "towers and battlements . . . bosomed high in tufted trees."

No wonder Windsor is considered the most regal building in the world. Kings and queens of England since William the Conqueror have made it their residence, and it is still one of the homes of the reigning monarch. Across the river from Windsor lies Eton, largest and most exclusive of all English public schools.

Shopping for food on a Thames boat trip is not too easy. The supermarket is not known in England, except in a few of the great cities. The chain store has not yet monotonized English towns. And even the chain grocery that does exist is by no means a supermarket. Its range of foods is strictly limited, and this is even more true of the small individual shops that have been kept as family enterprises down the years. The butcher whose father was a butcher and whose grandfather was a butcher would not think of branching out and selling milk as well as meat. The average butcher will not even sell chickens —that is the business of the poulterer.

To buy milk, meat, fish, paper napkins, cold cream, groceries, fruits and baked goods it is necessary to go to eight different stores rather than one. You will find milk only at the dairy, meat at the butcher's, napkins at the paper store, cold cream at the chemist's, fish at the fishmonger's, canned goods at the grocery, fruits at the fruiterer's or greengrocer's, and bread at the bakery. And in many a store it will be necessary to stand in line to be waited on. We developed great respect for the patience and endurance of the English housewife.

The salesmen and saleswomen we found always pleasant, accommodating and honest, and of course the prices are fixed, not vacillating as in many other lands.

Floodlit London

We saw our first tugs at Kingston, all boats above this point having been pleasure craft. This was the first sign that we were about to enter a quite different Thames, a river not of green splendor and postcard villages but of industry and great ships.

"Where are you going?" the lockkeeper at Teddington challenged.

"To Southend."

"But Bushnell never allows his boats to go downriver. Too dangerous."

I produced the owner's letter authorizing us to sail the *Goshawk* below Teddington if we took a pilot. Shaking his head, the lockkeeper let us through.

Now we were in the tidal Thames. Teddington is the last full lock on the river. Above this point the water is fresh. Below, it is brackish. Above, the level remains more or less the same except in flood. Below, the river restlessly rises and falls twice a day as the ocean tides make themselves felt seventy miles upstream. Just beyond the lock a stone marks the division between the Upper Thames, controlled by the Thames Conservancy, and the Lower Thames, supervised by the Port of London Authority.

Caution dictates that an experienced pilot be aboard every boat in the crowded lower reaches. This had been arranged, and Denis Hoolahan, licensed waterman, was waiting for us at the boathouse by the weir. He came on at once, and we sped downriver.

Denis was a pleasant and competent Irishman who began by asking for a cup of tea. This was the first of hundreds of cups he consumed on the way to the mouth of the Thames. Just as the engines ran on petrol, Denis ran on tea.

Passing through London at night was one of the great experiences of my life. Floodlighting has greatly enhanced the beauty of the city, and nowhere are the lighted buildings seen to greater advantage than in the black mirror of the Thames. Every illumination is doubled and at the same time given a wavering ethereal unreality.

Even the Battersea Power Station was a thing of beauty, its chimneys reaching up like giant arms, with their enormous smudges of smoke transformed into golden draperies against the black sky.

The gleaming white stone and bold statues of the Tate Gallery showed little sign that the famous building was severely damaged by air raids in 1941. The great clock dial of Westminster Palace, from which Big Ben counts the hours, glowed like an enormous moon. A light at the top signified that the House of Commons was in night session.

Most gorgeous was the façade of the stately London County Hall, illuminated in four colors. Festoons of light completed the picture, which gained contrast from the blackness underneath the bridges as we passed through.

Cleopatra's Needle, an ancient obelisk brought from Egypt with its twin which stands in New York's Central Park, was silhouetted in black against the two-color floodlit face of the skyscraping Shell-Mex building.

We passed under historic London Bridge and faced the grim old Tower of London. But now it looked more fairylike than grim under its whitewash of light, and we preferred to think of it as a palace for kings rather than as a prison and death house.

Like a climax to all this splendor, Tower Bridge soared into the air, the tips of its two Gothic towers lost in the mist, its twin bascules opened like a pair of gigantic jaws to allow the passage of a ship. We tied up below the bridge.

Treasures of Far-off Lands

The next morning as we dodged through the frantic traffic of the Pool of London, made more dangerous by morning fog, we understood why a licensed waterman was needed on board. This is perhaps the heaviest river traffic anywhere in the world. London, of course, was built here because the Thames was here; the city grew because the river brought the world to its door.

Canals led off from the river through locks into the port's great harbor system—the Royal Docks contain the largest area of impounded dock water in the world. Here lay ocean liners and freighters by the score, and great cranes picking off cargo or putting it on.

Here approximately one thousand ships a week come and go, more than fifty thousand a year. Nearly a quarter of a million passengers arrive or depart during the year. More than sixty million tons of cargo are handled in a year, half again as much as passes through the Port of New York.

In endless warehouses are stored the stuff of history, the treasures of far-off lands which evidence the trade that made England great: marble, mahogany, mother-of-pearl, ivory, tortoiseshell, indigo, spices, quicksilver, gums, rubber, silks and perfumes, grain and timber, sugar and tea by the ton, coffee and tobacco and wine, tallow and hides, frozen meat, and dairy produce.

We passed from west to east as we sailed by a vertical marker on the seawall indicating zero meridian. For here is Greenwich, from which point time and longitude are still reckoned. The lights of the city and the increasing smokiness of the atmosphere, though, have forced the observatory to move to new quarters in Herstmonceux Castle in Sussex.

Gravesend is in a sense Thames-end; it is here that an outgoing ship puts off its river pilot and takes on a pilot for the deepwater channel.

We sailed on, for though Gravesend may be considered the end of the river proper, we wanted to see the Thames improper, the unpredictable estuary, miles wide, sometimes savage under fierce winds, sometimes blinded with fog or chilled to almost arctic temperatures by storms from the North Sea.

It was nearly eight in the evening when we drew into Holehaven Creek (which was to prove no haven) and anchored in a channel barely two hundred yards wide between a mud flat and Canvey Island. We lay between two boats that were drying very fishy nets—with the consequence that we were promptly visited by flies.

Perils of a Dragging Anchor

A storm came up and gave us a bad night; we braced ourselves in our bunks to avoid being thrown out. A weird medley of bangs, rattles, smacks and cracks made the night hideous, and the morning light showed piles of crockery and tinware, cans and milk bottles chasing each other over the cabin floor.

The day greeted us with a chill wind and a tossing sea. The *Goshawk* tore at her anchor like a frightened horse. To go on, we needed petrol. Mr. Hoolahan and Herbert rowed away in the dinghy to get it.

Some time later I stepped out of the cabin and discovered that our stern was within twenty feet of a lee shore under a strong gale. And the lee shore was not soft—it was the solid stone dike. The anchor was dragging. Ten minutes more, perhaps five, and we would be pounding the rocks.

Could I fend off with the boathook? My strength would be
nothing against seven tons of boat and more tons of water.
Could I haul in on the anchor chain? Five men couldn't
budge the boat against that pressure of wind and sea. My only
hope was to start the engines. But engines won't run without
petrol. Hoping there might be a little left, I pressed the starter
button. There was only a melancholy buzz.

I tried and tried again. My wife reported that we were now
ten feet from the rocks. If we struck, first to be smashed would
be the twin screws. Then our last chance would be gone, the
boat would be broken up, and we would be lucky to clamber
up the steep wall without being ground to pulp between boat
and dike.

One engine coughed, sputtered, and took hold. I threw the
lever into full ahead. The engine stalled. Mary came running
forward.

"Only five feet," she said. "What do we do?"

"Be ready to jump," I said.

I tried the engines once more. The port engine refused abso-
lutely. The starboard engine started, stopped, started again.
This time it kept going. But one engine wasn't enough. We
were still inching toward shore, though more slowly. I saw Hoolahan and Herbert coming in the dinghy. They had seen what
was happening and Hoolahan was fairly tearing his arms out at
the oars.

I kept coaxing the port engine. Suddenly it responded. The
boat pulled away with tantalizing slowness from the murderous
stone dike.

Six Miles Wide

The sea became rougher. Herbert lost his breakfast and his
two false teeth over the side. His speech became flannelly.

"I'm thick," he complained.

"Sick!" exclaimed the irrepressible Hoolahan. "Oh, no! Come
help me fix the engines. That will cure you."

By next morning the wind had dropped and we were able to
get on to our last port of call, Southend-on-Sea, where estuary
and ocean meet. It was Sunday and trippers from London had

inundated the seaside resort. We parted regretfully from Herbert and Denis, who left to sail the *Goshawk* back upriver.

Southend is the British Coney Island. At night the waterfront bursts into millions of colored lights. The pier, one of the longest in the world, even has its own seven-car trains to transport people from shore to pierhead.

At the end the pierhead broadens to become a pile-supported island three stories high, populated with thousands of trippers. Here at the mouth of the Thames they visit shops and shows and concerts and enjoy the bravest illumination in England. They gaze open-mouthed at enormous fire-breathing dragons, a vast luminous mosaic of Queen Elizabeth I and her square-rigged ships, another of the present Elizabeth and her castles and palaces, a replica of the Statue of Liberty to please visiting Americans, a doll's theater, Mother Goose, Miss Muffet, Santa Claus and his reindeer, and many other characters from fact and fiction, all blown up to gigantic proportions and blazing with color and light.

There are cafés and bars and booths where you may nibble cockles and whelks and jellied eels. There are games of chance to suit any taste. And there are the people, with green, red, or blue faces, according to the colors that happen to be flashing at the moment, all struggling cheerfully to get past, under or over other people, all laughing and screaming and ignoring the grave old Thames which cannot smother this gaiety with its dark, silent mantle.

There is a place where you can get away from all the uproar, at the far end of the pier projecting darkly into the river. Here we were a mile and a third from shore and yet far short of the middle of the mighty stream, some six miles wide.

We stood in the dark and thought of the thousands of ships that pass this point in a year, thought of the fabulous port and the city of cities that owes so much of its greatness to this stream. We thought of all that the river has meant to England and the world.

It was hard to believe that this was the same Thames we had taken up on the tip of a finger at Thames Head.

10

The Bewitching Rhine

NAKED AS a jay, Dr. Potts strode through the village of Ober-
wesel-on-the-Rhine.

Male residents muttered in their beards. Females averted
blushing faces and peeped from the corners of their eyes.

Dr. Potts told me about it himself. That is not his name. He
is a reputable physician of Palm Springs, California. When I
appeared for my annual pre-travel checkup, he made conversation with:

"Well, where to this time?"

"The Rhine."

"Ah, the Rhine! I had an odd experience there once."

Between taps on chest and back, he recalled his Rhine adventure.

Adam Without a Fig Leaf

"I was hiking cross-country. I came down through the hills to the west bank of the Rhine just above Oberwesel.

"The shore road is very busy, as you know, but I crossed it and found my way out onto a quiet point. There I was all alone. Bushes screened me from the road. I was hot from walking and the river looked inviting, but I had no bathing suit.

"On the other side was another quiet point. It occurred to me that I might swim across to that point and back again without disturbing anyone. If a boat happened to pass, it wouldn't matter—only my head would be visible.

"So I stripped, tucked all my clothes under a bush, and dived in. The Rhine was new to me. I didn't realize how strong the current is.

"At first it was all right because there was a lazy back eddy in the lee of the point. But when I got out a bit, I was swept downstream. Try my best, I couldn't make the other point. I came to shore a good half mile below it. Since there was another busy road here around the base of the famous Lorelei Rock, I didn't come out of the water, but turned about and headed back.

"Now I was really worried. I had to make it against that current and get back to my starting point. Of course I couldn't do it. When I reached the left bank I had lost another half mile.

"There was a lot of traffic on the road. I didn't want to come out, but I was getting cold. So I crawled ashore, tore a branch from a bush in lieu of a fig leaf, and then walked as nonchalantly as I could up a mile of shore road and through the village of Oberwesel back to my clothes.

"The police were alerted but didn't catch up with me until I was dressed. They took me in custody, probably meaning to escort me to the police station and have me examined for sanity. But when I pulled out a U.S. passport they waved their hands as if to say, 'What can you expect of an American?' and let me go."

Dr. Potts went on to philosophize a bit. That experience, he said, gave him tremendous respect for the Rhine. He realized, as never before, what a living force it is. And the five castles that looked down on his swim—they took on life too. He could better appreciate the surge of events up and down this great waterway, the feuds between robber barons, wars of princes, tortures in black dungeons, duels, suicides of lovelorn ladies, events savage, dramatic, romantic, that made history and left behind a trail of fascinating legends.

Born in Paradise

A month later we stood, my wife and I, knee-deep in July snow, watching the birth of a great river.

The Rhine is born in Paradise. It rolls out from under the ever-melting, ever-renewed Paradise Glacier fed by the snows of the Rheinwaldhorn (Rhine Forest Horn, 3,406 meters) and the Rheinquellhorn (Rhine Source Horn, 3,200).

As befits its divine nature, the Rhine comes forth with authority. Even as an infant, it seems to know that it is destined to inherit the honorable title of "Father Rhine." From the glacier's icy womb it leaps out in full armor, flashing in the sunlight, roaring as if it were a real river and not merely a cascade four feet wide.

Its birthplace is the eternal white city of the Swiss Alps. On the south side the mountains drop down abruptly to the lush, tropical dreamland of the Italian lakes. These frosty peaks feed those lakes and through them the River Po.

That is the smallest part of their job. The Alpine Massif initiates most of the great rivers of Europe.

It has been called "unknown Switzerland"—this stretch of almost inaccessible pinnacles lying between the Julier Pass and the St. Gotthard.

Unknown—but its children are known, and famous. It sends them out in all directions—the Ticino to the south, the Rhône to the west, the Aare to the northwest, the Reuss to the north, the Rhine to the northeast, the Inn east to swell the Danube.

Mightiest of all these is the Rhine. I have said it issues from Paradise Glacier. But the gods were not content to trust this source alone. To insure the flow of the great river, they gave it many other sources almost as important. All are in the same mighty Massif.

Many Rhines

The one from Paradise is known as the *Hinter Rhine* (the Rhine Behind, so called because it starts far back among the peaks). But there is also the *Vorderrhein,* Forward Rhine, and between them the Middle Rhine. And as if that weren't enough, more ice water is supplied by the Gammer Rhine, Glenner Rhine, Valser Rhine, Julia Rhine, Albula Rhine, Cristallina Rhine, Rabiusa Rhine, Averser Rhine, Jufer Rhine and Madriser Rhine.

We followed every one to its beginning or as near the beginning as possible. One characteristic they have in common. They are all in a hurry. They rage down through savage gorges, tearing their hair, foaming at the mouth, battling with boulders, deafening the ears and making speech inaudible, churning and vaporizing, sending up clouds of writhing mist to the mountaintops.

If you stand on the bank and look upstream and squint, what you see is a troop of a thousand white horses bursting out of the sky and plunging toward you down a precipitous flight of stairs.

Incoming cascades and waterfalls rapidly swell the stream. Within a few miles the puling infant has become a brawny giant. It may be a hundred feet wide but still only ten feet deep. But when squeezed between cliffs ten feet apart, it must reverse its proportions, becoming ten feet wide and a hundred deep.

It savagely cuts its way through incredible barriers. Hell Gorge on the Middle Rhine slices into solid rock to make a slot a thousand feet deep. So abrupt are the walls that the road cut into the face of one of them is continuously overhung by rock and nine times disappears into a tunnel. It looks more like an elongated cliff-dwelling than a road. You can't help marveling at the temerity of Swiss engineers who dared even to imagine such a project, much less carry it out.

A wild rocky defile that Walter Scott would have loved cradles the "tempestuous Averser Rhine" whose waterfalls are more frequent than hydrants on a city street.

The Gorge of Schöllenen on the Reuss, a Rhine tributary, is so black and ominous and made so mysterious by blinding mist that it has long been believed to be a door to the infernal regions. A bridge was swung over it—but wayfarers refused to cross it because of the rumor that the devil in person presided over it and collected as toll the soul of anyone who dared put foot upon it. The bridge is still there, but unused.

The gorge of the Aare, another Rhine tributary, is only a yard wide in places, and on a catwalk suspended within it you may, by projecting your elbows, touch both cliffs. Here the water sneaking by beneath you plummets to unknown depths and the raging current sweeps away a sounding line before it can reach the bottom. As you look up, only a thin ribbon of sky is visible between the vertical cliffs.

At the bottom of the fearsome Tamina Gorge hot springs gush from the walls. For some centuries patients were lowered down the face of the cliff to the springs at the end of a rope. It was a harrowing experience, and many who looked down decided that, after all, they did not need a hot bath. The terror of the treatment effectively separated the truly ill from the hypochondriacs.

The Bad Way

Most grandiose of all is the gorge known as the *Via Mala*, Bad Way, on the Hinter Rhine. Here the resolute river has cut a cleft *sixteen hundred feet deep* through a schist escarpment, leaving two worse-than-vertical cliffs almost touching each other like two gigantic jaws.

They are very irregular jaws, twisting and curling, their top edges contorted like scornful lips. It's as if some mountain monster were diabolically snapping at the river, determined to bite it asunder.

At the bottom of the sixteen-hundred-foot chasm the river, narrowed and almost choked but deepening accordingly, boils its way through in white fury.

Its roar can be heard for miles, yet you can hardly see it because the twisting, bulging walls shut off the view except in some spots where they are more strictly perpendicular. Even there you must strain your eyes since the depths of the abyss are as dark as a moonlit night in spite of the noon sun above.

To get a close view you can go down uncounted steps until your legs turn into spaghetti. Then on a platform you stand close enough to be deafened and soaked, and escape with a sense of relief to the upper world.

Naturally there are local superstitions about the place, especially the bit known as *Verlorene Loch*, Lost Hole.

High above all this on a rocky peak stand the ruins of the castle *Hohen Rhätien*, "a sight worthy of an engraving by Gustave Doré." It is reminiscent of the Lorelei Rock on the Lower Rhine, but incomparably grander, much higher (3,117 feet as against 425), and bulging belligerently over the river instead of gracefully retreating in the fashion of the Lorelei.

I would not be guilty of detracting from the fame of the Lorelei, or any of the glories of the known Rhine. But would that more travelers might explore the Swiss Rhines, largely unfamiliar even to habitual visitors to Switzerland.

Fifteen Castles in Fifteen Miles

Take castles.

The castle just mentioned is but one of fifteen in a fifteen-mile stretch of the Hinter Rhine. Most are in ruins, some are still lived in. All are "teen-agers" built between the thirteenth and seventeenth centuries.

Their stories compete with the fascinating tales of the German castles. There is a rough humor in some of the stories—as in the account of the haughty lord who spat in the peasant's broth, whereupon the peasant ducked the lord's head into it, saying, "Eat the soup thou hast seasoned," and strangled him.

The castles are built high and low on projections of the mountain wall along the right side of the river. There is no comparison between this stupendous rampart and that along the known Rhine. Here the peaks rise to six thousand feet and more—there seldom over six hundred. There the river is soiled by ships and cities. Here there are no cities. The river comes fresh from snowfields and glaciers, and even the dirt in it is clean.

It is not transparent but opaque, carrying rock material that has been ground from the glacier bed. The resultant mixture has been described as "glacier milk" and has a lovely light aquamarine tint not found elsewhere, even on the reefs of the South Seas. But as the surf gleams white over the turquoise shallows of Pacific atolls, so the foaming rapids of the Hinter Rhine are snow-white against the aquamarine background.

No boat could live in these delightful but deadly waters. The same is true of all the mountain Rhines. There is no spot except behind a dam where a boat could be launched without being ground to bits at once. The swift current contorted by great rocks defies the most adventurous whitewater enthusiast.

Needless to say, no exploration by canoe or *Faltboot* was possible here. We followed the streams in a small German car rented in Zürich or, where there was no road, went afoot.

The Hidden Wonder

This latter means of locomotion, so unfamiliar to modern man, got us into occasional trouble. As when we searched through pathless woods over inconceivably rough terrain, above and under logs, around rocks, across ravines, crouching and crawling, to come out at last on the edge of the abyss into which thunders the highest falls in the entire Rhine system. It is called the Fumatsch Falls and over its brink the Middle Rhine drops ninety-eight feet—nearly twice the fifty-foot plunge of the much visited Rhine Falls below Lake Constance.

But whoever heard of Fumatsch? Not only is there no trail to it but there is no signboard on the nearest road. And even when we reached the edge of the precipice and the thunder told us the fall was only a few hundred feet away, we could not see it. To get a look at it and take a picture it was necessary to creep out precariously on a branch projecting over the gorge and operate the camera while the other member of the party steadied the photographer by clutching a dangling foot.

Mary never did see Fumatsch until the picture was developed.

The net result of this scramble was two lame backs which for six months thereafter kept alive the memory of Fumatsch. But it was a stirring memory of a truly remarkable hidden wonder in the privacy of the deep forest—a single sheer drop completely outclassing the three-step descent of the Rhine Falls little more than half as high.

The most sensational waterfall of the Rhine is neither of these. It is the Trümmelbach in the Lauterbrunnen valley. Shy of publicity, this waterfall performs its star act *inside* a mountain, roaring down through the dark in five terrific cascades. Its privacy has not been respected and manmade tunnels permit visitors to view this underground spectacle.

Marvels Underground

Switzerland has many underground wonders. The highest railway station in Europe is underground. The railroad tunnels its way up through the heart of the mountain to the terminus at Jungfraujoch, 11,342 feet. If you step out of the train expecting to have a vision of the snow-clad Jungfrau burst upon you, you are at once disillusioned. You might imagine yourself in the New York subway. You walk through a tunnel and come out into a small town, still underground, with hotels, research stations, post office and shops. But you get the view at last from the windows of a large restaurant or, after a lift of 367 feet through a vertical tunnel, from a view-terrace. You return underground to discover the Ice Palace, a skating rink laid out in the middle of the glacier.

All this is nothing new to the Swiss. There is much more in Switzerland than meets the eye of the tourist—it is hidden in the bosom of the mountains. There are dozens of subterranean forts, military installations with underground power stations, factories, hidden artillery and even airfields. Planes lie hidden, always ready to be hoisted to flying position by hydraulic lifts. There are underground hospitals, stores of food, enough ammunition to supply an army of eight hundred thousand men— all concealed behind innocent-looking mountain slopes studded with smiling flowers.

Across the valley from the subterranean waterfall is another phenomenon no less remarkable—the Upside Down Falls of Staubbach where the force of gravity is canceled by rising air currents turning the falling water into soaring spray. What goes up must finally come down, and the two falls join forces for the journey to the Rhine.

They say that if the mountains could be flattened with a hot iron, Switzerland would be the largest country in Europe. It may be so. But creased and folded like a closed accordion, Switzerland is so small that a plane can cross it in fourteen minutes.

One way that the Swiss can get more use out of their tiny country is to utilize the inside as well as the outside, and that they have done. Many mountain roads are half underground. The tunnels boring under the Alps all the way from Switzerland to Italy are unmatched in the world. The Swiss want to keep in touch with their neighbors but want also to be able to get out of touch promptly in case of war. They are willing and fully prepared to blow up these engineering masterpieces on a few moments' notice.

A Nation of Warriors

We think of Switzerland as a peaceful country. So it is, but no country is better prepared for war.

The saying goes: "The Swiss do not have an army; they *are* an army."

Throughout her history Switzerland has been war-conscious. Not that the Swiss have wanted to seize territory. On the contrary they have followed the advice of one of their great statesmen:

"Do not extend the frontiers too far!"

By limiting her ambitions, little Switzerland has remained at peace with the giants around her. But she has never trusted those giants and is ready to defend herself when and if necessary.

The Swiss enjoy a good fight, but they are too wise to involve their country in the fighting. For centuries Swiss soldiers hired out as mercenaries to the highest bidder. Their belligerent tradition may be traced back to the Helvetii whom Julius Caesar called the most courageous of all the Gauls.

In the War of the Spanish Succession two thousand Swiss fought with the Imperialists, three thousand with Milan, four thousand with Savoy, thirteen thousand with the Dutch and twenty thousand with the French—a total of forty-two thousand Swiss fighting on two opposite sides.

Four thousand Swiss fought in the American Civil War. During the First World War seven thousand Swiss died in the service of France. Many of the hardiest fighters of the French Foreign Legion have been Swiss.

Since 1927, volunteering in foreign armies has been forbidden by Swiss law. The only exception is service in the Vatican Guard, a polite formality involving no military action.

Industrial advance has made the sale of Swiss manpower unnecessary. But the military spirit remains. Every Swiss male is a soldier. He keeps his weapons always at hand and the entire Swiss army can be mobilized in three hours.

Liechtenstein, Pocket-Size Nation

A savage old castle at Reichenau looks down upon the final blending of the Swiss Rhines. From there on there is only *the* Rhine.

It is a grown-up river now but has not lost its youthful impetuosity. And for another seventy miles it remains unruly and unnavigable. Its wild aspect is enhanced by dramatic mountains crowned with castles.

Even better than looking up to these castles is the privilege of stepping back a thousand years to live in a castle and look down to the Rhine. It is one of the peculiar delights of a European journey, this opportunity to spend a night or a week now and then in a genuine castle, whose owners have succumbed to the high cost of living and have converted their ancestral home into a hotel.

From a tower room in the castle-hotel at Bad Ragaz we look out across the magnificently landscaped private estate to the hurrying Rhine and the dreaming blue of the mountain range beyond. The furnishings of the room take us back to the middle ages, but below, instead of a dungeon, is a sparkling restaurant serving the best Swiss, German and French dishes. Outside, waving above the ramparts, the banner of a robber baron has been replaced by the Swiss flag.

Not far downstream we see one of the finest castles in all Europe. It stands high above the right bank. We stand on Swiss soil and look up to it but the flag billowing above it is not Swiss.

This is the castle of the prince of the pocket-size nation of Liechtenstein.

We find the Swiss side of the border heavily fortified by tank traps of huge cement blocks garnished with barbed wire. Is Switzerland so afraid of invasion from tiny Liechtenstein? Not from it, but through it. Beyond lie great powers—Austria, Germany, Russia—and the Swiss have no confidence that the little principality would be able to stem an attack.

However, the tiny sovereign state has been successful in preserving the independence acquired in 1719. The extent of its territory is only sixty square miles and the population is fifteen thousand. And yet it has been happy and prosperous thanks to government by enlightened princes and the sale of corn, wine, fruit, cattle, cotton, leather—and false teeth.

Incidentally, the most significant collection of Rubens paintings in the world is that of the Prince of Liechtenstein, some of them displayed in a gallery in the town of Vaduz, the others in his castle.

Through a picturesque covered bridge across the Rhine we return to Switzerland and continue north.

But it is a different Switzerland now. The floodplain widens to ten miles between mountain ranges and makes room for fine residences and handsome public buildings.

So they appear at some distance. When we come closer, they turn out to be factories. But what strange factories! They do not belch smoke. There are no chimneys, no piles of slag and ashes, no cemetery of broken-down motor vehicles, no heaps of boxes, bales and rusty machine parts.

The buildings are not merely functional. They have grace and dignity and the grounds are beautifully landscaped. Go around a building and you will have difficulty deciding which is the back. The waste and debris that must exude from any industrial plant—where does it go?

Shocking Cleanliness

The cleanliness of Switzerland is shocking. The American visitor accustomed to roads bordered by beer cans feels a sense of loss. The Frenchman finds everything too precise. The Iberian and Italian visitors may feel that there is something unnatural in these always scrubbed faces and scrubbed streets. A visiting author expressed it this way:

"Switzerland is a clean country, an orderly country, but it is surely obvious that the predominance of these factors in a nation's life implies above all a concern for material well-being, a cult of comfort, which are likely to preclude those spiritual preoccupations that might distract it from its everyday routine."

Plainly stated, this critic's theory is that a man or nation must be dirty to be good.

The Rhine plays a large part in Swiss cleanliness. Six thousand power stations transform the energy of mountain torrents into electricity. They supply more than enough power for all Swiss needs, leaving a surplus to be exported to neighboring countries.

Not only are factories electrified, but the swift, sure and punctual trains climb some of the steepest railroad gradients in the world without the stink of diesel, carrying annually some 700 million passengers and 35 million tons of goods. One is thankful for the absence of smell and smudge when penetrating any one of Switzerland's 672 railroad tunnels. Very pleasant too is the silent operation of the hundreds of aerial cableways, chairlifts, skilifts, rack railways and funiculars.

But Swiss spotlessness is due to something more than the clean power contributed by her Rhines. The Swiss take pride in the appearance of themselves and their country. There are no billboards to mar the incomparable mountain views. Window boxes of geraniums give charm not only to chalets but to banks, stores and factories. Schools hold classes out of doors and teach the laws of mountains, valleys, trees and birds.

Wild flowers are jealously protected. Such signs as "Don't pick flowers," "Don't damage trees," are meant for visitors—the Swiss don't need them. Swiss children, usually shy, will muster the courage to reprove a stranger who wades into a meadow and plucks the blooms. And if you toss a scrap of litter from your car, you may expect to be overhauled and have it politely returned to you.

The Rhine Makes the Wheels Turn

Rhine-powered industries have made the Swiss preeminent in many fields. They are the wizards of chemistry, they invented and perfected vitamins, manufactured DDT, make the best dyes, are famous for their chocolates. Swiss architects plan New York's skyscrapers.

Used to spanning their own country's abysses, Swiss engineers are great bridge builders and the largest bridges of the world are the work of a Swiss firm.

And watches. The Swiss turn out watches that do everything but sing your national anthem. Their clocks are inordinately proud of themselves and continually remind you how good they are.

In the little village of Mörschwil in the Rhine hills we listened with amazement as the clock in the bell tower of the church struck twelve. One would vaguely suppose that twelve strokes would make twelve. But no. First there must be two strokes for each quarter hour that has passed since eleven—that made eight strokes; then twelve blows on a big bell; then, for listeners who might still be in doubt, twelve blows on a bigger bell. Thirty-two strokes in all!

We recalled Mark Twain's comment on Swiss clocks:

"We did not oversleep at St. Nicholas. The church bell began to ring at four-thirty in the morn, and from the length of time it continued to ring I judged that it takes the Swiss sinner a good while to get the invitation through his head."

Much liquor is brewed in Switzerland. Whether it is good is a matter of opinion. Mark Twain didn't think so, and he found it expensive:

"We bought a bottle or so of beer here; at any rate they called it beer, but I knew by the price that it was dissolved jewelry and I perceived by the taste that dissolved jewelry is not good stuff to drink." (I quote from *A Tramp Abroad*.)

Whether Mark Twain liked it or not, the Swiss are fond of pouring a little cognac or Kirsch on everything edible. At a formal dinner an Englishman tasted so much brandy in his soup that he lifted his cup of consommé and announced:

"Ladies and gentlemen: the Queen!"

In many Western countries there is a lack of skilled labor. In Switzerland the tables are turned—there's plenty of skilled labor, but unskilled labor must be imported. Each year about 400,000 seasonal foreign workers must be brought in to do the necessary unskilled work.

Ignorant and untrained Swiss are hard to find. This is no new thing. In the eighteenth century when most European peasants were illiterate, travelers were amazed by the high degree of education found even in the remote valleys of the Alps.

A discussion of Swiss education would take us far afield. For a devastating comparison of educational systems see Admiral H. G. Rickover's *Swiss Schools and Ours: Why Theirs Are Better.*

Main Street a Picture Gallery

The Rhine lays down its burden of glacial powder in a broad delta and emerges with deceptive calm into Lake Constance. It would appear to have reached sedate maturity. But it will rage and tear its hair again, though never with the same childish abandon.

Boats and even steamers may venture upon its waters now. We sail the length of lovely Lake Constance to the fine city of Constance and the alluring island of Mainau with its remarkable subtropical gardens of banana, citrus, datura, oleander, palm, lantana, bamboo, gingko, in an Italianate setting of terraces, balustrades and statues.

We have reached the less alluring part of the traveler's paradise. But Switzerland will not let us leave without a going-away present. It is Stein-on-the-Rhine, one of the most pictorial of all Swiss villages.

From our hotel window we look down a main street that is a veritable picture gallery, the façade of every house portraying in brilliant color paintings of life in medieval Europe.

Dining on a terrace over the river we watch the small boats coming through under a bridge that is quaintly arched like those of Japan. Above the bridge rises a full moon, casting golden reflections on the fast-flowing water which is now as black as ebony.

What a chameleon the Rhine is—milky aquamarine as it emerges from the glaciers, snow-white in the rapids, tan as khaki after plowing through the gorges, placid deep blue in Lake Constance, a vivid, lively, translucent green jade as it pours out of the lake, and now, black and gold.

The Rhine Falls

The Rhine Falls are not much compared with Victoria, Iguassu or Niagara but it is exciting to ride a small boat almost beneath them, flopping precariously through the waves to the great rock that blocks the falls at their center.

One may climb to the peak of this rock, water boiling furiously all about, rainbows appearing and disappearing in the spray, the tumult making conversation impractical.

Though only half the height of Fumatsch, the Rhine Falls do take the prize for noise and for volume, delivering more water than any other falls in Europe, an average of 25,000 cubic feet a second as against 2,500 a second for the Thames where it drops from the weir at Teddington.

A castle looks down from a precipice on the left bank and another looks up from the right below the falls. These castles give the visitor something more substantial than romance— they have both been converted into restaurants.

The fresh green river, adorned by swans and cygnets, now flows through a mild farming area—yet there are frequent signs warning motorists of the presence of deer. All is not lost to commercialism where deer still run wild.

Suddenly the jade Rhine stepping out daintily from between wooded islands is overwhelmed by the great black Aare. The Aare is twice as wide as the Rhine, and deeper, and why the entire river from this point on was not called the Aare is a mystery.

We have the same sort of mystery in America where the puny Mississippi joins the mighty Missouri, then the deep Ohio, and yet, though completely outclassed by either one of these rivers, continues to call itself the Mississippi.

Salt Baths from the Saltless Rhine

An astonishing feature of this stretch of the Rhine is that the saltless stream makes possible the strongest salt baths in Europe. A half dozen towns owe their existence to Rhine brine.

Hundreds of feet beneath the river are heavy salt deposits. Rhine water seeps down to them and the saline solution thus formed is pumped up and piped to hotels up and down the valley.

The salinity is 30 percent. Patients are advised to start with baths slightly saline, say 2 or 3 percent which is about the salinity of the ocean, making each bath a little stronger but never going above 8 percent.

One lady who suspected that this procedure was devised merely to prolong the treatments, insisted upon taking the brine full strength. She changed her mind after two baths—it nearly took the hide off her.

According to the spa prospectuses, there are few ailments that the baths are *not* good for. They are said to cure or relieve heart affections, high blood pressure, faulty circulation, thrombosis, varicose veins, venous affections, hardening of the arteries, nervous diseases, gout, rheumatism, catarrh, anemia, bladder trouble, irregularity, diseases of the liver and gall bladder—and even sterility. Has anything been forgotten? If so, notify the spas, and they will doubtless add it to the list.

We think of Switzerland as a landlocked nation buried far away from all oceans in the dry heart of a continent.

But the Swiss city of Basle is an ocean port. Seagoing ships from all the world dock at these piers. Half of Switzerland's imports of 10 million tons a year come to her by water—up the Rhine. Switzerland owns 300,000 tons of Rhine shipping. Her world trade places her third among all countries in proportion to population.

Nothing could be better evidence of the prosperity of the Swiss. They buy from all the world because they have the means to buy. Switzerland has the world's fourth largest national income per capita, exceeded only by the United States, Canada and Great Britain. She can afford to buy from every land under the sun and, thanks chiefly to the Rhine, she does.

Gangling Youth Becomes Gangster

We have now covered about half of the Rhine's total length of 850 miles from Alps to sea.

The second half is quite unlike the first. The river has lost its boyish exuberance. That doesn't mean that it is tamed. It is an adult gangster, bearing a heavy burden of traffic but doing it sullenly, wrecking craft on shoals and rocks, flooding lowlands when unprotected by dikes, mindful of the volcanic origins of its valley and a willing collaborator with earthquakes such as the one that in the fourteenth century killed sixteen thousand inhabitants of Strasbourg.

Not only in terms of strength, but in terms of time, it is now an adult river. No other river is richer in history and legend. If you lift your eyes from the barges to the castled heights, you are in a dreamland of romance and high adventure.

To relate the rest of our Rhine journey in chronological order would leave the reader in a state of complete confusion. It was not simply a matter of proceeding from Basle to Rotterdam. It was a most intricate itinerary involving four months of travel, first on the world's newest and finest riverboat, *Helvetia*, all the way down and back, then by car from village to village along one shore and back on the other, plus endless interweavings to work in certain points of interest that did not fall neatly into the schedule. For example, the castled stretch between Bingen and Bonn was traversed seven times.

Rather than retrace all these meanderings, let us imagine a simple trip from Basle to the ocean, noting what may be seen along the way.

The river drops 450 feet between Basle and Strasbourg, descending through five deep locks of the *Grand Canal d'Alsace*, a manmade waterway broader than Suez or Panama.

Below Strasbourg shipping follows the river itself but never without risk. You sail, or drive, through what seems like placid farming country, but you observe that all towns are built well away from the river and on high ground where they hope to be safe from floods when Alpine snows melt in June.

College Cutups and Bloody Blades

It is not until you reach the inflowing Neckar that you feel the hot breath of romance down the back of your neck. Here is castle-crowned Heidelberg in whose ancient university many bloody duels have been fought.

At the end of World War II the Allies occupying Germany outlawed dueling. Now that the Occupation laws have lapsed, 379 dueling fraternities have again come to life. Not only in Heidelberg but at the universities of Munich, Stuttgart, West Berlin, Göttingen and others, double-edged sabers three and a half feet long with razor-sharp tips are flashing.

Four thrusts are allowed to each round and the fight continues until one of the duelists is too bloodied to continue or until the limit of thirty rounds is reached.

The right of students to carve each other up has been confirmed in the German courts. Yet there is much public opposition. The most recent protest to date comes from fifteen West German university professors who declare that student duels are "often used to disguise real blood duels. They are a violation of the morality of civilized peoples."

Face wounds are welcomed by fighters because they leave plainly visible scars, proof that the bearer has been through a university. After all, one cannot go about flaunting a diploma. That would be immodest. But a scarred face is a modest reminder to all and sundry that you are a highly educated man, and a brave one to boot. Face wounds are sometimes picked open to delay healing and leave as ugly a mark as possible.

We talked with a student whose face was so completely bandaged that only his eyes could be seen. He was quite happy about it and would accept no sympathy.

"It's a custom as old as that castle," he said, waving a hand toward the magnificent floodlit towers and battlements on the mountainside. "We like to preserve our old traditions. We like to think there's something left of the age of chivalry."

"But can't you have your age of chivalry without slaughtering each other?"

"Do you do any better?" he retorted. "You've had three boxers die within a year. And every football season more than a dozen of your students are killed."

I let him win the argument.

Every Castle Has Its Tale

The age of chivalry—sometimes more distinguished by knavery than chivalry—is encountered wherever you turn in the Neckar Valley. Every castle has its tale. Sometimes it is pure history, sometimes pure legend—more often a blend of the two.

Fairly factual is the story of the castle above Heilbronn which was besieged until starvation forced surrender. The defenders begged for leniency, but the attacking prince declared he would spare none but the women and children—every man must die. The women came to him on their knees begging for the lives of their husbands.

"No," said the prince. "Not a man shall escape alive; you yourselves shall go with your children into banishment; but that you may not starve I grant you this one grace. Each woman may bear with her as much of her most valuable property as she is able to carry."

The women returned to the castle. Presently they emerged carrying their husbands on their shoulders.

The besiegers, angry at having been thus outwitted, rushed forward to slaughter the men. The prince stopped them.

"Put up your swords," he said. "A prince's word is inviolable."

The castle of Dilsberg was saved by bees. When the marauder Tilly and his forces succeeded in scaling the steep hill, placed their ladders against the castle walls and began to climb, defense would have been hopeless if one of the defenders had not thought of the bees.

All of the beehives within the castle courts were collected, thoroughly shaken to enrage the bees, then dumped upon the climbing invaders who tumbled to the ground and made off in headlong flight down the mountain, wildly flailing their arms.

A foundling boy, child of an illicit union, grew up ignorant of the burial place of his mother and father. His search at last turned up a clue. He was told by a Carmelite friar that he would find his parents within a wall of the castle of Hirschhorn where they had been buried alive by the girl's outraged father as punishment for their misdeeds. The son joined some men doing repairs within the castle and, after much probing and dislodging of stones, found within the wall the standing skeleton of a woman and that of a knight in full armor.

There is no particular reason to doubt this story since such a form of punishment was not uncommon in "the age of chivalry."

To swing to pure legend, but legend with a surprisingly modern touch, we are told that the spectacular ruin of Eberbach used to be the home of a fire-breathing dragon. He would issue forth and devastate the countryside, burning houses and destroying crops with blasts of flame. And how do you suppose he was conquered? A doughty knight climbed the hill and waited in ambush at the castle gate. When the dragon came out, pouring forth flame as usual, the knight unslung a cylinder from his back, pointed the hose down the beast's throat and pressed a lever. The spray that shot out extinguished the fires and the dragon curled up and died. Mixing the mythical and the modern, the villagers soberly explain that the device used by the knight was simply the common fire-extinguisher.

Swimmers die in the Neckar. Again there is something legendary and something modern in the explanation. Old folks will tell you that the *Neckargeist* lives at the bottom of the river and will pull down anyone who dares enter it.

Some of the more scientific-minded blame detergents. Writes Roger Pilkington, in *Small Boat to Bavaria*:

"The locks are so filled with detergent foam . . . that a deck-hand falling overboard will almost certainly be smothered before he can be located below the mass of froth and hauled out. People have in fact been drowned in the Neckar precisely in that way."

Skeletons, Dragons and Billygoats

Emerging from the Neckar, we pass on down the Rhine to Worms which, on a plaque near the cathedral, gives itself this legitimate praise:

This is one of the most memorable sites of the Western world. Here was the holy temple area of the Romans, the royal fortress of the Nibelungen, the imperial palace of Charlemagne, the court of the lord bishops of Worms. More than a hundred gatherings of empire and earldom were held on this spot, and here there stood before the emperor and empire, Martin Luther.

On the riverbank is a giant figure, not of Charlemagne or Luther, but of the wicked Hagen who cast the treasure of the Nibelungen into the river. Every year someone who refuses to

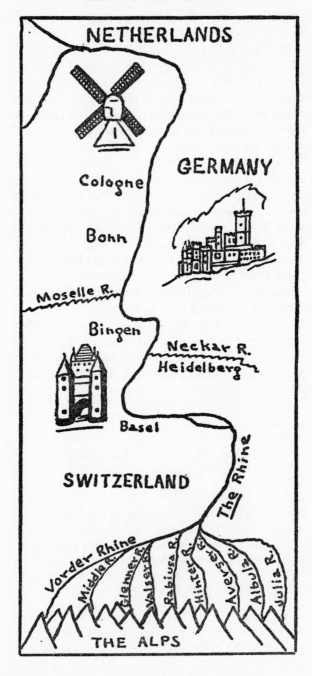

accept the story as pure legend dives here in search of gold and jewels.

The scrotum of a billygoat, *Bocksbeutel* in German, has been made famous by the River Main for it was in this natural container that Main wine used to be bottled. Now glass is used, but one gourmet assured us that the wine lacks that special something that only the smell of a he-goat could give it.

In Mainz a man born with the name Goose-flesh, which he wisely changed to Gutenberg, printed his Bible while Satan, resenting some unkind things the book had to say about him, stood by and did his best to upset the molds and gum up the machine.

In gay, wine-bibing Rüdesheim one drinks more than is good for him, secure in the knowledge that Wiesbaden with its healing waters is nearby.

Bingen too has a reputation for hard drinking, giving rise to the English expression "go on a binge."

Nowhere, Castles like These!

Now we come to it—the greatest parade of castles in all the world.

Nowhere else, not even in Wales or Scotland, are there so many strongholds assembled in such close order. In a single day's journey between Bingen and Bonn we count thirty-one castles.

This is the most magnificent stretch of the Rhine. The river narrows and swirls dangerously between rocky precipices or vine-clad hills topped with the grim keeps of robber barons long gone.

What a story they tell of the days when Germany instead of being one country (or two) was a nation divided against itself into petty kingdoms, dukedoms, bishoprics, free cities, every one of them semi-sovereign, each suspecting and fearing its neighbor. Such political units were especially numerous along the Rhine because it was the one great highway, because it was a region of great beauty, and because of the tolls that could be extracted from passing ships.

How well I remember my first visit to this magic land. Just escaped from college, making a 2,000-mile bicycle trip from Rotterdam to Naples, quite innocent of the wonders of Europe, I could hardly believe my eyes when the storybook castles of childhood actually took solid form and their quaint and curious stories gripped my imagination.

The Mouse-tower and the Wicked Bishop

Just below Bingen on a rocky island in the middle of the Rhine stands the Mouse-tower, so named in honor of the mice who devoured the wicked Bishop Hatto.

It was in the famine year 969 that starving countryfolk came to Bishop Hatto, lord of this island castle, pleading their inability to pay the taxes he demanded and beseeching him to lower the price on the corn that filled his barn. Annoyed by their entreaties, the bishop said testily, "Go into the barn. Take all you want. It will cost you nothing."

They entered the barn—whereupon the malicious lord locked it and set it afire. The screams from within were music to his ears.

"Listen," he said, "how the mice are squeaking among the corn. This eternal begging is at an end at last. May the mice bite me if it is not true!"

Then history, in search of a climax, resorts to legend. It is said that Heaven heard the bishop's prayer. Thousands of mice swarmed from the burning barn, entered the castle and devoured the evil Hatto.

Many a castle housed a languishing maiden whose unfeeling father tried to force her into an unwelcome marriage. Such a castle is the next one, beautiful Rheinstein, perched on a lofty rock beside the river. In this case the maiden was saved by a sympathetic gadfly which stung the horse of her suitor causing it to plunge over the precipice to death for both steed and rider on the stones below.

The Robber Baron and the Blind Archer

The splendid castle of Sooneck recalls the story of its robber baron who took a rival lord prisoner and clapped him into the dungeon. Then he summoned his friends to a banquet, promising them some rare entertainment. When they had assembled he had the prisoner brought before them and said to him, "You are reputed to be a great archer, so great that you can shoot a mark with closed eyes. You shall shoot for us—but since you do not need your eyes you will not mind if we extinguish them."

He called men to bring hot irons. The eyes of the prisoner were burned out.

"Now," said the lord of Sooneck, "I shall throw down a goblet. When it strikes the stone floor the sound will tell you where it is. Then shoot, and if you hit it you will go free."

Bow and arrow were placed in the prisoner's hands. The goblet rang as it struck the stone and Sooneck cried, "Shoot now."

Guided by sound but not that of the goblet, the archer shot. Pierced through the mouth, the robber baron of Sooneck fell dead.

Another remarkably picturesque castle stands in mid-Rhine. It is Pfalz, shaped like a stone ship. Flanking it on the left bank is the castle Stahleck, and on the right bank, Gutenfels.

The maiden Guta of Gutenfels fell in love with a gallant stranger who sought shelter for one night in the castle but declined to give his name. He declared his love for Guta and promised to come back for her.

Five months went by. The lovelorn Guta gave up hope. Then the stranger returned, but with a great retinue. He solicited the hand of Guta, declaring that she must share his throne. For he was Richard of Cornwall, just elected Emperor of Germany.

It is recorded that Guta decided he had been worth waiting for.

Seven rocks make the Rhine hazardous below the castle of Schönburg. There lived seven beautiful maidens who treated their suitors so scornfully and cruelly and were in general so stony-hearted that a vengeful Heaven finally tossed them into the river and turned them into rocks.

How can one doubt the story, since the rocks are still there to prove it?

Live in a Castle and Like It

To get to know a castle, it is necessary to live in it. Already we had sampled several including the *Jagdschloss* on the mountaintop above Rüdesheim—a castle built in the eighteenth century as a hunting lodge for the Duke of Nassau who left the walls practically buried under the heads and horns of his trophies. The place is now quite modernized as a fine hotel.

But it is even more interesting to spend some days in an unmodernized castle, and such is Schönburg, home of the seven stony-hearted maidens.

It would not be proper to say that it has been converted into a hotel. It is still pretty much as it has always been, and it is the guest who must be converted. He must adapt himself overnight to life as it was lived a thousand years ago before hot water could be had by turning on a tap, or heat by switching on an electric stove, or service by picking up a telephone.

We drove up the steep, tortuous road from the Rhine-side village of Oberwesel and came to a halt at the edge of a chasm. This was a nature-made moat for the castle which loomed above.

From here we proceeded on foot, crossing the abyss on a slightly uneasy wooden bridge, then clambered up a stony trail which led at last between the castle walls to a small door.

There was no sign over the door, nothing to indicate that strangers would be welcome within these forbidding walls. It took some temerity to jangle a bell, and considerable jangling before the door creaked open and a pretty girl who might have been a descendant of one of the beautiful seven admitted us.

She led the way as we carried our suitcases up endless stone steps through dark passages and finally entered a stone-walled room with ceiling so low that we instinctively crouched. A narrow casement window in a wall five feet thick admitted a pencil of light.

Curbing an impulse to inquire whether this was the dungeon, we put down our suitcases. They looked ridiculously out of place in this medieval setting.

The girl waited for us to say something. Mary looked about, trying to pierce the half-gloom in search of anything worthy of a compliment.

"Oh," she said. "It's charming—it has so much—atmosphere."

After all, that was why we had come. For atmosphere. A telephone or a radio or a private bath would have spoiled the atmosphere. Even the washbasin and tap running only cold water seemed a desecration.

The view from the window made up for any small inconveniences. We looked out to cobbled courts, crenelated ramparts, massive towers slitted for crossbow fire, sentry walks where you could easily imagine the sentries themselves ever watchful against attack, ravens circling the banners that waved above. Far below rushed the Rhine between the charming village of Oberwesel and the Lorelei Rock on whose summit one could clearly imagine the tantalizing water nymph combing her golden hair.

But if this was not the dungeon, it would do no harm to inquire where the dungeon was. We did inquire.

"You wish to see it? Come."

Through more dark passages, then out into a sunlit court past a picturesque stone tower.

"How old is that?" I asked, estimating that it might date back to the eleventh or tenth century.

"It was built in pre-Christian times by the Celts. The rest of the castle was constructed in the tenth century and has been restored since." She led the way to another tower. "This is the dungeon."

The black interior was thirty-five feet high without a single window.

"Prisoners were lowered into it from the top at the end of a rope," the girl said. "They could never escape unless they were hauled out in the same way. Many never made it. When this door was cut in the base of the tower, sixteen skeletons were found inside."

Much more cheerful was the dining hall with splendid vistas and excellent food. The cost for meals and lodging was so nominal and the spell of this place which carries memories of all the days of A.D. history was so strong that it was hard to resume the journey among upstart castles only a millennium old.

Combing Her Golden Hair

Peculiarly dangerous is the swirl of the river around the boldly projecting Lorelei. This sharp treacherous bend is the graveyard of so many wrecks that it was only natural for legend to blame them on the golden-haired maiden who sits atop the rock, flashes her jewels in the eyes of sailors, and lures them to destruction.

As we sailed past the Lorelei on the *Helvetia,* the sound system gave forth the familiar melody matched to Heine's poem. It was a thrilling moment for lovers of legend—made piquant in my own case by the fact that on my first Rhine journey my bicycle had broken down on the road directly beneath the Lorelei, an accident which I naturally charged up to the baneful influence of the golden girl. I knew Heine's verses by heart in the original German and they ran through my mind with the music as we passed under the shadow of the rock and out again. It was a moment of enchantment.

At the next table in the lounge four tourists, with their backs to the Lorelei, were discussing Topeka, Kansas.

"Yeah, there's been a lot o' changes. That theater was made over into a movie house. Say, I wish they'd turn off that loudspeaker. You know, they took down the old firehall. And we have a real good turnpike now."

Still sadder was the case of the lady who had come all the way from South Africa to see the castles of the Rhine.

Her timing was off, and she came on deck just as the last castle faded from view and a factory with smoking chimneys loomed ahead.

A retired British colonel undertook to console her. He pointed to the factory and said, *"Schloss Aktiengesellschaft,"* which would mean roughly "Castle Incorporated."

The lady brightened at once and said, "Oh, good, at least I can tell people I saw that one."

A teen-age girl whose parents had taken her on a tour of Italy was asked, "Did you go to Florence?"

"I don't know," she said. "Papa bought all the tickets."

It is a common sin and we are all guilty of it, every one of us. We spend thousands of dollars, cross the ocean, then talk Topeka. We miss 90 percent of what the far places of the world have to give us.

The Maus Devours the Katz

One thing we missed was the annual "Rhine in Flames" celebration at the next village, St. Goar. It occurs in September and is said to be one of the most spectacular sights of the year. The illuminations bathe the river in fire, floodlighting Rheinfels, the greatest of all Rhine castles, and, on the other shore, the highly pictorial Burg Katz and Burg Maus (not to be confused with the Mouse-tower already mentioned).

History has it that the lord of Katz declared he would devour Burg Maus as a cat devours a mouse. They went to war but the result was not as expected. The mouse devoured the cat.

We may bemoan the state of the world today—but is it any worse than in that former age when every hilltop was at odds with the next?

The cat-and-mouse feud was matched on two nearby hills where two brothers devoted to each other had built their castles. Falling in love with the same girl, they became bitter enemies and built a wall between their castles. This did not prevent them from coming in combat and both were killed.

There on the heights still stand the ruined strongholds known as The Hostile Brothers with a high wall between.

In an upper story of the castle of Marksburg is an arsenal of torture instruments including an iron headpiece for singeing the tongues of common scolds.

Fact stranger than fiction characterizes the magnificently battlemented and turreted castle of Stolzenfels and the nearby quaint ruin of the Königsstuhl, King's Chair.

A Crown for Six Wagons of Wine

Here the emperor of the Holy Roman Empire traded his throne for six wagons of wine, and considered it a good bargain.

It was the Emperor Wenzel who preferred Rhine wine to the onerous duty of ruling an empire. Believing that wine tasted better at the place of its origin, he frequently came to visit Prince Rupert, lord of Stolzenfels. One day, quaffing delicious Assmannshäuser, he was twitted by the prince for his neglect of his public responsibilities. He responded genially, "What is a throne? I offer you mine if you are able to place before me a wine better than this Assmannshäuser."

The prince ordered a servant to bring up from the cellar a cask of Bacharacher. The emperor tasted the fiery vintage and declared, "This wine is worth more than a thousand crowns!"

He kept his word and ceded the throne to Rupert who, in his turn, made the emperor a present of six wagonloads of Bacharacher wine.

"The Gibraltar of the Rhine" is the still usable fortress of Ehrenbreitstein at Coblenz.

Here the Rhine is joined by the dreaming Moselle, famous not only for its wines but for Trier, oldest city in Germany. There appears to have been a settlement here as far back as 2500 B.C. A Celtic town dates from 400 B.C. It was conquered by Julius Caesar in 58 B.C. The Romans made much of the place, called it "The Northern Rome," built enormous palaces and baths, and some Roman emperors deserted Rome itself to make their home here.

The parade of Rhine castles ends where

> *The castled crag of Drachenfels*
> *Frowns o'er the wide and winding Rhine.*

The castle which so inspired Byron stands where the legendary dragon made it a habit to devour a few people daily between 2:00 and 2:30 P.M. until Siegfried killed it and, indulging a peculiar whim, bathed in its blood. More blood flowed in World War II when the almost unscalable peak was the scene of a bayonet charge by the American 78th Division.

And so, on this note of modernity, we leave the "chiefless castles breathing stern farewells from grey but leafy walls, where ruin greenly dwells."

Skipping a Millennium

Bonn, despite the fact that it has been the home of Neanderthal Man, Beethoven and Konrad Adenauer, is a sparkling new city of concrete and glass, fine government buildings, big hotels and plush restaurants. In the washroom of our hotel I puzzle over a marble trough set higher than a wash basin and equipped with a handle on either side so that you may hang on firmly as you use it. The attendant explains its purpose. It is for the vomit of the guest who has dined too well.

It is a far cry from the austerity of feudal castles to the abundant life of machine civilization, and one cannot emerge from the Rhine of the Past into the Rhine of the Future without a peculiar feeling of dislocation. It is like the jolt of waking to find that in crossing the 180th Meridian you have skipped a day —but in this case the day is a millennium.

At the close of World War II the cities of the Lower Rhineland were heaps of rubble. Factories were dismantled, blast furnaces were silent, all bridges were down, the black hulks of burned ships lay rotting at the piers. Hungry people poked among the ruins and combed the countryside for food.

Yet in only twelve years the Ruhr came back to life and was once more the industrial heart of Germany. There were several good reasons for the miracle. Of course the Germans are a hardworking and thrifty people. The Marshall Plan came to their aid to the tune of three billion dollars. Since their industrial plants were ruined they had to build new ones and install up-to-date equipment, more modern than the average in use in America or elsewhere. Since rearmament was forbidden, money that formerly went into arms was now spent for machinery. It was not necessary to go far for coal and iron—they lay directly underfoot.

With plenty of resources, plenty of skilled manpower, brand new and efficient plants, and plenty of hard work, Germany has swiftly become the strongest industrial power on the continent and the focal point of her power is the Lower Rhine. Supreme among the advantages of this region is the river itself.

Second Busiest River on Earth

The Rhine is Germany's most important single artery of trade. It carries 150,000,000 tons of goods a year. Ships of a dozen nations ply its waters. Once blocked by customs barriers, the river is now open to all. It has become, after the Mississippi, the busiest river on earth.

Duisburg is Europe's largest inland port. The harbor has twenty-seven basins and twenty-eight miles of quays. Through it move 30,000,000 tons of cargo a year.

The Rhine flows upstream, cargo-wise. Downriver cargoes are relatively light. But upstream barges carry imports from all the world and, particularly, the products of Ruhr factories, to most of Europe, thanks to an elaborate canal system fanning out through the continent linking the Rhine with the Rhône, the Seine, the Marne and the mighty Danube.

As a Rhine port, Duisburg is surpassed only by Rotterdam at the river's mouth. This Dutch port is the world's most active, surpassing both New York and London.

A completely new harbor area is now being added. It has been named Europoort or Gateway to Europe. It will be equipped to handle vessels of 100,000 tons. Rotterdam already handles more tonnage than *all* French ports combined.

By Barge to Rotterdam

We sail down the final stretch of the great river into Rotterdam harbor on a barge.

The word "barge" doesn't do it justice. It is a brightly and always freshly painted craft, as neat as a pin, thanks to the fact that the skipper's wife is aboard—his children too if not away in boarding school.

The family quarters are as comfortable and homelike as a home ashore. Frau Siemel shows us her refrigerator, washing machine, radio, hi-fi and TV. Her table groans with good food, much of it brought alongside by store boats which do a thriving business, since as many as two hundred barges may round the bend in fifteen minutes.

As the stream broadens to become Rotterdam harbor, the water seems to be steel-plated, so many are the ships. There are vessels of all nations, as indicated by their names: *African Lord, Viking, Sudan, Zermatt, Hanoi, Bogotá, Utrecht, Hamburg, Antibes* and *Panagiotis*.

Ships lie three abreast beside the docks. Gantry cranes with enormously long arms easily reach out over two vessels to service the third.

Seven towers house radar scanners that will enable ships to find their way in the densest fog.

Barges turn their cargoes over to oceangoing giants bound for far ports.

"What's the greatest export?" I ask Skipper Siemel.

I expect him to have something to say about German motor cars, or Ruhr coal, or Dutch tulip bulbs.

But the skipper is something of a scholar. "You want to know the chief shipment ever made from this port? It was the love of liberty."

"How do you make that out?"

"The Pilgrim Fathers sailed from here in 1620."

11

The Storied Hudson

"EASY DOES IT," warned Chief Bosun's Mate Richard Terhune as I prepared to jump from the dancing Coast Guard cutter to the heaving lightship.

With each swell the two steel-clad vessels separated, then came together in a resounding crunch. If a man happened to be between the steel jaws at that moment, he would go home in two pieces.

"Now!" yelled Terhune. I leaped from the deck like a ballistic missile, two husky sailors serving as boosters. Even they could not insure that I would grab the rope ladder. Luckily I did, pulled my feet up out of the way of the closing jaws, and clambered to the deck of the Ambrose Lightship. Her commanding officer, Max Trepeta, was waiting.

"Glad you came on a good day," he said. "In bad weather, getting aboard is quite a trick."

A Lighthouse Afloat

As we climbed to the bridge he explained the purpose of the Ambrose Lightship.

"You'll see many lighthouses on your way up the Hudson. This is number one. But this lighthouse happens to be floating rather than stationary. That's necessary because of the depth of the water and exposure to storms—we're actually about twenty miles out to sea from Manhattan."

It is the Ambrose Lightship, and not the Statue of Liberty, which first welcomes the visitor to America. The approaching ship may ride in on the Ambrose radio beam and her captain may talk with the officer on the bridge of the lightship over the radiotelephone.

"Want to go to the top?" We climbed the swaying tripod foremast to the platform and looked in at the great lamp. "Five and a half million candlepower," said Trepeta. "Visible for thirteen miles at this elevation."

The rocking of the ship was quite noticeable at this height, yet the pillar of fire balanced itself like an acrobat standing on the back of a galloping horse. "Mounted in gimbals, so it always rides erect no matter how much the ship pitches or rolls."

We went through the crew's quarters. They were comfortable, and need to be, for every man must live on board for two weeks at a stretch. He has the third week off. There were TV and radio sets all over the ship.

Don't Send Books

And books! Trepeta opened closet after closet, stacked from top to bottom with books. Some newspaper story had stated that this was what the boys wanted most—books—and in came an overwhelming flood of literature.

If you want to do something for the shipbound lads on the Ambrose, don't send books. Not that they don't like them, but their present supply should be enough for the next hundred years.

Back to the bridge. The skipper had called this the first light on the Hudson. There was no sign of a river—nothing but open sea all around us.

Yet I knew that the Hudson was below us. At my request Trepeta spread out a chart.

River beneath the Sea

There it was, the famous "Hudson Canyon," a submarine gorge extending more than two hundred miles out to sea!

The Continental Shelf was once dry land. Through it the Hudson cut a tremendous canyon, in some places three miles wide and a thousand feet deep. Then the land was submerged. But the channel is still there, a drowned Hudson in which Beebe descended to discover extraordinary lantern-carrying fish, and a Woods Hole expedition in 1949 explored for 225 miles out to sea where the ocean floor is 12,000 feet below the surface and the canyon floor is nine hundred feet deeper. The gorge ends in an undersea waterfall eight times the height of Niagara.

Invisible from a ship's deck, this fabulous canyon can be seen from a plane as a dark stripe through the lighter green of the waters on the Continental Shelf.

When it emerges to become a visible river, the Hudson still keeps its canyon character. It is walled in between the 500-foot Palisades on one side and the skyscrapers of Manhattan on the other. For much of its 315-mile length from the Battery to Tear of the Clouds its banks are high and rugged, and its waters unusually deep for a river, reaching a maximum of 216 feet near West Point. At New York the Holland Tunnel had to dive nearly a hundred feet to get beneath the riverbed.

As Hudson Saw It

By car, Coast Guard cutter, tug, paddlewheel steamer, barge, freighter, millionaire's yacht, lamplighter's launch and often by means of our own thirteen-foot, 45-pound Grumman aluminum canoe, we traveled up the Hudson.

We were beginning our exploration of the river at the seaward end, for it was here that Henry Hudson had begun. We would follow his route, seeing wonders that he saw and other marvels of which he never dreamed.

The concrete-and-glass cliffs on the east shore would amaze Henry Hudson if he should return today. But the Palisades across the way are about as he saw them in 1609.

They are built to last. They were forged in fire. Liquid lava boiled up into an immense crack in sandstone. The lava cooled and hardened into a vertical wall from 350 to 550 feet high and some forty miles long. The sandstone on the river side gradually fell away, exposing the magnificent cliff of brown basalt crystallized by fire into magnificent prismatic six-sided columns of a sort seen in only two or three other places in the world, notably the Giant's Causeway in Ireland and Fingal's Cave in the Hebrides.

All this happened long before Hudson sailed by in the *Half Moon* seeking a water route to India. It happened even before the days of the dinosaurs whose bones and footprints have been found in the sandstone back of the cliff.

Beware the Pukwidjinnies

The first Indians must have seen the rock much as we see it today. It inspired awe and superstition. Back of it, they believed, was the land of the gods. Now it is less poetically known as New Jersey. From the cliff's edge the goddess Miniwawa hurled down thunder and lightning upon any who dared come too close. From here Mishemokwa swooped down to eat bad children. From here the pukwidjinnies, "little men," came down to do mischief. The Great Spirit himself had thrown up this rampart to keep meddlesome man out of the gardens of the gods. On its edge he stood guard, ever watching the river.

He is still there. It takes little imagination to see him in the great stone face that keeps a stern eye on Yonkers across the way. Today it is called the Indian Profile. It is amazingly clear-cut, with aquiline nose, deep-set eyes, high straight forehead, sharply chiseled mouth, spearlike chin. Mary, standing on its head to show its proportionate size, seemed to be about one-seventh its height. This would make the great stone face of the Hudson some forty feet long. From its crest one looks straight down half a thousand feet to the river shore.

The face is particularly fine against a ghostly curtain of fog. But a clear day has its advantages—the panorama below stretches away like a gigantic relief map. Far downstream is the George Washington Bridge, third longest suspension bridge in the world. It takes thirty men four years to paint it.

Beyond it are the city's towers and a harbor that vies with the port of London. One ship every twenty minutes ties up at its docks. Nearly as much goes on under the river as above it. Approximately one hundred thousand vehicles pass beneath it every day. The Lincoln Tunnel is the world's first triple-tube underwater roadway.

Wherever you look you are apt to encounter some reminder of the *Half Moon* and her master. Below the Palisades is the Henry Hudson Drive, still as wild and lovely as the road along the shore of an Adirondack lake. You look across the Hudson River to the Henry Hudson Parkway, the miraculous bypass that whisks you from city to country more quickly than it is possible to escape from a city one tenth the size of New York. And across Spuyten Duyvil Creek soars the Henry Hudson Bridge.

To Spite the Devil

Spuyten Duyvil, bounding the isle of Manhattan on the north, gets its name from the tale of the doughty trumpeter who swore he would swim the swollen stream *"en spuyt den Duyvil"* (in spite of the devil). Halfway across he was dragged down by said devil, but blew a defiant blast on his trumpet just before he sank.

"His ghost still haunts the neighborhood," wrote Washington Irving, "and his trumpet has often been heard of a stormy night."

Directly across the river from the Indian Profile is Yonkers, so overshadowed by New York that few realize it is the fifth largest city in the Empire State. Its name may not seem musical, but it is noble. It derives from *jonker,* "his young lordship," referring to Van der Donck, first patroon of this region.

North of it are the fine riverside mansions that caused this lovely shore to be called the Gold Coast. Most of their owners have long since surrendered to the tax collector and the great houses have been taken over by tax-exempt institutions.

Upstream is Dobbs Ferry, named for one Dobbs who lived in a shanty on the beach and ferried passengers across the river in his dugout. The name was too plain for some prideful citizens who tried to get it changed to Livingston, or Paulding, or Greenburgh. Some stood out for Van Wart. The sarcastic opposition suggested that the Van be dropped and the place be called Wart-on-the-Hudson. Common sense finally prevailed and Dobbs Ferry kept its unusual and colorful name.

It was off Dobbs Ferry that a British warship at the close of the Revolution entertained the American Commander in Chief George Washington on board and fired seventeen guns in his honor. It was a gallant gesture, the first British salute to the new nation.

The precipice below us is an enduring monument to John D. Rockefeller Jr. and other public-spirited citizens who stopped the defacement of the cliffs by quarrymen and made possible the Palisades Interstate Park. A beautiful parkway stretching forty-two miles from George Washington Bridge to Bear Mountain runs through woodland so wild that motorists must be warned to watch for deer crossing the road—and this within sight of a city where people must live as much as a hundred layers deep for lack of room.

Flight in a Doorless Plane

Speeding up the parkway, we arrive at Nyack in time for a gay regatta on historic Tappan Zee. Here the Hudson has broadened into a lake three miles wide.

Nearly a hundred sailboats take part in the race. I fly over them in a Piper Tri-Pacer. The door has been removed to make picture-taking easier.

"Better not take your gadget bag," the pilot suggests before we take off. "It might roll out. And no jacket—the wind might whip it out. No lens hoods—the wind would tear them off. And look out for your glasses—if you put your head out a little you'll lose them. Keep your safety belt tight. I had one customer plop into the river."

Stranger things have happened in the Tappan Zee. It is a highly temperamental stretch of water. Many of the oldtime sloops and early steamers were lost here. One long-sunken Dutch vessel known as the *Storm Ship* or *Ghost*—a sort of river version of *The Flying Dutchman*—is said to scud across the sea during every gale and woe betide anything that gets in her way.

And here a young roisterer named Van Dam, who danced and drank all Saturday night and into Sunday, set out to row home though his friends warned him that it was a mortal sin to row on the Sabbath. He never got home but was doomed to row forever up and down the Tappan Zee.

But how could the Tappan Zee escape romance since it was here in the village of Irvington that the great romancer, Washington Irving, had his home. And just above Irvington rise the hills of Tarrytown where Ichabod Crane sang in the old Dutch church, courted Katrina Van Tassel, and was vanquished by the Headless Horseman.

Here history and legend are inextricably intertwined. There never was an Ichabod, but the church was and is very real, set among the tombstones of Sleepy Hollow Cemetery, one of them Irving's own. The church is one of the oldest still in use in America. It is still the scene of weddings and funerals, though regular services are held elsewhere.

Ichabod, says Irving, used to sing in the choir and "there are peculiar quavers still to be heard in that church, and which may even be heard half a mile off, quite to the opposite side of the millpond, on a still Sunday morning, which are said to be legitimately descended from the nose of Ichabod Crane."

Babbling through Sleepy Hollow past the church and under Headless Horseman Bridge, Pocantico Creek widens to form the afore-mentioned millpond. Reflected in its surface is the stone "castle" of Philipse, once lord of a manor that extended all the way from Manhattan to Croton. The great house famous for three centuries as Philipse Castle or Philipsburg Manor was confiscated by the Revolutionists because Philipse was a Tory. It was later the home of many notable persons including the lively actress, Elsie Janis. Now it has been beautifully restored by Sleepy Hollow Restorations, a Rockefeller project also responsible for the preservation of Van Cortlandt Manor and the home of Washington Irving.

The special Rockefeller interest in this area may be due to the fact that this is home ground. The Rockefeller estate, "Pocantico Hills," with its sprawling mansion, thirty-five hundred richly wooded acres, one hundred miles of roads and bridle trails, lies just outside Tarrytown.

I Go to Prison

Ossining means "Singing Stones." The musical name suits this attractive city but hardly the grim walls of the state prison. Sing Sing lies below the town along the waterfront. With its administration building, cellblocks, mess hall, schools, library, chapel, shops, power plant, hospital, gymnasium, playing field, recreation yard and gardens, the institution covers fifty-five acres.

It is almost as hard to get into Sing Sing as to get out. I was questioned for half an hour by the guard at the gate, questioned again through the barred entrance of the administration building. When admitted I was received by six armed guards who instructed me to sign a register, then to spread my arms and be frisked from head to foot. "Is that a film in your pocket?" I drew it out and it was confiscated, along with my cameras, to be returned when I left. No pictures may be taken inside the walls—they might show a prisoner, who thereupon would have the right to sue the state.

I was escorted upstairs to the office and asked to see the warden. Ah, but—I was told—the proper procedure is to write a letter asking for an appointment later . . . perhaps in a week or so. "But I can write the letter now if you will give me a piece of paper." I wrote the letter, requesting an appointment an hour later.

"In the meantime, may I see the prison?"

A sergeant took me in charge. He led me through five iron gates, each unlocked by a guard and locked behind us. Of most interest to me were the schools. Here inmates are trained for after-prison life. Men were at work in a well-equipped machine shop, an automobile shop, a radio and TV department, a print shop, a typewriting class, and many courses in academic subjects.

A Prison with No Illiterates

"There are no illiterates in this prison after a year," said the sergeant. "Learning to read and write is compulsory." More than this, technical training turns drifters and mischief-makers into skilled mechanics and electronic engineers.

There is a radio control room and the selected program may be heard in every cell through earphones. There are two first-run movies every week. Prison teams play outside teams in the large playing field.

It's like a small town—many buildings, broad open spaces, a large garden with trees, rose and peony beds, plenty of work and plenty of companionship—but of course hardly normal, every move prescribed, no female companionship, no home life or home comforts, not much likelihood that a man will enjoy it so much that he will wish to stay for life.

A heartwarming touch: in a courtyard on a small gravestone, "Chowder at rest," in memory of a prison dog.

Back in the administration building, I was received by the warden, Wilfred L. Denno. He is a far cry from the brutal and sadistic warden of Victorian fiction.

He explained the modern philosophy of Sing Sing, which lays less stress on punishment, more on reward and incentive. The prisoner gets time off his sentence for good conduct. There is no corporal punishment. The only punishment is by deprivation of privileges.

On entering Sing Sing a man is automatically placed in the "first class" where he has maximum privileges, such as recreation, movies, permission to write frequently to relatives, visits from relatives and friends. Bad conduct demotes him to second class, his privileges being decreased, and worse conduct puts him in third class with next to no privileges. It takes six months of good conduct to put him back in second, and six more to restore him to first. This system makes a man think before misbehaving.

I had a sense of relief when the last iron gate opened and closed behind me. My wife was waiting outside the barrier. As we drove away, she told me of her conversation with another waiting woman, who had told her:

"My sister's nephew is in there and she's gone in to see him
. . . Who *you* got in there?"

Mary said, "My husband," but went on to explain that she
expected me out soon.

"Oh, that will be nice," said the other. "On parole for good
behavior, I suppose."

Goblin of Thunderbolts

When is a river a lake called a bay? When it is Haverstraw
Bay, which is no bay, but a lake more than three miles wide.

Some writers have compared it to Como, but perhaps they
have not seen Como. Likewise, the Hudson has been dubbed
the American Rhine, an insult to both the Rhine and the Hudson. In such cases comparisons really are odious. Both rivers are
fine but in a quite different fashion, and handsome Haverstraw
Bay is no more like lovely Como than Hercules is like Venus.
Why not let American splendors stand on their own feet? They
do not need the crutch of comparison with any other splendors
on earth.

Haverstraw Bay is the broadest and finest sea in the entire
course of the Hudson. The town of Haverstraw looks down to
it on one side and Croton on the other. Croton Point Park
attracts thousands of picnickers and boatmen; and swimmers
too, for the pollution of the Hudson, though a real problem, is
not so great as to preclude bathing.

Bold precipices line the western shore, culminating in High
Tor and higher Dunderberg. Between Dunderberg and Anthony's Nose the river narrows into a dangerous channel subject to sudden storms, which have been attributed to a bulbous-
bottomed Dutch goblin who sits atop Dunderberg and gives
orders through his speaking-trumpet to the winds and thunder-
bolts. Only by lowering their peaks in homage to the goblin
could sloop masters hope to pass safely.

Legend has it that even Captain Kidd lost his ship here. And
when an iron cannon was discovered in the riverbed at this
point, the legend was taken so seriously that a stock company
was formed to dive for Kidd's treasure. It was never found, but
the story lives on.

Anthony's Nose

The aquiline promontory called Anthony's Nose was named
for a Dutchman, Anthony Van Corlaer, who had a nose compared with which that of Cyrano de Bergerac was a mere wart.
The nose was not only great but shiny, and its owner used to go
fishing with it; the sun reflecting upon it killed as with an electric shock the eight-foot sturgeon which used to lurk in the
waters off this point. The mountain stands there as proof of this
story and an everlasting memorial to a noble nose.

Why did the Dutch, usually so practical, people the Hudson
with monsters, goblins and ghosts? Probably because, after the
flat landscape they had known in Holland, these precipitous
mountains, deep gorges, dark forests, hidden savages, thunder-
bolts hurtling from peak to peak bred mystery and spurred imagination.

As one goes north into the "Highlands of the Hudson," the
mountains multiply and so do the legends. Viewed from the top
of Bear Mountain, the mountains march northward on both
sides of the river like a double procession of elephants. From
Bear Mountain to the tip of Anthony's Nose the river is
spanned by a suspension bridge 155 feet above the river, so
delicate a mesh of cables that on a misty day it looks as insub-
stantial as a cobweb. In its shadow on a summer Sunday dock
no less than three great paddle-wheel steamers, having brought
some fifteen thousand trippers from New York for a holiday in
Bear Mountain Park.

It is well to look twice at this phenomenon for you will see it
nowhere else on the Hudson. Nowhere else and at no other
time will three of the splendid, old-fashioned side-wheelers be
found together.

Indeed even one of these graceful ladies of the river is a rare
sight nowadays. And in a matter of a few years they will have
disappeared forever.

To Albany by Teakettle

The first of their breed were not so graceful. With their paddle wheels exposed and their awkward machinery much in evidence, they excited derision and contempt.

When Fulton's *Clermont* first snorted and puffed and clattered its way upriver on that historic summer day in 1807, the craft was aptly described as a "devil in a sawmill." Fulton, said his critics, had a notion he could go "to Albany by teakettle."

The boat moved a short distance, then stopped. Derisive voices came from the shore, "Hire a whale to tow your boat"— just as in a later era skeptics were to yell at the embarrassed automobilist, "Get a horse!"

But the contraption got underway once more and moved against the current at the rate of five miles an hour. The fat pinewood used for fuel sent up a flood of sparks and warranted the newspaper report, "It was a monster, moving on the river, defying wind and tide, and breathing flames and smoke."

But it got to Albany. The Scottish engineer celebrated so liquidly that he was fired. Fulton was happy until he saw the newspapers. The feat was dismissed as a freak: perhaps the wind had blown the boat upstream, perhaps it had floated up on the tide. Anyhow it couldn't do it again, and even if it could, of what value was it? Sails were better and always would be.

But the side-wheelers were soon outstripping the fastest sloops and at the same time passing from awkward youth into well-groomed maturity. In time the floating palaces of the Hudson became "the most elegant in the world." They boasted plush carpeting, crystal chandeliers, Corinthian columns, carved figureheads, private parlors, orchestras, dining salons capable of serving three hundred persons at one sitting. Their calliopes made the gorge of the Highlands resound with "The Belle of the Mohawk Vale" and "Way Down Upon the Swanee River."

Queen of the fleet was the *Mary Powell*. She had three hundred feet of clean sweet lines and was the fastest thing on the Hudson. It was said that her builders must have mixed whale's grease in her paint to make her slip so easily through the water.

Competition became intense. The passenger fare between New York and Albany dropped to ten cents. Speed rivalry grew. Steam gauges were plugged, safety valves tied down, and steam pressures increased to a dangerous point.

Floating Volcanoes

Boilers exploded. Passengers became painfully boiler-conscious. Some steamers boasted copper boilers which were said to be safer than iron boilers. Many an iron boiler became a "copper boiler" overnight, thanks to an application of copper-colored paint. Some operators sought to mollify the public by the quite unscientific claim that their boats had "no boilers!"

The *Swallow,* during a race, struck a rock called Noah's Brig and broke in two. Fifteen lives were lost.

The *Oregon,* racing the *Cornelius Vanderbilt* for a stake of a thousand dollars, ran out of fuel. Yet she won the race by twelve hundred feet—by stoking her boilers with benches, chairs, furniture and even stateroom partitions, much to the discomfort and annoyance of the passengers.

Public protests reached a peak when the racing *Henry Clay* broke into flames and ran aground with such impact that passengers were hurled from the promenade deck into the river. Sixty people lost their lives.

"The passenger walks and sits and sleeps almost in contact with the volcano that in an instant may blow him to atoms," said a Poughkeepsie paper, starting a campaign to end racing. The campaign culminated in a Steamboat Inspection Act that made steamboat racing unlawful.

That was a little more than a century ago. During the past hundred years side-wheeler travel on the Hudson has been swift, safe and lovely. And yet the steamboat has been superseded by the automobile, and the Hudson waterway by the New York Thruway. The lone survivors of the steamboat era lie below us as we look down from Bear Mountain. Only two of them, the proud and beautiful *Alexander Hamilton* and the slightly smaller streamlined *Peter Stuyvesant* are strictly Hudson River craft. These white swans are the last of the Hudson River Day Line. The third boat, the yellow-painted *Hudson Belle* is a visitor from down the Atlantic Coast brought in for the Sunday excursion.

The Night Line to Albany was discontinued in 1940. The Day Line quit service to Albany in 1950. The Day Line still operates a daily service, but only up to Poughkeepsie.

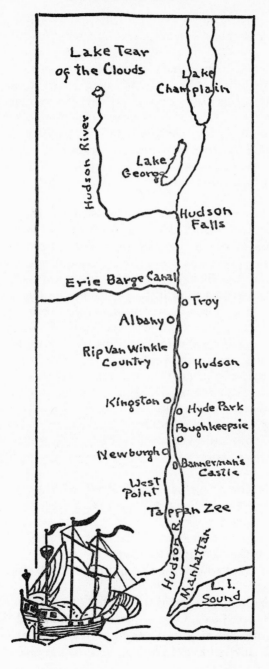

We later made the journey downriver to Manhattan on the Day Line's *Alexander Hamilton*. The big ship was a floating carnival. Juveniles occupied the bow where they got all the wind and excitement; agelings the sides and stern; teen-agers in love, the top deck. The snack bar and dining salon were continuously busy, and an orchestra played for rock 'n' roll dancing in the ballroom. An ever-changing panorama of mountains and towns slid by and handsome bridges passed overhead. History unrolled its brilliant and bloody pages.

The Mothball Fleet

History is still being made on the Hudson. You have only to look at the "mothball fleet" of several hundred war vessels rusting away at Tompkins Cove and the atomic power plant being built across the river at Indian Point to realize how rapidly the face of history has changed in only the last ten years.

But no matter how fast history spins by the Hudson keeps its old-time charm. The mountains of the Highlands are there to stay, the broad seas are as fine as ever, the cliffs of the Palisades defy change, and on the eastern shore the towns are so hidden by trees that one might suppose it to be quite uninhabited, except perhaps by a few Indians. Then at last, by way of contrast, the incredible towers of Bagdad on the Subway.

We made the return trip on the same boat a few days later. Venturing into the wheelhouse, we talked with Captain Dewitt Robinson, who had been a captain for half a century, and the First Pilot who is also a veteran of the river, Captain John Burlingham.

The *Hamilton* now has power steering. A touch on a small steam-driven wheel directed its course. There was also a great wheel but it stood motionless.

"We use it when the steam-driven wheel fails," said the skipper. "But it takes four men to move it."

Like the great wheel, the two old men of the river may soon come to a standstill.

"Can't be long now," said the master. "Getting uneconomical to operate these boats. Only a question of time and they'll have to be laid up. Fewer passengers every year. A pity, because it's still the nicest way to travel."

West Point

Nowhere is river travel more definitely superior to road travel than through the Highlands of the Hudson. The Highlands are not actually very high by Rocky Mountain standards, but rising directly from sea level with every foot of their flanks visible from water to sky, they are more majestic than many a higher mountain obscured by foothills.

Their crests are crowned by picturesque seminaries or academies such as Ladycliff at Highland Falls, castlelike mansions, or very real castles such as Dick's Castle still lived in, where a teenage daughter of the family does an enterprising business receiving sightseers at twenty-five cents a head.

The stone walls of the United States Military Academy at West Point look sternly down upon one of the sharpest and most hazardous bends in the river. Washington called this contorted defile "the key of America." It was here that the great chain spanned the river to bar the northward progress of British ships during the Revolution.

If Benedict Arnold had been successful in his plot to surrender West Point to the British, and if British troops coming north had been able to join those on the way south, the story of America might have been quite different. The key did not turn; the lock held fast.

Bannerman's Castle

The most authentic castle of the Hudson is set on a romantic island at the northern gate of the Highlands. It has towers, turrets and crenelated battlements, vaults and dungeons, even a real drawbridge and an iron portcullis—everything a castle should have.

It is in full view of passengers on New York Central trains, and its warning signs such as "Bannerman's Island Arsenal," "Danger," "Explosives," "Keep Out," give it an aura of mystery bound to excite the liveliest curiosity. Yet few of those who pass ever learn its story.

While the Bannermans chose to call it Bannerman's Island, it appears on government charts as Pollepel Island. It was so

named for Polly Pell, who according to legend was courted by a
minister and a farmer. One day she and the minister drove out
over the ice in a sleigh, bound for the island. The sleigh broke
through the ice, and the two would certainly have been
drowned if they had not been rescued in the nick of time—by
the farmer! So Polly married the farmer. The minister, with as
good grace as he could muster, conducted the ceremony.

There have always been and still are people willing to believe that Pollepel is haunted. Its reputation as the home of evil
spirits is borne out by its forbidding appearance and dark
woods and the savage peaks that loom around it: Storm King,
Crow's Nest, Breakneck, Butter Hill, Mt. Beacon, and Mt.
Taurus. Taurus was first called Bull Hill, but the early English
who settled hereabouts had an aversion to the word bull. Why
a bull is less a bull when he is a taurus is something for the
English to explain.

The sinister air of this spot is not relieved by the fact that the
Hudson is here joined by Murderer's Creek, which once ran
red with the blood of settlers slaughtered by the Indians.

So malicious were the ghosts and goblins of this area that
skippers of sailing ships used to toss their apprentices overboard
as a sacrificial offering to the unseen mischief-makers. The
spirits were evidently satisfied with this gesture for they seemed
to have no objection when the apprentices were hauled aboard
again.

Now it so happened that in 1692, in the massacre of Glencoe,
a young Scot gallantly rescued the banner of his clan and was
rewarded with the name of Bannerman. A later Bannerman
came to America and in 1865 found himself attending an auc-
tion sale of Civil War armaments.

He bought heavily and started a business selling arms and
ammunition to anyone who fancied them as souvenirs,
antiques, lawn ornaments, or whatnot. He was not responsible
if some of them eventually found their way into South American rebellions.

At the close of the Spanish-American War the firm bought
nearly 95 percent of the surplus war goods from the American
and Spanish governments. To preserve this great mass of material larger and safer storage space was needed. In 1900 Frank
Bannerman bought Pollepel Island, built a medieval

stronghold, and stocked it to overflowing with war goods. Because of the explosive nature of many of the articles, a strict keep-away policy had to be enforced.

Of course buyers are welcome, but their access to the island is not made easy. There is no bridge from the mainland, no road leading to the shore opposite the island, no place to launch a boat, and even if you should contrive to reach the island, there is usually no one on hand to sell you anything. Your best bet is to write first for an appointment.

Canoe to the Island of Mystery

A mile below Pollepel we carried our canoe across the railroad tracks, barely escaping a remarkably silent northbound train, and eased it down to the water over a steep embankment of boulders. We had no intention of landing on the island but merely wished to get a closer look at it.

But as we neared the castle we saw a man sitting under a tree at the foot of the battlements. The water between us was posted with forbidding signs. Reefs and chunks of masonry lay just below the surface and the canoe must proceed with the greatest caution. We learned later that a man had been drowned here some months previously when his powerboat struck a sunken wall.

We passed through a water gate flanked by stone towers, keeping our eye on the man, expecting him at any moment to leap to his feet and wave us off. But he seemed quite placid. We came within speaking distance.

"Go easy," he called. "Pretty shallow there."

He didn't sound too formidable. Dodging a couple Bewares, we came alongside the wooden dock. We exchanged remarks about the weather, the river, and the castle. Mention of *National Geographic* got us an invitation to come ashore.

"Are you alone?" we asked, failing to see any other signs of life.

"All alone. I'm the caretaker. My name is Sexton—Walter Sexton."

"But I suppose you go home at night to be with your family."

"I have no family. No, I stay here right along—except once a week or so when I must go to town for groceries."

"But don't you get lonesome?"

"Not me. This is a pretty nice place after all."

One man, living all alone in a castle big enough to hold a regiment, and liking it!

"But the owners," I said, "don't they have to be here to run the business?"

"It's more a hobby than a business. Oh, they still sell war goods, but only by special arrangement. It's run now by the grandson of the Bannerman who built the place. He drops in once in a while. Some of the family come to stay for a few weeks in summer. Sometimes they're marooned here longer than they expect if the river is rough. Once a housekeeper they brought along with them became ill. She couldn't be taken ashore by our boat. The fire company at Beacon sent a larger craft and got her out. I've been isolated here many times. But I don't mind that. It's quite a place—would you like to look around?"

Drawbridge, Portcullis and All

The small boy that is in every man was thrilled as we passed over a real drawbridge, then under a real iron-grill portcullis, through a stone gate from the top of which boiling oil could readily be poured upon an intruder, then up a dark-walled passage to the broad steps ascending to the main entrance. Within was a great hall fitted out in medieval splendor. The hilltop garden was smothered in weeds and bushes, the paths were blocked by honeysuckle and roses run wild. All this would be hastily cleared before the annual family visit.

We descended to the dark vaults and dungeons smelling of mold and gunpowder and so extensive that our voices echoed mysteriously from distant walls. Sexton's flashlight picked out great piles of war goods—pistols, muskets, mortars, unexploded shells, mountains of cannon balls, thousands of bayonets black with blood that once flowed red in the War between the States and the Spanish-American War, old uniforms, army boots. . . .

"That's sold," Sexton kept repeating, pointing to one item after another. A big wooden gun carriage—"Sold"—coffins as stout as battleships left over from the Civil War—"Sold"—

articles lying about in such confusion that it was necessary to step carefully, yet although none were tagged he knew exactly which were sold, which still for sale and which not for sale.

"Mr. Bannerman doesn't want to sell that," was a frequent remark.

We emerged into the lower garden. Here too one stepped gingerly over explosives and cannon balls. A huge cannon commanded the river.

"It's sold," said Sexton, "but the buyer didn't reckon on the cost of taking it away. A lighterage firm has given him an estimate of $2,100 for transportation. He's shopping now for a lower price."

A great deal of the ammunition is still live, even though it may date back to Civil War days. Sexton pointed out a battered balcony on which stood the wreck of a daybed. A woman had been lying on the bed just before a store of black powder beneath exploded. The balcony and bed were ruined, but not the lady, who fortunately had left the spot ten minutes before the explosion.

We picked our way over live shells to the shore and were relieved to get back to the relative safety of the canoe. Now we learned how it is possible for occupants of the castle to be marooned by bad weather. It was only with difficulty that we paddled downstream against an upstream storm and hauled the canoe up over boulders that were being lashed by surprisingly big waves.

The Man Who Bought a Mountain

"Will you sell me all the land I can see?" said Francis Rombout in 1663. The Indians agreed and a price was fixed. Then the wily Rombout climbed Mt. Beacon where his view encompassed eighty-five thousand acres. The Indians, though indignant, kept their promise.

The mountain did not get its name until more than a century later when beacon fires were lit on its summit to warn of the approach of the British. Now an incline railway, said to be the steepest of its length in the world, runs to a height of fifteen hundred and forty feet where holidaymakers dance and dine in a large casino.

One of the last of the Hudson ferryboats carried us across the river to Newburgh. It was soon to be replaced by the New-burgh-Beacon Bridge. That marked the end of an era. This ferry has operated continuously ever since it received its charter granted by King George in 1743.

The ferries that used to enliven the river from the Battery to Albany and were most numerous between Manhattan and Jersey are no more. The ferryboat was always one of the delights of the river. How pleasant it used to be after a day within office walls to stand on the deck of the ferry and enjoy the wind on your face and the smell of water. Now the commuter steps into a bus and is whisked under or above the river to his home with scarcely a chance to take one good breath of fresh air. It is progress—but at a price.

Aboard a Buoy Boat

By courtesy of the Coast Guard, the Coast Guard Cutter *Beech* came from Staten Island to pick me up at Newburgh for a tour of "the aids to navigation"—the buoys, bells, lights and lighthouses that make river travel as far as Albany safe even for ocean vessels.

The smart, clean-lined little craft drew up to the Newburgh dock and the skipper, Chief Petty Officer Walter Lewis, took me aboard and introduced me to the twelve men of his crew.

"We call this a buoy boat," he said. "It's one hundred and one feet long with a displacement of two hundred fifty-five tons. We have some larger ones, running up to one hundred eighty feet. Come into the wheelhouse."

Here was the most modern equipment—radar screen, radio-telephone, shore telephone for use at docks, echo sounding instrument whose fluttering illuminated figure gave the changing depth beneath the bow.

We sailed downriver to "Lower Hudson River Light 34" near Pollepel Island on which loomed the castle of Bannerman. To thwart the goblins who used to bedevil shipping at this point, a light tower stands on a rock base. A motorboat put off from the *Beech* and men replaced the batteries in the tower and repainted the iron standard.

We went on to "World's End." It actually appears on the

chart under that name. It is the deepest spot in the entire Hudson. The depth indicator registered more than two hundred feet. Here during the Revolution the great chain was laid across the river to bar British advance.

Flirtation Walk and Kissing Rock

A fact more interesting to West Point boys is that here, winding down the steep bank through the trees, is Flirtation Walk. Over the path hangs Kissing Rock. If a cadet passes under it with his best girl and fails to kiss her the rock will fall and crush them. So the story goes, and where is the cadet who cares to prove it false?

On the shore is a light tower at the base of which is a fog bell. If a boat groping through the fog blows its whistle, the blast actuates a switch that starts the bell ringing and it continues to ring for ten minutes.

At least that is the way it *should* work. The *Beech* blew a terrific blast but the bell did not answer. Again—no effect. Lewis got on the radiotelephone.

"Cutter *Beech* to Stony Point, Cutter *Beech* to Stony Point."

A voice replied, "Stony Point to Cutter *Beech*."

"Mr. Kerr, the bell isn't ringing at 27. Do you know why?"

"No—it was ringing okay last night."

"We'll put a boat over and see what's wrong."

The chief ordered out the boat. "I think it's probably just the sensitivity control that's out," he said. Two men took off in a skiff and rowed to the light. In twenty minutes they were back. The whistle blasted again. The bell rang. Lewis called Kerr.

"Sensitivity was nine and a half. We put it at ten and it's all right now."

"Thanks a lot," from Kerr. Stationed at Stony Point, Kerr tends the shore lights in these reaches.

The Lighthouse That Talks Back

There is one other "lighthouse that talks back." Unfortunately it talks too much. It is 37, located at what the Dutch called the Devil's Dance Chamber. A noisy railroad and a noisy steam generating plant keep it ringing most of the time.

We pulled up beside a can buoy, it was hoisted up out of the water, some repairs were made, and a sextant was used to determine exactly where it should be let down.

"Buoys don't just stay put and keep working," said the chief. "They require frequent attention. A barge may catch on a buoy and drag it out of position. A freighter may damage it with its propellers. Floating ice can do a lot of harm to a lighted buoy, perhaps push it under and break the lens—the lantern on a lighted buoy costs $500 independent of the clockwork. Some people deliberately shoot the lenses out of light buoys."

The boat serviced one more light buoy. "Open up the lantern; check the voltage of the lamps." Two of the four lamps were replaced. The arrangement is most ingenious—the four lamps are one on each side of a square box. If one goes bad, the box automatically turns another into position. It is most unlikely that all four will go bad before the Coast Guard makes a check.

We later visited Lamplighter John J. Kerr whose voice we had heard over the *Beech*'s radiotelephone. His house is perched on the crest of Stony Point which during the Revolution was called the "Gibraltar of the Highlands."

"Can you storm Stony Point?" Washington asked Mad Anthony Wayne.

The impulsive and daring young general replied, "I'll storm hell, sir, if you say the word."

"Better try Stony Point first," said Washington quietly.

The nearly impregnable stronghold was taken in one of the most daring night attacks in history.

At the river's edge stands Stony Point light, one of the tallest of the Hudson light towers.

I expressed a desire to see the lantern.

"All right, but watch your step."

There was frequently little more than toehold on the rungs because girders of the tower crowded them, and twice it was necessary to squeeze through a "lubber's hole" where momentary absentmindedness would mean a cracked head against an iron bar, the jolt loosening one's grip and dropping him to the rocks beneath. There was not much space to stand at the top, but what a view over Haverstraw Bay! To make the scene perfect, the beautiful side-wheelers *Alexander Hamilton* and *Peter Stuyvesant* glided by, taking the Sunday crowd home from the Highlands.

Kerr opened the lantern. Clockwork lights it in the evening and turns it off in the morning. There is a smaller beacon just below it. If the big light fails the small light clicks on and remains until the big one is functioning again.

At the base of the tower is a great fog bell. It is not left to the uncertain promptings of a ship's whistle but is started by means of a switch in the house up the hill.

Kerr had been here only a month. Before that he and his family lived in a lighthouse three thousand feet from either shore.

"It's at Esopus. That's something you must see. It's unique—the only lighthouse on the whole Hudson to be still lived in."

The Last Lived-In Lighthouse

Some telephoning got us an appointment at the Hudson's only manned lighthouse. The three young men stationed there are good cooks—we could testify to that after dinner with them.

This is no iron tower, but a real house topped by a beacon. There are many others like it on the Hudson but they are empty and their lights are controlled by switches on shore.

"Why is this manned while all the others have been made automatic?"

"Because this is a mighty bad stretch of river," said Officer-in-Charge John F. Monahan. "It's very shallow between here and the west shore. The ship channel is on the east side of the lighthouse, but smaller yachts often try the west side, neglecting to study the depth figures on their chart, and get grounded and need help. But I don't know how long we can stick it out. The old house threatens to fall down on our heads—it makes me nervous."

In every room he showed us yawning cracks, some of which

had developed only during the last few days. The whole structure was listing like the Leaning Tower of Pisa.

"That happened last winter," said Monahan. "The ice piled up fifteen feet high against it and pushed it out of plumb."

Lamplighter Perry M. Peloubet took us out in a launch to the Hudson City light. This also is a real lighthouse, eight rooms and basement and tower. The lighthouse keeper with his wife and five children lived here for more than ten years. The children used to go to school by boat. Now the light is automatic.

"But I come out every week or so to see that everything is okay."

This is not always easy or safe. The mountains around provoke severe storms. In winter Peloubet walks across the ice to the lighthouse. An electrician came up from New York to fix the wiring—Peloubet took him across. They came to a tide crack four or five feet wide. Peloubet bridged the gulf with a small ladder and walked over. The electrician was horrified.

"Do you expect me to walk across that thing?"

He did it, quaking, but said, "Never call me again unless you have solid ice."

Peloubet, an ardent duck hunter, took us ashore to his duck camp where his wife had spread a chicken dinner on a long table under the trees within a few yards of the river. About twenty persons sat down to table. The warmhearted Peloubets like children as well as ducks. They have fourteen children, one of them their own, the rest "welfare children."

The oldest lighthouse on the Hudson River we visited with Light Attendant C. B. Glunt, who is responsible for twenty-three Hudson lights. Saugerties light bears the date 1869, and a sign placed during the 1959 celebration of Henry Hudson's visit in 1609 announces:

"Saugerties celebrates 350 years of river travel. Welcome."

It is best not to take this welcome too literally, for the reception committee consists only of the ghosts of long-gone lighthouse keepers.

The historic old lighthouses must disappear, but thanks to the Coast Guard and the U.S. Corps of Engineers the Hudson has never been so hazard-free as it is today.

Shakespeare on the Hudson

Poughkeepsie, beautiful college town, owes its name to the Mohegan word *apo-keep-sinck,* "a safe and pleasant harbor." It boasts a number of firsts. The first United States flag was made here, the white stripes from the shirts of soldiers, the red stripes from the petticoats of their wives, the blue from an officer's blue cloak. It was here that the colony of New York voted to become part of the American republic. Here the first telegraph wires were strung by an inventor named Morse. Here two gentlemen whose bearded faces are familiar to anyone who has ever had a tickle in his throat pioneered in the cough drop business. And here a wealthy brewer, Matthew Vassar, built himself an enduring monument—the first college in the world devoted exclusively to the higher education of women.

Chief gem of the unusually beautiful grounds of Vassar College is Sunset Lake with an open-air theater on its shore. Second choicest gem is the Shakespeare Garden abounding in the flowers mentioned in Shakespeare's plays.

The Vanishing Canoe

For many years Poughkeepsie was host to the annual Intercollegiate Regatta, most famous of American shell races. There is no shell to be seen now, and even the canoe has almost disappeared. The Pirate Canoe Club once housed eighty canoes— only two remain, and they are not used. The club retains its name, but its yards and docks roar and smoke with the servicing of powerboats.

Many citizens do not remember the old Poughkeepsie for they are refugees from terrorized Hungary. They appreciate American liberty but are astonished that Americans work so hard. Said one employee in a busy factory, "We work harder here than we ever did at home. We had rather supposed that Americans picked up money off the streets, so the help America sent to Europe was not fully appreciated. But when we see how hard Americans have to work to send help abroad, we understand for the first time how goodhearted the people of this country really are."

No Boots in Bed

A few miles north in Hyde Park is the Franklin D. Roosevelt home, open to visitors. Eleanor Roosevelt was not to be found there but lived in a woodland hideaway from which she emerged during our visit to attend St. James church on the occasion of a revival of oldtime customs and costumes.

Also open to visitors is the proud palace erected by millionaire Frederick W. Vanderbilt. On the other shore is the home of naturalist John Burroughs, and the difference between the two men is revealed in their houses—one full of costly and showy treasures, the other the workshop of a man who liked sticks, stones and birds.

Not far west of the river are two of the loveliest small lakes in America, Mohonk and Minnewaska, each overlooked by a fine old Quaker hotel.

And speaking of hotels, what traveler can afford to miss the Beekman Arms at Rhinebeck, oldest hotel in America. The guest in this hostelry must observe certain rules which were laid down before the Revolution and are still in force. The most important is that no boots can be worn in bed.

I photographed an old stone house in nearby Rhinecliff. The lady of the house came out and said, "You know, this house has fire insurance, and it doesn't cost us a cent. When the house was built, a colonial on one side threw a bottle of whisky over the roof to an Indian on the other side. If it broke, the house was destined to be burned down. If it didn't break, fire would never touch the house. The Indian caught the firewater—so there has never been a fire."

Pioneers Worked for the Indians

Thriving Kingston has long since forgotten the days when pioneers were forced to work for the Indians. "The savages," said Governor Stuyvesant, "compel the whites to plow their maize land, and when they hesitate, threaten, with firebrands in their hands, to burn their houses."

The harassed settlers resorted to prayer meetings held from house to house, each householder to supply the liquor that would encourage full attendance. One householder, when it came his turn, asked the dominie to excuse him—he couldn't afford to pay for the drinks!

Just outside of Kingston is quaint Hurley, "more Dutch than Holland" said a visitor from the Netherlands. But it must be noted that the citizens no longer take their cheeses to bed with them, as was their wont so that the heat from their bodies might hasten the ripening process.

The shade of Rip Van Winkle hovers over Catskill. The illuminated Rip Van Winkle Bridge, particularly when the rising moon keeps it company, is one of the prime beauties of the Hudson. And on a mountaintop back of the town is Rip's Retreat where Rip is supposed to have had his long siesta and where the architecture and arts of his day have been authentically and lovingly reproduced by antiquarian Harold Hargreave.

The town of Hudson, believe it or not, was once a whaling port. Because Nantucket was exposed to attack by British ships, a group of Nantucket whalers sought refuge far up the great river and in a few years Hudson had twenty-five whalers on the high seas.

The Dogs Barked in Dutch

Dating back to 1614, the capital of New York State, Albany, is one of the oldest cities in America. It was founded before the pilgrims landed at Plymouth. It had reached such maturity by the Revolution that a French nobleman said of it: "I almost incline to think that young people here are old born."

The Dutch folk clung to their own ways under British rule. Even the dogs, it was said, "barked in Dutch." Garbage was tossed into the streets for the half-wild pigs—a custom which one critic described as "more Dutch than decent." Today we should consider it neither decent nor Dutch.

More characteristically Dutch was the annual street-scrubbing by housewives. The custom persists to this day. Once a year the ladies of the City Club, wearing Dutch costumes and wooden shoes and armed with brooms and buckets, go through the motions of cleaning the already spotless State Street. Hudson Valley residents are proud of their history and slip into costume on the least provocation. In three fine old mansions open to the public, Schuyler House, Tenbroeck and Fort Crailo, ladies regown themselves in a style two centuries old and bring back the glamor of the past.

Seaport 150 Miles from the Sea

But reminding us that Albany and its neighbor cities have more than kept up with the times is the busy Port of Albany, a seaport 150 miles from the sea, berthing ships from all over the world.

It received its first oceangoing vessel in 1609, when Henry Hudson dropped the anchor of the *Half Moon*. The shallowing stream convinced him that this was no water road to the Orient. Bitterly disappointed, he put back to sea.

During the days of the clipper ships, many of them put in here to deliver exotic wares from the Far East and Europe. But when steam replaced sail, the port died, since steamboats demanded a deeper channel than the Hudson afforded.

Half a century later the port was reborn, thanks to the channeling of the Hudson to a depth of twenty-seven feet in 1932. Now Albany is one of the largest inland seaports in the United States. It berths some two hundred ships a year, handles annually about $75,000,000 worth of cargo.

We saw thirteen ships loading and unloading.

"Step aboard," came a shout from the bridge of the *Andros Citadel*, discharging lumber. We climbed to the captain's cabin and enjoyed sweet sedimentary Greek coffee with Captain S. Sarris and Chief Officer K. Makris.

Here was a good example of the international character of Albany's contacts. The coffee cups were decorated with paintings of Japan's Fujiyama, the two officers were Greek, the vessel was a Liberty ship built in New Orleans, it flew the star and stripes of Liberia, and it was unloading lumber from British Columbia!

The captain said his home was in Athens, but perhaps his home was his ship. He and his mate were thoroughgoing seadogs.

"Always eager to get home," said Captain Sarris, "but in a couple months I'm fretting to be off to sea again."

"I don't speak the same language as my family," said Makris. "I find myself calling the floor a deck, the wall a bulkhead, the window a porthole."

With Captain Frank Dunham Jr., general manager of the port, we went to see the chief import, blackstrap molasses, piping ashore into huge tanks with the largest molasses storage capacity in the country, 17,000,000 gallons. It comes from the West Indies and will ultimately be mixed with grain to make cattle feed. A tank truck, looking exactly like those used for gasoline, was filling with molasses from a tank as high as a house.

Asphalt was pouring ashore in hot fluid form. It would be kept in insulated tanks and delivered in the same hot and flowing condition to customers.

An oil tanker with four black tentacles reaching to the dock was piping off four different kinds of oil at the same time.

And one of the largest single-unit grain elevators in the world was swallowing carloads of grain at the rate of one every six minutes.

There are gloomy predictions that the St. Lawrence Seaway may increasingly take over the cargo that formerly reached the sea through Albany. On the other hand, the port's best days may be just ahead, for the 27-foot Hudson is soon to be deepened to 32 feet and the giants of the world's fleets may safely sail to Albany.

Just above Albany is one of the most remarkable meetings of waters in the world. Here six water routes converge—the Hudson, the old Champlain Canal now abandoned, the modern Champlain Canal which for the most part follows the Hudson, the old Erie Canal used now only as a spillway, the modern Erie Barge Canal, and the Mohawk River.

Ocean vessels may not go above this point. But tugs and barges transport cargo to and from the Great Lakes and throughout the elaborate canal system of New York State as well as northward through Lake Champlain to the St. Lawrence. The upper part of the last-mentioned waterway is shallow but there are plans to deepen it so as to tie the Hudson to the St. Lawrence Seaway and speed ore from the new mines of Labrador by an inland water passage safe from submarine attack to American steel mills.

It is good to have a friend who owns a 42-foot Chris Craft Commodore yacht. Lionel Beakbane, Glens Falls industrialist, took us on a fifty-mile round trip on the Champlain Canal. Aboard was Frank Dwyer, superintendent of the canal.

From Waterford and Troy north to Fort Edward the canal is for the most part simply a trench dug in the floor of the Hudson, maintained at a depth of twelve feet and marked by buoys. Every time the river is interrupted by rapids or a fall, the canal deserts it and joins the river again at the higher level.

When the Hudson turns sharply westward the canal leaves it and goes forth on its own, making connection with the southern end of Lake Champlain at Whitehall.

Amphibious Cows

One of the unique sights of the canal is a herd of amphibious cows belonging to farmer Charles Wright. These handsome Jerseys graze on one side of the canal, voluntarily swim across in the evening to be milked, stay in the barnyard to be milked again in the morning, then swim back to pasture.

The distance from shore to shore is about 150 feet. Calves a few hours old swim close to their mothers—for a calf can swim as soon as it can walk. So each generation learns easily and the habit is passed on. Wright has never heard of another lot of cows that swim home to be milked.

The highest waterfall on the Hudson is probably that at Hudson Falls, although it has a very close competitor at Corinth, a little farther upstream. Both measure eighty feet or better. The height of a waterfall is not always the same, varying according to volume and the draw-off for industrial purposes.

At Hudson Falls cascading waters drop into a deep and almost inaccessible gorge. On the brink of the gorge stands the Sandy Hill Iron and Brass Works which makes machinery for the many paper mills scattered along the Upper Hudson. When we asked its president for permission to go down the eighty-foot cliff to take pictures of the falls from below, he said, "That should be interesting. So far as I know it's never been done. I'll lend you two men to help get your canoe down."

A hundred-foot rope was strung down the declivity and with its help we inched the canoe to the bottom of the gorge. Said one of the men, "I've lived here all my life and I've never been down here before."

Canoe among the Haystacks

There was the thrill of the mysterious in this echoing canyon full of sound and fury. We slipped the canoe into a quiet back-water and paddled out to the swirl of tumbling "haystacks" near the base of the waterfall. There we were attacked by two currents, one coming from the main fall, another rushing in on the right from a side fall. This conflict of interests made treach-erously choppy waves. The water was churned white, and the thunder of the falls made conversation out of the question. The steady little aluminum canoe took it all as a matter of course and we regained the shore with nothing worse than a wetting from flying spray.

The hardest trick fell to the men who must climb the cliff by rope, hauling the canoe, which is as much at home as a seal in water but awkward as a walrus on land.

Pushing farther north into the Adirondack forest we found the rangers complaining about wild beasts. Bear have been in-creasing rapidly.

"Now there are more bears than people," said ranger Chuck Severance. "A hunter is still allowed to shoot only one bear a season. The bears are big blacks, some as large as grizzlies and weighing as much as six hundred pounds. They do a lot of damage, especially on summer homes while folks are absent. Just recently one tore off the corner strip of a house, pried out the planking, went in and ransacked the place, leaving broken beds, chairs, lamps, kitchen cabinets all in a heap on the floor. Coyotes have been multiplying too although there is a bounty of fifty dollars on each. They gang up like a pack of wolves on deer, drive off ten or a dozen, surround them so they can't get away, and slaughter them at their leisure. And bobcats—the bounty of twenty-five dollars just isn't enough to keep them down."

One of the great cares of every ranger, of course, is to protect all animals, including bears, coyotes and bobcats. But to pre-serve the right proportion of each to offset the imbalance caused by man is the problem of a Solomon.

Teddy Roosevelt's Wild Ride

We came upon the trail of Theodore Roosevelt at Aiden Lair Lodge. The Scotch name means "haven of rest" or "king's rest"—and it was something like that on the night of September 13, 1901, when Vice President Theodore Roosevelt, already President in effect though he did not know it, paused to change horses and driver on his race to get to the bed of the dying McKinley.

The new driver was Mike Cronin, proprietor of Aiden Lair His daughter, Rose Cronin, still lives in the house by the side of the road and we were her guests for several days. On every wall of the lodge are mementos of that famous night, including a horseshoe stating that it is *not* one of those worn by the team that made the final dash.

"The story is," said Rose, "that my father did a big business selling those eight horseshoes—in fact, sold barrels of them. But the truth is he loved a joke and started the story himself. He never actually sold a single shoe."

The midnight ride has a bearing on the Hudson, for it was at Lake Tear of the Clouds during T.R.'s descent from Mt. Marcy where the river has its beginning that he was notified of McKinley's relapse. Night had fallen before the party reached the foot of the mountain. The ride was made through complete blackness and heavy rain.

"It was the darkest night I ever saw," said Mike later. "I couldn't even see my horses. . . ."

Edging a cliff, Mike suggested they slow down. "Not at all," said Roosevelt. "Push ahead." He held his watch in his hand all the while and kept continually asking how far they had yet to go. Upon arrival at North Creek railroad station he was met by his secretary, William Loeb, who informed him that McKinley was already dead and he, Theodore Roosevelt, was President of the United States.

The Hudson becomes steadily more wild and wonderful as we press up through the mountains of the Adirondacks. This is a land of lovely lakes. Superb Lake George is connected with the Hudson by way of Lake Champlain and the Champlain Canal. Lake Luzerne, instead of resembling Lucerne, looks quite Japanese when the mists roll down from the mountains into the tall pines on its boat-shaped island.

A most important contributor to the Hudson is the Sacandaga Reservoir which by means of its dams controls the river's flow and makes impossible a repetition of the Hudson flood of 1913, which scourged Albany with a typhoid epidemic and left schooners stranded on State Street.

Lake of the Drifting Islands

To find the source of the Hudson we must penetrate the wildest and least frequented part of the Adirondacks. At Newcomb a roadside sign announces "Source of Hudson River." This approximation may do for the motorist, but the canoeist and hiker will find the real source, or sources, some ten to twenty miles back in the mountains. Of course no river has but one source.

After seeing the open-pit titanium mine at Tahawus we paddled up the dwindling Hudson through the region of the High Peaks, tallest of all Adirondack mountains, the ultimate retreat of bears, coyotes, raccoons, deer and beavers. The bottom steadily climbed toward our keel and at last we definitely scraped to a stop. A little farther is Henderson Lake which claims to be a source of the Hudson. However that may be, I should say that when the Hudson becomes so shallow that you run aground, you may properly say that you have reached the end of the river.

But only one of the ends. Another is the highly romantic and almost unknown Elk Lake, surrounded by the High Peaks, sprinkled with some fifty islands. Thirty-seven of them are stationary. The rest are floating islands which drift here and there according to the direction of the winds.

The loon has disappeared from most Adirondack lakes but it still laughs and cries above Elk. There is no sound more weird and lonely, more in keeping with the mystery of woods and waters uninvaded by man. The loon here prefers to make its home on a floating island, which will rise when the water rises, keeping the nest high and dry.

In this too noisy age, Elk Lake is a relief. The birds can actually be heard. There is not one motorized boat on the lake.

We glided over a still mirror as dusk deepened into night, not daring to speak, plying the paddles in complete silence without removing them from the water. The spell of the luminous lake, the velvet-black islands against the lighter gray of the largest cluster of high mountains east of the Rockies, transformed the experience into a dream, an unreality that might be dispelled by one bump of the paddle against the gunwale.

Elk Lake is privately owned, but its proprietor opens his lodge to guests provided they are willing to live in log cabin simplicity.

Lake Tear of the Clouds

Another source of the Hudson and with best claim to be regarded as *the* source if the highest body of water feeding a river shall be considered its true head, is Lake Tear of the Clouds.

It is cradled 4,322 feet high in the crater of a triangle formed by Mts. Marcy, Skylight and Gray. Mt. Marcy is dean of the High Peaks, 5,344 feet, highest in the state.

From tiny Tear flows Feldspar Brook which tumbles into the Opalescent River which joins the Hudson.

We paddled up the Opalescent until our keel and the riverbed met. True to its name, it is clear as crystal, and its bed is set with jewels. Through the glasslike water, hornblende, mica and feldspar sparkled in the sun.

But this glittering road of colored prisms has to be abandoned for a brown woodland trail punctuated by lean-tos if you would reach Tear of the Clouds. After you get there, it is a pond like any other.

To appreciate its wild setting among the peaks one must look at it from above. We had already followed the river by car and boat. Now we were to get the bird's-eye view. Returning to Albany, we made a flight to the peaks and back in an amphibious Otter, Roy Curtis, pilot, by courtesy of the State Conservation Commission. But the trip was authorized only after a mysterious period of hesitation which we were not to understand until later.

Every inch of the way we followed the Hudson, getting a new perspective on its character and beauty. Above Luzerne there is a dramatic change in the river. It is no longer tranquil and slow, punctuated only occasionally by a fall. Now it falls all the time, steeply, swiftly, swirling around great boulders, twisting through a narrow gorge between steadily rising mountains.

We are uncomfortably conscious of these mountains, for their tops are higher than our plane and we dodge one only to be confronted by another. But the pilot is merely following our request that he keep to the river as closely as possible.

The roar of the engine is deafening. We converse by gestures alone. I try to trace our route on the Geological Survey chart. The mountain names are intriguing. Many of the names in this region were pinned on by lumberjacks, and no other breed of men has more fertile imagination.

We fly over Deer Leap Mountain, Three Sisters, Kettle, P Gay, Baldhead, Bad Luck. Deep in the glens are gleaming gems of water, Mink Pond, Dunk Pond, Stonystep Pond, Big Bad Luck Pond, Whortleberry Pond, Squirrel Pond and O K Slip Pond which empties into O K Slip Brook!

More and more water, until the mountains are interlaced with it. The Indian River empties into the Hudson, then the Cedar River, then the Goodnow flowing down from Vanderwhacker Mountain.

Past the small mountain-girt village of Newcomb and up to the isolated titanium-mining works at Tahawus. We catch sight of a group of black bears on a hillside. At night they come down to raid the garbage cans of the village, and residents discreetly stay indoors.

Dodging the High Peaks

Now the real excitement begins. We head up into the High Peaks. There are forty-six Adirondack peaks over four thousand feet. Most of them are clustered right here in the heart of the Adirondack State Park which, by the way, covers some six million acres and is the largest park, state or national, in the country.

This is its wildest, most rugged, and most inaccessible region. There are no roads, no lodges, nothing but an occasional lean-to to shelter mountain climbers.

On the left is Henderson Lake, one of the Hudson's recognized sources, and on the right, Elk Lake where the solitude-loving loons nest on the floating islands.

Rising higher, we can see the divide between the Hudson watershed and the lakes and rivers that flow north to the St. Lawrence. Among the latter are lovely Lake Placid at the foot of Whiteface Mountain, the Saranac Lakes, Long Lake, Blue Mountain Lake. The sawmills of Tupper Lake are visible, for the lumberjack has not completely disappeared from the Adirondacks and each year a notable tree-felling contest is staged on the shore of this lake.

But where is the highest source of the Hudson, Lake Tear of the Clouds? Since it is little more than a large pond it easily escapes detection. We fly low to search it out.

It might seem a simple matter to follow the Opalescent River and Feldspar Brook straight to Lake Tear. But both streams are buried deep in evergreens. Seldom do they give a hint of their presence.

We pass over a small lake between high cliffs. The pilot points down and nods. I shake my head. Lake Tear is not walled in by cliffs. Another lake appears below. Consulting the chart, we dismiss it as Lake Arnold.

Lake Tear is southwest of Mt. Marcy, but which of these peaks is Marcy? The highest, of course, but it is not easy to pick the highest when you are not far enough away to get them in perspective.

We shoot about like a runaway meteor among some two dozen cloud splitters, all over four thousand feet. The map shows Marcy, Haystack, Basin, Gray Peak, Skylight, Nippletop, Saddleback, Gooseberry, Gothics, the two Wolfjaws, Armstrong, Sawtooth, Pinnacle and many others—the most savage herd of mountain monsters in the Eastern United States.

But which is which? How can one tell while engrossed in dodging about among them? We are not over them, but within their grasp, always lower than their crests.

Finally Roy selects one of the grimmest of them as the Cloud Splitter and circles it at a distance of about a mile which according to the map should be right.

Clouds have gathered, a thunderstorm is brewing, and the plane bumps, leaps and drops in the crazy currents as if the black giants were tossing it about. Stomachs have long since left their usual habitat and are glued to the ceiling.

Then we see it—Lake Tear. There is no doubt about it this time. It is in the right relation to Marcy. It has low shores shadowed by conifers, and the eastern end is a brilliant and jaundiced green. From it descends a sparkling stream, soon lost in the trees. That will be Feldspar Brook. Closely guarding the lake are Gray Peak and Marcy on the north while five peaks crowd in upon it from the south.

Thunder is crashing now and strong winds are rushing up and down the slopes. To get a last look at the cradle of the Hudson I have Roy circle again and again around Tear, Marcy, and its neighbors. I assume that he as master of the ship will deny my requests if he thinks them unwise. But every circle I make with my finger he follows with his plane, and so willingly that I am led to believe there is no particular danger after all in ducking and dipping among the peaks, tossed by stormy winds.

At last I signal "enough" and we streak away in a direct line some ninety-seven miles to Albany airport.

We crawl down from the plane and find ourselves a little unsteady on our feet. Also almost stone deaf.

Over a cup of coffee I begin to wonder why Roy had seemed so uncertain about the location of Tear and Marcy.

"I suppose you have often been up there before," I remark.

"Never. It was all new to me."

"But I thought you Conservation men had to know every inch of this territory."

"Some do. But not the fliers."

"Why not?"

"Because the Marcy area is no place for planes. Too much chance of a downdraft throwing you into one of those peaks."

Now he tells me!

12

Mississippi Miracle

HE STOOD his ground, snarling, trying to make up his mind what to do. I blocked his path. The river behind him cut off his retreat.

I took another step forward. Like a flash, the bobcat wheeled, fled to the river's edge, spanned the river in one great leap and disappeared in the forest.

The river was the Mississippi. Since we all know that the Mississippi thinks nothing of being a mile wide, to leap across it would seem to be a feat possible only to Paul Bunyan's mythical Blue Ox.

But at the point where we stood gazing across the stream after the vanished bobcat, the Mississippi was only ten feet wide. It was just a babbling brook, with very little to babble about, for it was not old enough to know much. Two minutes ago it was born. A hundred yards back it had issued from Lake

Itasca past a wooden marker designating this spot as the source
of the Mississippi.

Forest-girdled Lake Itasca lies in northern Minnesota not
very far from the Canadian border. Its discoverer, Henry
Schoolcraft, fixed upon it as the true source of the Mississippi.
Searching for some name that would suggest True Head, he
came upon the Latin words *veritas caput.* That would be too
long a name—so, with skillful surgery, he chopped off the first
and last syllables and came out with Itasca.

It had a pleasantly Indian sound. In fact, ethnologists have
ever since been trying to trace it back to the Chippewa language. One went so far as to imagine it the name of the tribal
god's unhappy daughter whose falling tears formed the lake.

But the question was settled once and for all when a scholar
happened upon a letter written by Schoolcraft to a Galena newspaper on July 25, 1832, twelve days after the discovery, stating
plainly that the name Itasca was devised from *veritas caput.*
This habit, by the way, of shaping names from Latin origins was
quite the fashion in those days.

A Crow Starts the Mississippi?

But is Itasca the true head of the Mississippi? Sceptically, we
explored the lakeshore in our canoe. At the far end we found
the source of the source of the Mississippi—a small stream flowing into Lake Itasca.

The stream was too shallow for the canoe, so we picked up
the craft and portaged a few hundred yards to find that the
creek flowed out of a smaller lake which appeared on the map
as Elk Lake. Again we explored the shoreline and found an
incoming stream from Little Elk Lake.

It illustrates the futility of naming any one patch of moisture
the true source of a river. Where should one stop? The stream
entering Little Elk comes from a pond higher up, and the pond
from a spring still higher. According to the humorous specula-
tions of author Holling C. Holling, above this spring is a tree,
and on top of the tree sits a crow with the rain pouring upon its
back and running off both ends; one has only to learn which
end of the crow is higher and that is the true source of the
Mississippi.

The way out of this absurdity was offered by a ranger we met in Itasca State Park bordering the lake.

"The truth is," he said, "that all the lakes in the Itasca region are interrelated by underground seepages and springs so that it is impossible to specify any one as *the* source of the Mississippi. The whole system is one big sponge. You can only say that the source is the Itasca basin."

Most Fickle of Rivers

The signpost which pinpoints one spot as the source of the Mississippi makes another doubtful assumption. It announces the length of the Mississippi from this point to the mouth as 2,552 miles.

The fact is no one knows the length of the Mississippi—and if he knew today he would have to revise his figure tomorrow. The river channel is constantly changing. Blocked by a sandbar, it may go several miles out of its way around islands. Where it makes a thirty-mile loop it may suddenly gather its strength and cut through the neck of the loop, reducing the river's length by thirty miles. It is the crookedest great waterway in the world and the most fickle. Even the Army engineers whose business it is to control the river cautiously use the word "approximately" when they estimate its present length at 2,434 miles.

The fame of the Mississippi draws many visitors to the spot where the infant river creeps over the lip of Lake Itasca and starts on its long journey to the sea. Boulders serve as stepping-stones across the stream, and if you slip from one of them the result is not too serious, for the rivulet is ordinarily only ankle deep. It is hard to imagine that this puling infant is to become the Father of Waters.

This timid little creek will grow to be the greatest river in North America; the greatest in the world with the exception of the Amazon. It will gather to itself more than 100,000 tributaries, large and small. It and its affluents will provide 15,700 miles of inland navigation.

The vast Mississippi water-web will drain 40 percent of the United States, not to mention 13,000 square miles of Canada. It will draw water from thirty-one states, and some of the fingers of its longest arm, the Missouri, will reach seventy miles into a Canadian province.

Its drainage area will stretch to a maximum of 1,900 miles in longitude and 1,400 miles in latitude and will cover 1,243,700 square miles.

That, as Mark Twain chose to interpret it, "is as great as the combined areas of England, Wales, Scotland, Ireland, France, Spain, Portugal, Germany, Austria, Italy and Turkey."

The river exacts tribute from states as far east as New York and as far west as Montana. No wonder that the explorers, hearing Indian stories of the great river, dreamed that it would carry them to China.

Some authorities consider it the longest river on the globe, measuring from the source of the Missouri to the Gulf, about 4,-200 miles—but, again, this is a variable figure due to the river's habit of stretching and contracting like a temperamental caterpillar.

"When God made the world," said the Mississippi orator, S. S. Prentiss, "he had a large amount of surplus water which he turned loose and told to go where it pleased; it has been going where it pleased ever since and that is the Mississippi River."

God's surplus pours into the Gulf of Mexico at the rate of 785 billion cubic yards a year. It delivers three times as much water as the mighty St. Lawrence, twenty-five times as much as the majestic Rhine, 338 times as much as the Thames.

America's Backbone

The Creator seems also to have had more mud than he could use. The Mississippi has been industriously carrying it off at the rate of five hundred million tons a year.

Long ages of such mudslinging have had an astounding result. Enough mud has been thrown out to make a country the size of Portugal. Generous portions of Missouri, Tennessee, Arkansas, Mississippi and Louisiana came from Minnesota, Iowa, the Dakotas, Montana and Canada. That is a debt the South owes to the North!

The Mississippi once poured into the sea at Cairo, Illinois. The Gulf of Mexico extended up to this point. Deposits of sediment pushed the Gulf farther and farther south, laid down a mud plain twenty to eighty miles wide and lengthened the river by a thousand miles.

The Mississippi is America's backbone from which proliferating spinal nerves pass to the sense organs, muscles and glands of the body politic from the Rockies to the Atlantic. The agricultural Midwest and the industrial East are linked with New Orleans and, through that second greatest of all America's export outlets, with all the world.

The greatest such port, New York, is also a part of the system. From the Mississippi by way of the Great Lakes and canals, cargo may be waterborne all the way to New York or Montreal, there to be transshipped across the Atlantic or around the globe.

During the steamboat era Mississippi tonnage was greater than the entire tonnage transported by all the ships of the British Empire. In 1849 there were a thousand big packets plying the river. The end came rather suddenly. After the Civil War the steamboats were eclipsed by the railroads.

Mississippi Reborn

The Mississippi was dead. Progress had passed it by. No one dreamed it would ever come to life again. It was only natural to suppose that slow transport must always give way to rapid transport. Improved roads allowed trucks to compete with the railroads. Both began to yield to the airplane. There could surely be no return to the plodding riverboat.

But during the two world wars the government, as an emergency measure to relieve transportation congestion, revived river traffic. From December 1941 until August 15, 1945, the amount of petroleum alone transported on American inland waterways (mostly on the Mississippi network) was the equivalent of seven million carloads.

"If our waterways rendered no services beyond that of transporting petroleum and its products during the war," stated the Office of Defense Transportation, "they would have amply justified their improved existence."

But Mississippi traffic did not stop when the war stopped. The lesson had been learned—heavy goods such as oil, metal, grain, building materials, salt, sulphur, chemicals, ores and scores of other products could be carried far more economically by water than by land—and in some cases almost as rapidly, thanks to the evolution of that marvel of water transport, the diesel-powered towboat.

Since the war tonnage has increased year by year. To take a single dramatic example, in a ten-year period the Port of St. Louis has seen her river trade grow from 1,839,483 to 6,810,940 tons.

And yet the possible use of the river has only begun. There is plenty of room left on the great highway. It is still a lonesome river. You may sail it for hours without seeing another craft.

It is still a wayward and rebellious monster, only half-tamed. Millions of dollars and thousands of men are constantly working to improve its habits.

In view of the possibilities of better control, better boats, perhaps atomic power, the Mississippi, already the most heavily loaded river on this planet, may be only in the early stages of its useful career.

Buggered Up

"You can get pretty buggered up in there."

That was a farmer's comment when we mentioned our plan to canoe down the first reach of the Mississippi River.

We did get pretty buggered up. In spite of the fact that I had the able assistance of two lusty lads, it was rough going. Fortunately the Grumman Aircraft aluminum canoe drew only three inches. It was thirteen feet long and weighed but forty-five pounds, therefore was light to carry around obstructions. But when you have almost nothing but obstructions for eighteen miles and repeatedly find yourself with a three-inch-draught boat in two inches of water, you are inclined to give this part of the river back to the mosquitoes.

We started out in high spirits. My wife had departed with the car to a point where the road crossed the river. There she would wait for us. Considering the wiggle of the little stream on the map, we estimated that the trip would take an hour.

It took five. We had scarcely left the lip of Lake Itasca when a disjointed old stone bridge, perhaps dating back to lumbering days, blocked our way. It was smothered in brush. We must pull the canoe out, beat a passage through the prickly brush, and carry around to the stream below the bridge.

We repeated this performance at four more bridges, all of them slumped too low to permit the canoe to pass under. Even when the canoe was in the water we were seldom in the canoe. We were wading alongside, hauling or lifting the boat over pebbly shoals or rocky ledges. The shallows now and then gave way to deep holes, and we were soon soaked to the hips.

Then the forest fell back on both sides and the stream meandered through a great swamp a mile wide. We could stay in the boat now. The water was some twelve inches deep. But there was no discernible current to help our paddling.

At times there were several possible channels through the reeds and only the most learned debate could decide which we should take. My son, Bob, was a lawyer, therefore his arguments were not to be dismissed lightly. Jonathan was fifteen years old and had all the bright intuition and assurance of youth. I had the calm wisdom of maturity, not too much respected after I had steered the party up several culs-de-sac. Thus we whiled away the sunlit hours while Mary sat and waited.

Buffalo, Bear and Timber Wolf

The sinking sun found us still staggering about in the bewildering swamp. We were alone with our problem. There was no sign whatever that any other human beings inhabited the planet—no house, bridge or road, nothing but swamp a mile wide backed by forest.

The swamp had its own peculiar beauty. Brown cattails, blue iris, tawny reeds, yellow water lilies were reflected in the sleeping water. Below us, what looked like pine forests in miniature rose almost to the surface, chambers of mystery like beds of coral.

The solitude was a lively solitude, ringing with song, for what could be a better bird paradise than this forest-bordered open swamp full of bugs and free of humans?

The red-winged blackbird's *gug-lug-gee* suggested perfectly the gurgle and ooze of the swamp. The purple grackle twanged his piano wires. The cedar waxwing gave a subdued imitation of a peanut-roaster's whistle. When we neared the trees we could hear the tinkling wineglasses of the wood thrush and the tremulous spiral of the veery who never seems quite able to make up his mind whether to play a jew's-harp or an accordion.

Muskrats and beavers swam out of our way. Deer stood at the edge of the woods. Woodland sounds were untranslatable, but we had already been told by the foresters that the animal population of this northernmost of all American states is still considerable.

The buffalo has vanished, but the majestic moose still roams the northern edge of the state, changing his nationality every few days as he crosses and recrosses the Canadian border. Moose are actually increasing in number.

The big gray timber wolf, which we think of as belonging to the far past of the western pioneers or at least to the era of Jack London, is also increasing in the northern woods. In winter he ventures out on the ice of lakes and is hunted by plane for a bounty of $35. A farmer's wife looked out of the window one day in 1957 to see a big timber wolf trotting away through her garden with a lamb in its jaws. In the Wildlife Museum at Bemidji one may see a wolf that was killed within three miles of town.

It is said that the wolves are increasing because their important food supply, the deer, are increasing. The bobcats also prey upon deer. They too are growing in number, not only because there are more deer available, but because the bounty of three dollars on bobcats is, with inflation, no longer an inducement to the trapper.

The grizzly is gone, but the black bear continues to be a source of amusement to visitors and distress to campers and rangers who have difficulty in guarding their food supplies.

We were to encounter skunks frequently in this wood-and-water country, and veteran trapper Henry Guertin of Deer River told us how to catch one: just seize it by the tail and lift it from the ground.

"The skunk can't spray unless it's gripping the ground with its front feet."

We took his word for it and made no experiments.

Slow Work in Fast Water

The river had no interest in the shortest distance between two points. It looped back and forth upon itself, tripling and quadrupling the distance to our objective. We longed for a straight course and a fast one.

But when we got just that, we were far from satisfied. The river finally left the swamp, became straight and swift, and plunged down a chute several miles long between high banks supporting tall trees that met above to form a near-tunnel.

Though the river was now fast, we could not be because the rapids were too shallow for navigation. We waded through the rocks, hoisting the canoe over the worst of them, stumbling into holes, feeling our way through the half-dark. Dusk had brought out the mosquitoes in millions. They eagerly lapped up the repellent we had spread on every inch of exposed skin. Every few dozen yards, a fallen tree blocked our way. We must carry around it through almost impenetrable underbrush.

When we had begun to think of spending the night on a bed of leaves under a blanket of mosquitoes, the trees suddenly parted and there was the road bridge. The yellow car waited patiently and Mary a little less so. We flung the canoe on top of the car and drove to Bemidji State Park where our 21-foot travel trailer stood within a few yards of the north shore of Lake Bemidji.

Travel and Stay Home

The river flows out of Lake Bemidji in a noble stream two hundred feet wide, contrasting strongly with the ten-foot rivulet in the first reaches.

It is now navigable for small craft. No longer need we carry the canoe—it will carry us. So begins a 400-mile canoe trip down one of the most delightful of rivers. The journey is pretty soft compared to those of the early voyageurs. We do not camp out. At the end of the day's stint we find the car waiting for us and drive back to spend the night in our mobile home.

This means there must be a driver to bring the car. After the boys have flown home to Massachusetts, a visiting sister takes over for a few days and thereafter we must find someone, perhaps at a garage, to perform this service.

The day's routine is simple, at least in theory. Our helper huddles with us over a map to decide where he shall meet us. It should be a point about twenty-five miles downstream. That is an easy day's paddle, allowing time for picture-taking, lunch, inquisitive side trips, perhaps a portage or two. Our driver is to have the car at the meeting point at 5 P.M. Having fortified ourselves with a good breakfast, Mary and I embark. The trip that takes us all day takes our driver half an hour. At 4:30 he steps into the car, drives it down to the rendezvous, picks us up and we return to our trailer. Every few days the trailer is moved another hundred miles downstream.

On the whole, it works well. But there are a few things that can happen, and do.

The driver forgets, or happens to be busy at 4:30. Or the point of meeting has been misunderstood. He waits at one spot, we wait at another. He concludes that we have been picked up by someone else and goes home. We spend the night on pine needles under the canoe.

Or we have been dumped in the rapids. Wet and shivering in a cold wind, we would much rather go back to headquarters at once than wait until late afternoon. If there is a farmhouse and a telephone handy, we are in luck. But there is more likely to be solid forest flanking the river on both sides. We must wring ourselves out as best we can and go on.

But, barring accidents, the plan provides one great luxury that the explorers never knew: home at the end of the day. The modern trailer is a model of convenience and comfort, and takes most of the travail out of travel.

Unknown Mississippi

The Mississippi is a secretive river. It is almost unknown to many people who live within a few miles of it. Over some stretches the road hugs the shore and magnificent views may be had of the river and its maze of islands. But for the most part the highway does not attempt to follow the river's meanderings. You may drive from the Canadian border to the Gulf following the general route of the Mississippi and scarcely be aware of its existence. If you are determined, you can reach it by small side roads, often unpaved. And, of course, it can be seen from the bridges.

But by far the best way to see the Mississippi is over the bow of your own boat. Lacking the inclination to take your own, you may hire boats, motored or motorless, at many points along the river.

It is easy to imagine oneself a Joliet or Marquette while paddling down this undiscovered river. It flows today as it flowed then between unbroken walls of dark green conifers and snow-white birch. It slows in lilied swamps or speeds down narrow chutes between threatening boulders. It embraces charming islands and swirls rudely around rocky capes.

It is clear and pure for hundreds of miles before its confluence with the turbid Missouri, and when it pauses long enough to smooth the wrinkles from its forehead, its clean surface reflects the flight of kingfishers and herons and black terns. You may paddle for half a day without sight of a bridge or a house or a human. It is your river, for your boat alone. If after long hours of solitude you see another boat, you are surprised and a little indignant.

Bath, Finnish Style

At one of the rare waterside farms we saw on the beach a small square cabin belching both smoke and steam from its chimneys. Could this be a Finnish *sauna*?

We disembarked and examined the cubicle. It was almost as windowless as a fort and the door was closed. We walked up to the farmhouse. From a radio inside the house came talk in a strange language, then song, equally strange. It was certainly not German or Scandinavian.

Our knock brought a big, cheerful rosy-faced man to the door. He spoke English without accent, yet he had been listening to a foreign-language program. He welcomed us in, then turned off the radio.

"Was that a Finnish program?" I asked.

"That's right. They call it the Finnish Hour."

"But can you understand it? You weren't born in Finland."

"No. I was born right here. But my parents and grandparents

spoke Finnish, so of course I picked it up. There are plenty of Finns in Minnesota, you know. And a lot of them still speak Finnish."

"And take their baths Finnish style?"

"Oh, you saw the *sauna*. Yes, that's one Finnish custom we won't give up. I suppose you've seen how it works."

We confessed that we had not. He took us down to the cubicle on the beach. A girl, completely nude, was just coming out of the door. Her whole body radiated steam as if she were walking in a mist. Quite undisturbed by our presence, she ran across the beach and plunged into the water.

We went inside. First there was a small dressing room. Beyond it was the steam room fitted with a bench where the whole family and perhaps a few guests could sit, soap themselves and swelter in the steam. To increase the effect, they might beat each other with switches of prickly oak leaves or birch twigs. When they could bear no more, they would run out and dive into the river.

Across from the bench was a wood stove. On top of it was a huge pan filled with rocks. The rocks gave off tremendous heat. But there was no sign of a boiler or other steam-producing equipment.

"How do you make the steam?"

"I'll show you." He took up a wooden bucket, filled it from a large tub, and threw the water over the stones. The water fell on the hot rocks with a noise like machine-gun fire. A dense cloud of hot steam immediately filled the little room. We choked and backed out.

But the proud Finn would not be satisfied until at least one of us had tried it. With grave doubts I disrobed in the dressing room, went into the steam room and closed the door. The fire was burning briskly and the stones glowed. Sitting on the bench, I found myself already dripping wet, thanks to the humidity.

After soaping myself, I flung a bucketful of water on the stones. The sudden steam made me gasp for breath. More and more water went on the stones, and more and more I progressed towards a state of complete suffocation.

Perspiration streamed out of me like juice from a squeezed orange. In ten minutes I felt as wrung out as a rag. For five years in Japan I had taken a daily bath in water three feet deep, heated to one hundred and twenty degrees, but it was nothing like this. The steam went up the nostrils and down into the lungs and I felt baked from both the inside and the outside. My head seemed about to explode.

"Out already?" said my Finnish host as I burst through the door and ran to plunge my stewing body in the river. Later the ceremony was completed with a mug of mulled cider in the farmhouse. Now I was feeling the afterglow. It was like sinking into a featherbed a mile deep. Every muscle, every nerve, was relaxed. A shoulder that had become paddle-lame was now perfectly at ease.

"It's good for neuralgia," said the farmer's wife. "And colds."

"You take these baths in winter too?"

"Certainly."

"But then you can't go in the river. It must be frozen over."

"Yes. We roll in the snow instead. A drift six feet deep forms against the north wall of the *sauna*. We have great fun in it."

As in Japan, the two sexes bathe together in the nude and take their cooling-off together in the water or the snow. A boy may come to see his girl and bathe with her and her family. And yet at other times strict propriety is observed. At the bathing beaches, even though swimming suits are worn, it is Finnish custom for men and women to bathe separately.

The difference lies in the fact that the bath in the *sauna* is not just a bath. Traditionally it is a ceremony.

"The bathhouse is a kind of temple," writes Arthur Reade in *Finland and the Finns*, "and the bath has the nature of a ritual. The church and the bathhouse are holy places, says a Finnish proverb. The place has grave and lofty associations of another kind also. It is to the bathhouse that the mother retires when a child is about to be born and the temperature is made as high as possible in order to ease her delivery. To it also sick people are taken as to a hospital."

Disappearing Lumberjack

There's a long carry at Grand Rapids. A dam has taken the place of the rapids that gave the town its name, and above the dam the river is surfaced with several acres of logs waiting to be ground into pulp and turned into paper in the mill of the Blandin Paper Company.

This is one of the longest of the fourteen carries around dams on the way to Minneapolis. There navigation for large craft begins and every dam is supplemented by a lock. From Minneapolis to the Gulf, one need never take one's craft out of the water.

The logs awaiting pulverization remind us that lumbering is not yet dead on the Mississippi. To be sure, the logs are rarely floated downriver as they once were, but go by truck and train. Six million acres of commercial forest lie within easy reach of Grand Rapids. The days of wholesale slaughter are gone. Now cutting does not keep up with growth. Forest surveys show that only a half to two-thirds of the allowable cut each year is harvested.

White rapids tumble over unseen rocks as we near Brainerd. We slide along with toboggan speed. The current is full of whirlpools with doughnut holes in their centers—but though they sometimes twist the boat out of control for a moment they are never powerful enough to upend it and suck it down as the whirls in the lower river sometimes swallow logs.

Great blue herons and kingfishers sail from one forest wall across to the other. Deer come down to the shore to drink. If deerflies are any indication of the presence of deer, there must be great herds in these woods.

The deer flies sail round and round our heads and we have to be continually dropping our paddles to swat them. Our conversation is punctuated with impolite exclamations, the whang of dropped paddles, and resounding slaps on tortured skins.

Repellent seems to have no effect, unless it actually attracts the flies. They calmly sit in puddles of the stuff and proceed to bite. We seek reassurance by reading the label on the bottle. It shows beautiful pictures of flies, but the text mentions only black flies, sand flies, stable flies, not deer flies.

The regional distribution of insects is curious and hard to understand. We had had no deer flies on other stretches of the river, only mosquitoes. Here there is not a single mosquito, but clouds of deer flies.

They are stupid as well as vicious. They get tangled up in one's hair, blunder into ears, eyes and mouth. But they do not lack talent when they bite.

Tough Going

We rounded a bend into the wind and presto!—there was not a single fly. But we had no sooner congratulated each other before we encountered the hardest job in all our canoe experience.

It looked so easy. The current was strong and we expected it to carry us along with little or no effort on our part.

But a violent headwind developed. Many travelers down the Mississippi have complained of the prevailing south wind. Generally it is only a breeze; this time it grew into a gale.

It was like trying to paddle through a stone wall. The opposition was so strong that if we stopped paddling for an instant the wind promptly blew us upstream against the current. The blasts all but whipped the paddles out of our hands. Many times we ran into sea-size waves as the result of upstream wind against downstream current. They showered over us and nearly swamped the boat. The river was in places a half mile wide— much too wide for comfort in a strong wind. A helicopter from nearby Camp Ripley returned time and again to see if we were still above water.

Whenever the wind battering our eyeballs would let us, we realized that the river was beautiful. Hundreds of islands lay between the low shore on the right and the high rugged bank on the left. Deer looked out from the island woods. It is said that they take refuge there because the mainland has become too busy—though we went many miles without seeing a house.

But it was often difficult to pick the most direct channel through the islands. At one place there were five broad passages to confuse us.

We ran into rapids repeatedly, nine times within one period of six hours, and the rapids were full of ugly rocks.

The wind and waves were so noisy that, sitting only ten feet apart, we could not hear each other speak. The waves curled and broke over us, the surface was churned into whitecaps, and we seemed to be afloat on a sea of whipped cream.

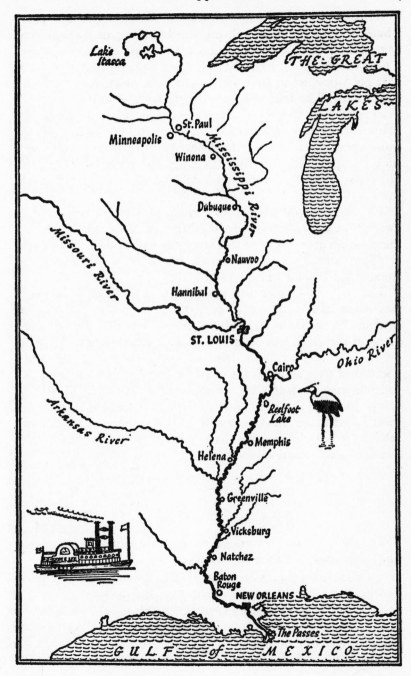

We were quite willing to give up the struggle. But then what? A night on an island, the wind chilling us through our wet clothes? If we could just find a house, we could telephone. There was no house. Even the helicopter had deserted us.

It got worse when the river began to broaden into a lake at Little Falls. The lake was one roaring rush of water, the wind dead against us. But there at last was a small pier. We pulled in behind it, walked half a mile back through the woods until we came upon a farmhouse and telephoned our driver to come and pick us up. It was the first time we had fallen short of our objective, but we acknowledged defeat with the greatest pleasure.

The canoeist paddles through much of Minneapolis scarcely aware that the city exists. In the heart of Minnesota's greatest metroplitan area the river still struggles to maintain its privacy. It passes through a sylvan canyon closed in on both sides by wooded banks some hundred feet high.

The gorge is a quiet bird sanctuary and probably about as it was when man first saw it, except that it is now crossed by bridges. These are so high above that they hardly disturb travelers on the river. For long stretches no houses are to be seen, yet we find later when we drive along the river roads that only a screen of trees shuts off beautiful residential districts from the solitude-loving river. An unimportant-looking little stream comes in from the right, but this trivial trickle is one of the most loved waters in America. It is Minnehaha Creek, immortalized by Longfellow. We disembark to see the bronze of Hiawatha about to bear his sweetheart across the stream.

> *Over wide and rushing rivers,*
> *In his arms he bore the maiden;*
> *Light he thought her as a feather,*
> *As the plume upon his head-gear.*

Then the stream plunges over the precipice to the delight of daily thousands of admiring visitors.

> *Where the Falls of Minnehaha*
> *Flash and gleam among the oak trees,*
> *Laugh and leap into the valley.*

A little after the advent of the famous creek, we pass under old Fort Snelling, for more than thirty years the northernmost post of the U.S. Army. Here the Minnesota River quietly joins the Mississippi.

As if this reinforcement gave the river the courage to face the world, the Mississippi now flows through the busiest part of St. Paul, fully exposed to view and affording docking facilities for large river craft.

So far as commercial traffic is concerned, the Mississippi begins at the Twin Cities. There the Falls of St. Anthony block off the upper reaches.

From Basket to Steamboat

We have now come to the river of big boats. The Mississippi from the Twins to the Gulf was once famous for its floating palaces, with great side-wheels or stern-wheels, with tall chimneys crowned with iron plumes, with murals and chandeliers and sumptuous cabins and good food and a deep whistle and gay music on the calliope.

There are a few of the old steamboats left. We boarded one, the *Avalon,* at a St. Paul dock for an excursion downriver. Away aloft a steam calliope was playing "Cruising Down the River."

We spotted the captain, introduced ourselves, and asked permission to visit the top deck where normally no passengers are allowed. We wished to photograph the calliope and its player.

"Certainly—and you'd better hurry. He won't play after we start."

The high-pressure music was intended to attract customers and must surely be effective for it could be heard anywhere within a half-mile radius.

We climbed to the top deck. The musician proved to be 22-year-old Clark Hawley, first mate and musician.

"This calliope and one on the *Delta Queen* are the last still in use on the Mississippi," he said. "The *Admiral* has one but has nobody to play it—so they use recordings, some of them mine."

"How old is this instrument?"

"About half a century. It was made a little before 1900."

The calliope consisted of a row of steam whistles, each connected with a valve, every valve governed by a key on a keyboard like that of an organ. As each key was pressed the corresponding whistle let off a shrill note and a jet of steam.

Mary asked, "Is it like playing the piano?"

"Well, it's harder. You see, there are fifty-five pounds pressure on each valve."

It takes strong fingers and a strong back to play the calliope, and ears that will stand more violent sound waves than a hundred symphony orchestra instruments could produce.

The fascinating history of boats on the Mississippi begins with baskets, like the coracles still used on some rivers in Wales. The basket was round, some five feet in diameter, made of a wicker frame covered with a buffalo's hide. The boat usually carried only one person, two at the most.

When white fur-traders invaded the valley, they adopted the Indian craft but enlarged it. They called it a "bullboat" because of the use of skins of buffalo bulls. These made a sort of rawhide armor plate that would stand a great deal of chafing against the rocks of the river bottom without abrasion. The hides were sewn together into one great sheet which was thoroughly soaked, then placed over the framework where it dried and shrank until it was as tight as a drumhead.

Early white explorers used the pirogue. It was a canoe, but all in one piece, carved from a huge cypress log. Famous pirogue makers could make a pirogue in two days. Said one such expert, "It's easy to make a pirogue from a fine log like this. You just chop away the wood you don't need and there's the pirogue. It was inside that log all the time."

Home on a Raft

The timber age brought in the lumber raft. It was a way of getting the logs to market. Several thousand logs were bolted together to form a floating island some two or three acres in extent, and shanties were thrown up on it to serve as bunkhouses and cookhouse for the crew who must row the raft to its destination.

Cooking was not easy on a raft. Supplies were sometimes hard to get and the meals were not as bountiful as in a lumber camp.

On a raft commanded by the fabulous Whisky Jack the crew complained about the meals. There was no variety. It was the same old stuff every day. Captain Whisky Jack asked the cook, Big John, why he didn't use a cookery book.

"I got one," said Big John, "but I can't do anything with it."

"Is it too fancy for you?"

"Sure is," replied Big John. "Every recipe begins the same way, 'Take a clean dish.' That stumps me."

The Wisconsin Folklore Society has resurrected this amusing item on Whisky Jack:

Whisky Jack was no scholar. He didn't care to read, and he could not write. When he signed the payroll or any other document at the sawmill or lumberyard offices, he signed with a big X instead of his name. He did this for a long time. But one day he signed with an XX instead of just an X. The bookkeeper wondered at this and asked him why he signed with two X's instead of just one. And Whisky Jack explained that he and a milliner lady in one of the river towns had just got "spliced," and he thought that now, being a married man, he ought to change his name.

On some rafts the men took turns doing the cooking. One man cooked until somebody complained. Then the man who complained had to take his place.

A certain temporary cook, Jem Wilson, determined to do the job so badly that the men would get sick of his cooking and let him go back to the oars. He made a batch of biscuits and dumped in enough salt for a barrel of pork. When the men bit into the biscuits one exclaimed, "Great guns, these here damn biscuits is saltier than hell!"

Suddenly realizing that a complaint would make him the next cook, he hastily added, "Best I ever ate!"

Later came the keelboat, some seventy feet long. It would go downstream easily enough but had trouble getting up. After discharging its cargo at New Orleans it turned about and struggled back upstream. The oars were supplemented by sails which sometimes consisted only of blankets or a screen made of boards. Poles were used in shallow stretches. When the boat hugged the shore the crew laid hold of bushes and branches and pulled the boat along. This process was called "bushwhacking." If there was a path along the shore, the crew "cordelled" the boat by walking up the path, pulling the boat after them at the end of a rope.

The tale is told of an Irishman who wanted to get from Ste. Genevieve to St. Louis. He asked the captain of an upbound boat if he might work his passage. The captain consented and the Irishman took his carpetbag aboard and settled down for a comfortable journey. But he was promptly ordered ashore and put at the end of a rope with the rest of the crew. After three miles of trudging and sweating under the hot sun he complained, "So you call this a boat trip. Faith, I'd about as soon walk."

Who Invented the Steam Engine?

But something was happening that would soon make oars, poles, sails, bushwhacking and the cordelle unnecessary.

The age of steam did not come suddenly. Nor did it begin with James Watt and his teakettle. The ingenious Greeks in the second century B.C. devised a steam engine and used it to open and close the heavy doors of temples. Leonardo da Vinci was one of many who experimented with steam. In the sixteenth century a Spanish captain devised a steamboat and sailed it in the harbor of Barcelona. In the seventeenth an Italian engineer made a steam windmill. A mining engineer used steam to drain the mines of Cornwall.

It was another century before Watt, studying the behavior of his teakettle, improved the steam engine by adding a separate condenser.

Fulton, Fitch and Shreve evolved the steamboat.

It was Shreve who made the steamboat queen of the Mississippi. He initiated a style of travel that was practical; it was also good fun. Before this a river journey had been an uncomfortable experience. But Shreve's *Washington* was luxury afloat: the public rooms were elaborate with carved woodwork and mirrors, soft carpets and fine furniture; the meals were as good as could be had in the best hotels and were served with a fine flourish.

Other builders took their cue from Shreve and went on to outdo him. Boats rapidly grew longer and lovelier. Their saloons glittered with cut-glass chandeliers and glowed with oil paintings. Bronze and marble statues lent an air of culture. The dining room gleamed with solid silver and as many as two dozen stewards were in attendance. A typical menu was two feet long and offered thirteen desserts.

The *Eclipse* eclipsed its predecessors by providing forty-eight bridal chambers, a grand piano and provision for the lordly planter who wished to take along a full retinue of servants.

"The steamboats were finer than anything on shore," wrote Mark Twain in *Life on the Mississippi*. "When a citizen stepped on board a big fine steamboat he entered a new and marvelous world."

Travel on a Mississippi steamboat was not only sumptuous, it could be highly exciting. One never knew when the boiler would blow up. Between 1810 and 1850 there were four thousand steamboat casualties, most of them due to boiler explosions. Mark Twain's brother, Henry Clemens, was one of a hundred who lost their lives when four of the *Pennsylvania*'s eight boilers exploded. Boats foundered on snags or sandbars. Or someone dropped a cigarette and the wooden structure loaded with bales of inflammable cotton went up like a torch. The average life of a steamboat was reckoned at four to five years, and it could be fairly sure of coming to a violent end.

There was always an argument between railroadmen and rivermen as to the relative safety of their professions. A Negro railroad porter clinched the argument to his own satisfaction with this comment, "If you is blowed up on the railroad, there you is; but, good lord, if you is blowed up on a steamboat, where is you?"

Why did the exciting and luxurious packet boats of the Mississippi disappear?

The impatient age arrived, people were in a hurry, roads and railroads offered faster transportation.

The golden age of the steamboat lasted only some eighty years. Even as early as 1874, a former pilot, who had known the river in its thrilling heyday, noted its dreary return to primitive emptiness.

"We met two steamboats at New Madrid," wrote Mark Twain. "Two steamboats in sight at once! An infrequent spectacle now in the lonesome Mississippi."

Miracle of the Towboat

A miracle brought the Mississippi back to life. The great river now does in a day what it formerly did in a year. For the Mississippi's new usefulness we must thank the towboat.

The towboat is misnamed. The word "towboat" gives no idea of the nature of this remarkable craft. One is apt to confuse it with a tugboat—the busy little beetle that hauls barges across New York Harbor or presses its padded nose against the bow or stern of an ocean liner hugging up to a North River dock.

The towboat is nothing like that. It is one of the marvels of the transportation age. Instead of one deck it may have five or more. Instead of one engine it is likely to have four. Instead of one rudder it has ten. Instead of a few hundred horsepower it will deliver four to eight thousand. Instead of nudging an ocean liner it will push a fleet of barges carrying the load of two great oceangoing freighters. Instead of carrying a crew of two or three men it requires seventeen or twenty. Instead of costing a few thousand dollars, its owners consider it cheap if they can get it built for a million.

The towboat is not really a towboat. It is a pushboat. It tows nothing.

In the long-distant past it did haul its barges behind it and was properly called a towboat. The name has stuck, although the method of handling a tow has changed.

A string of barges trailing out behind could not be controlled. It whipped about like a crocodile's tail. Crosscurrents or crosswinds threw it onto the rocks or into other boats or against bridge piers.

So the barges were put in front instead of behind. Barges perhaps three abreast and numbering a dozen or more were tied together so rigidly by steel cables that they became one unyielding raft and this tow (still called a tow although it was to be pushed) was locked in place before the towboat and so firmly integrated with it by steel cables that the entire fleet became a single unit subject to the slightest touch of the pilot upon the steering levers.

Push towing, thanks to the Mississippi example, is now being initiated in lands as far apart as Laos, Germany and Argentina. Mississippi captains have been called abroad to teach the new method on the Mekong, the Rhine and the Plata.

The barge, like the towboat, is too humbly named. The Mississippi barge is a floating warehouse. One jumbo-size barge costs $90,000 to build. A standard barge weighs about three hundred tons and will carry a thousand in cargo.

Recently built barges dwarf these figures. A hopper barge now in operation has a capacity in excess of twenty-five hundred tons. A single barge will carry the load of three or four of the large packets of steamboat days. And one towboat may push twenty or more such barges!

One grain barge will carry a hundred thousand bushels. One tank barge will take a million gallons of oil. (By comparison, a railroad tank car has a capacity of ten thousand gallons.)

An integrated tow, the entire unit lashed together to make one streamlined vessel, may stretch to twelve hundred feet—longer than the largest ocean liner afloat. The *Queen Elizabeth* stops at 1,031 feet, the *Queen Mary* at 1,019.

Such a tow can carry two hundred thousand barrels (thirty-five thousand tons) of oil, the equivalent of the load of two oceangoing tankers.

This fabulous development in the history of transportation began during World War I. Half a century before, the railroads had banished the steamboats. The river was rediscovered in 1917. The demands of war overwhelmed the railroads. The government commandeered the few barges and towboats that could be found on the Mississippi, hastily built a fleet of new boats, and formed what became known as the Federal Barge Lines.

Great stores of war materials began to move. Private investors saw the opportunity and formed barge lines of their own. The government, having demonstrated what could be done, sold the Federal Barge Lines to private investors in 1953. The firm retained the same name but was now on its own and had plenty of competition. There were now more than 150 privately-owned barge companies on the Mississippi system. There was plenty of business for all and it continues to grow spectacularly year by year.

We Board the Huck Finn

Through the courtesy of the Federal Barge Lines we are put aboard the towboat *Huck Finn*. She was originally steam-powered but has now been converted to diesel.

People who confuse towboats with tugboats should see this vessel. It is only of average size, yet instead of the single deck of a tugboat, there are six levels in the *Huck Finn*—the radar deck on top, the pilothouse level, the texas deck, the boiler deck, the main deck, and the below-water engine-room deck.

But she has to be big and powerful to push the equivalent of a heavily loaded train four miles long, and that's about what her twenty thousand tons of cargo would amount to. That is only a modest load for a modern tow. In the pilothouse I pick up today's paper and happen to see an item concerning a tow of twenty-four barges, 126,000 square feet or almost three acres, now being pushed on the Tennessee River by the towboat *Robin,* 3,200 horsepower. Three acres on the move! I read the item aloud to the pilot. He says, "Imagine how hard it would be to stop it." He is peering anxiously ahead because this is Sunday and the small boats are out in force. They skip across the river in front of our tow.

"They have a lot of confidence in their motors," remarks the pilot. "If their power failed while they were ahead of us, nothing in the world could prevent us from running them down. We could reverse our engines, but with the momentum of twenty thousand tons plus the force of the current we couldn't stop in less than a quarter of a mile."

Half an hour later the pilot's fears are borne out. A motorboat flashes in front of the tow hauling a water skier who loses his balance and falls in the path of the oncoming barges.

The pilot immediately throws the engines into reverse and blows a thundering blast on the whistle. There is nothing more he can do. The raft of barges plows on remorselessly toward the struggling skier.

To the people in other boats it must look as if we are deliberately running the man down. They blow their horns and shout at us, the men angrily, the women hysterically, unaware that the boat's engines are doing their best, though vainly, to check the speed of the fleet.

The man disentangles himself from his skis and begins to swim. He is a good swimmer but he will never make it. The oncoming barges are too broad for him to get out of their path in time.

Close Shave

But there is a man in one of those speedboats who can do something besides blow his horn and shout. He sends his boat roaring into the path of the approaching tow. He slows just long enough to seize the swimmer and haul him aboard.

If his motor should stall now there would be two deaths instead of one. It does not stall and the boat shoots across the front of the barges and into safe water.

Onlookers cheer the rescuer and curse the towboat pilot. The floating skis disappear beneath the raft. They will not look like skis any more after a quarter of a mile of pummeling under the barges and towboat.

The pilot's face is tight and white. He is the one who should have been cursing through this entire episode but he has not said a word. Now he flips the engines back to full ahead and calls for a cup of coffee.

He smiles over his coffee. "Nearly went to jail that time."

"Who, you? It wasn't your fault."

"The law doesn't look at it that way. The least that could happen would be a trial and a fine and perhaps discharge. One pilot I know has been waiting trial for three months for running over a motorboat. Just last week he had the bad luck to run over another. I'd hate to be in his shoes when he goes to court. It's tricky, this business. Too many things you can't control. To be a pilot you need ten percent skill and ninety percent luck."

Over his radiophone the pilot chats with the master of some other vessel, perhaps miles away, perhaps just around the next bend but still unseen. It is important that an upcoming and downcoming tow should not take each other by surprise. They compare notes.

Chatting with the Unseen

"I'm close to the right bank but the current is swinging me out."

"Okay. I'll hug the sandbar and give you a wide berth."

But the talk is not limited to official matters.

"How's that bad tooth of yours? Did you get to a dentist?"

"How could I get to a dentist? No, I just tied it to a door-knob and slammed the door."

In a dense fog the tow keeps on going. The radar screen shows the river and its shores. When another boat appears on the screen the master picks up his telephone. He cannot see the boat, he cannot even see out to the front end of his tow, but there is the boat on the screen and here is the master's voice coming over the phone. They talk things over, decide what to do, where to pass.

In this respect the modern riverboats are far ahead of most oceangoing vessels. Many of the latter are not equipped with telephones for ship-to-ship or ship-to-shore calls. Many sea disasters are due to this lack of easy communication. If the *Andrea Doria* had been able to chat with the captain of the *Stockholm*, the collision that took more than fifty lives might have been avoided. Ocean vessels come up the Mississippi as far as Baton Rouge and are a menace to other shipping when they cannot be reached by the human voice.

The master uses another phone if he wishes to talk to the engine room. He has still another connected by a wire running out along the barges to the front of the tow. This is called the teletalk or, more commonly, the "tattletale."

Time was when the captain would shout through a megaphone to the men on the barges. The second mate would megaphone back. Every word had to be clearly pronounced and sung, not spoken.

As tows became bigger and longer, it did not work so well. With the "tattletale" there is no need to sing or shout. Words almost whispered are amplified into thunder. Both the teletalk and the radiophone make a mouse a lion. Soft-spoken men have their mildest remarks come out with a roar like the blast of a trumpet.

The River Changes Its Sex

The Mississippi changes its sex at Cairo. Here it is joined by the Ohio which contributes a far greater volume than the Missisipi itself. From this point we have a quite different Mississippi.

The charming upper river was unmistakably feminine. The big brute of a lower river is just as certainly masculine.

It is no longer a sweet river; it is grand. It is no longer pretty; it is majestic. It has lost its friendliness; now it is to be feared rather than loved.

It is erratic, power-crazy, a half-tamed giant capable of carrying enormous commerce to man's benefit, but guilty of devastating floods, savage eccentricities, sinkings and drownings without number.

It was on these lower reaches that the Indian and Negro nicknames, Old Big Strong, Old Man River and Old Devil River were born.

Superstitious sailors believe that its presiding demon is Old Al, the River King. He is said to be a male alligator bigger than a barge. He bears a gold crown on his head and holds a huge pipe of tobacco in one of his scaly paws. With his other paw he takes delight in scooping up a sandbar to block a passage or plucking men off barges for his dinner. With his tail he switches currents this way and that to throw a tow up against a bridge pier or smash a levee or toss floods over farms and villages.

This is no longer a small-boat river. Except for two or three hazardous experiments, we leave our little aluminum eggshell safely on top of the car until we shall reach the quiet bayous of the South.

But, full of menace though it may be, the Lower Mississippi is the most significant river on the planet in the value of its cargoes, and one of the most exciting to the traveler.

We pieced out the thousand miles from Cairo to the Gulf in every imaginable sort of craft capable of riding the whirling waters—towboat, houseboat, patrol boat, workboat, snag boat, passenger boat, showboat and shantyboat. Then went over the distance by hydroplane, and again by car.

How to Conquer a Giant

The most stirring story to come out of the Mississippi Valley is the story of the conquest of the Father of Waters by the U.S. engineers. It is a conquest not yet completed but well on the way. The most terrible disasters of the past are not likely to be repeated.

The flood of 1927 drove 800,000 people from their homes. Terrific currents chewed holes in the levees and poured through to inundate towns, carry away houses, and bury farms in muddy water as much as eighteen feet deep. The river broadened in some places to a width of eighty miles. Many people were trapped and drowned. Animals fled to the high places—mounds, trees, chimneys. They forgot their animosities. Old enemies huddled together in terror; rabbits, muskrats, herons, chickens, possums, snakes, foxes, raccoons and deer. Horses swam away until they were exhausted or found refuge, but the cattle stood impassive in the water until they drowned or starved to death.

In this grim picture there were glints of comic relief.

When the town of Greenville was inundated, ten thousand Negroes were evacuated to temporary camps on the crest of the levee. They were divided according to precincts and each person had to go to the medical tent of his precinct to get typhoid shots. One woman who came to the wrong place was told, "You don't belong here. You've got to get vaccinated in your precinct."

"Lor' God," she said, "this is a funny country. You white folks get vaccinated in your arm and you tell us we got to get vaccinated in our precinct."

Greater Than China's Great Wall

The Corps of Engineers, U.S. Army, has pulled the teeth of Old Al, the River King. Where the river formerly wound back and forth in great loops, the engineers have straightened it by means of cutoffs. The straightened river does not cut into its banks so severely as when it had to swing around curve after curve. In times of flood the swollen waters are not blocked and turned aside in loop after loop, and thereby compelled to spread out over the country, swamping towns and farms. The water is carried directly and swiftly toward the Gulf of Mexico. Thus the runoff may be able to keep up with the rainfall.

The engineers have corsetted the river between levees, their total length twice that of the Great Wall of China.

True, even these huge earthen battlements a hundred feet thick at the base and three or four stories high, are not completely invulnerable.

So small a thing as a pocket gopher may destroy them. A gopher, rat or armadillo makes a small burrow, then perhaps an internal system of runways, side branches, chambers for storage and nests. Some day the water rises, enters the burrows, and gradually reduces the solid bank to a mound of mush. The slopes slough off and slide down. The seepage comes through to the inner side and there is no small boy handy to stop the drip of water with his thumb.

The drip becomes a dribble, the dribble becomes a continuous stream, the hole broadens with amazing speed and the stream is a torrent. The earth above the hole drops and is washed out, and the result is a crevasse through which a Niagara pours into the back country sending people upstairs or into boats or to seek precarious refuge on the crest of the remaining levee.

Only eternal vigilance can prevent such catastrophes. The levees are usually kept clear of vegetation so that fiddler crabs and other borers can be more easily seen and destroyed. Burrows must be filled. During high water guards must walk the levee and watch for "boils," small geysers marking the beginnings of breaks.

A constant preoccupation of the engineers is the maintenance of a channel twelve feet deep and three hundred feet wide all the way up to Minneapolis. Where dredging is required, a "dustpan dredge" with a sucking mouth thirty-five feet wide may be used if the bottom is soft. Where it is hard, a many-bladed "cutterhead" is used to mince up the clay and gravel which is then sucked away by a gigantic vacuum cleaner and passes through a tube a thousand feet or so to the shore. The dredge is like an oversized elephant with a huge trunk stretching across the river.

The word "dredge" may call up an image of something small, smelly and noisy, the sort so often seen hoisting mud into barges. The Mississippi dredge is a different breed. We spent a day on the dredge *Rock Island* which, according to the captain, cost $750,000 to build in 1936, and would cost $3,000,000 to replace. It is the floating home of fifty-two men, also of two women who run the kitchen, is equipped with every civilized comfort, and is as spick-and-span as a millionaire's yacht.

No one can tell what next will pour out on shore from the end of the elephant's trunk—sometimes doubloons from the days of the conquering Spaniards; sometimes cannon balls of the Civil War; sometimes buffalo horns reminiscent of the herds that used to swim the Mississippi, delaying steamboats for hours; sometimes the skeletons of unfortunate rivermen.

Paving the River Bottom

Another vessel unique to the Mississippi is the snag boat. Snags are among the chief perils of the big river. Undercut by the current, a bank will cave in, hurling big trees into the river. The roots of the tree will sink to the bottom because they are heavily embedded with dirt. The top of the tree, being lighter, will float on or near the surface and the current will point it downstream.

The snag that stays in a fixed position is called a "planter." One that keeps lowering and raising its head is a "sawyer." Either may stave in a boat coming upstream, but the sawyer is the more dangerous. Its rhythm may be very slow so that it is out of sight for many minutes at a time. The steersman looks out upon perfectly smooth water only to see a monster rear its head ten feet above the surface when it is too late to avoid it. *Chicots*, the teeth of the river, the French used to call these snags, and they can bite a hole through the toughest hull. It is the business of the snag boats to pluck these obstructions out of the channel.

We rode the big stern-wheeler snag boat *Charles H. West* from Greenville to Vicksburg. From a lofty A-frame on the bow of the vessel dangled a gigantic pair of tongs which could grip and haul out a log as easily as a dentist pulls a tooth.

We seemed to be making for a small stick projecting from

the water. It was only as big as my arm and rose but a few feet above the surface. Surely this huge tooth-puller would not trouble to give its attention to such a trifle.

The *West* slowed up to the stick and the tongs descended and bit in. Up came the stick, foot by foot. It grew thicker and heavier and still it came, ten feet, twenty, thirty and still more until the top of it rose above the lofty pilothouse and the roots rested on the deck. It was a cottonwood log no less than one hundred feet long. The men cut it into short lengths with power saws and dumped the pieces overboard to float harmlessly away.

One of the most extraordinary feats of the engineers is the paving of the riverbed. The Lower Mississippi over much of its length is now a paved street. The paving usually does not floor the central channel but covers the bank where the current and wave action would otherwise wash it away. It may extend six hundred feet or more from each shore toward the middle of the stream.

This flooring used to consist of trees bound together with wire into mats sometimes a mile long. Today the mats consist of reticulated slabs of concrete. These blocks are linked together with stainless steel wire, the whole forming a flexible mattress. Such a mat will usually last twenty or thirty years.

The Strange World of the Delta

The last of the steamboats to take overnight passengers, the *Delta Queen,* carried us from Natchez to New Orleans. Behind it, a great stern-wheel threw up big waves and carried an aura of spray all about it like a veil. The *Delta Queen* is a floating hotel in the old tradition of deep comfort and fine food, but has one agreeably modern feature, air conditioning in the staterooms.

New Orleans is vaguely supposed to be at the end of the Mississippi. But there are 110 miles of river below it and this is one of the most fascinating stretches of the entire river. Here the Mississippi has laid down its modern delta—modern in comparison with the alluvial plain it has deposited over the ages from Cairo south.

The deep delta country is a strange and fabulous region, the like of which cannot be found in many places on this planet. It is a bewildering mosaic of twisting channels, lakes, bayous (from the Choctaw *bayuk* meaning a small sluggish waterway), swamps and sloughs, rising to dry land near the river and culminating in the levee hugging the shore. The levee is the highest land anywhere, yet it is seldom twenty feet above the water. The river is broad and tranquil in its old age, but still has enough force to carry its tremendous burden of silt on toward the Gulf.

The marshes are full of islands and every fairly solid island bears houses or even villages, perched on posts. There is nothing entirely solid in this world. This is "trembling earth." Here geology can be seen at work. Nature has not yet quite decided what to do with all the mud poured out by the great river.

The land suddenly sinks beneath the feet, or suddenly swells up into a small hill. Land under water may rise to a height of nine feet or more above it. These "mud lumps," as the deltans call them, have not been completely explained. They may be caused by gas and oil bubbling up from deep deposits. They are quite possibly due to the heavy weight of silt delivered by the river which by bearing down upon the soft clays in one area causes a push-up in another.

The folk who make this strange region their home were described by a visitor a century ago as "aquatic men, with fins like fishes', noses like alligators', feet like ducks'." We did not see any who answered to this description, but certainly it does take a peculiar talent to make a life and a living in such surroundings. Lafitte and his fellows did well as pirates and smugglers. Even today a manhunt through these marshes is considered practically impossible. Forbidden cargoes still find their way through the delta.

There are many reminders of the great days of piracy. We launched our canoe on Barataria Bayou and noted that the bayou, the larger bay, the town, the lighthouse, and the pass, all bear the name "Barataria" because of their association with the smugglers and pirates who made this locale their headquarters. "Barataria" is an old Romance word meaning "deception." It is romantically reminiscent in some connections but seems a bit odd when used on a church which announces itself as Barataria Baptist Church.

Another sign, "Lafitte Elementary School," seems to accord more honor to a robber and killer than one would expect an institution of learning to pay. More harmless and amusing is a sign over a tailor shop: "Pants pressed while you hide."

Winding Waters and Writhing Mists

Launching our canoe, we paddled up a twisting offshoot of Barataria Bayou so narrow that the trees sometimes met overhead. Ghostly curtains of Spanish moss waved in the wind. That beautiful pest, the water hyacinth, bordered the banks with purple bloom.

It was an ideal home for big snakes. A five-foot cottonmouth crossed our bow in one direction at the same instant that an unknown serpent just as large came straight for the boat from the opposite shore with the apparent notion that this thing was a log on which he could crawl out and bask in the sun. A paddle fended him off.

A fisherman strung his net from shore to shore completely blocking the waterway and soon there was a tremendous splashing—the man paddled his pirogue to the spot and hauled out a four-foot gar.

We became temporarily lost in the labyrinth of channels. Now it was easy to understand why the pirates had chosen this water-maze as their retreat.

This ghostly land of winding waters and writhing mists, where aged trees

Bearded with moss, and in garments green, indistinct in the twilight,
Stand like Druids of eld, with voices sad and prophetic,
Stand like harpers hoar, with beards that rest on their bosoms

deserves this description far better than does the "primeval forest" of Acadia which Longfellow had in mind when he wrote these lines.

The really colossal wealth of the delta is in its oil and gas. We flew over the oil rigs that stand in the marshes and in the Gulf itself as far as thirty miles from shore. All personnel are carried to and from the rigs by helicopter. On our plane radio, like that of a taxi, we overheard constant instructions to the drivers of these air taxis.

Weather is a serious subject to the oil-rig men since they are in a very exposed position. When a hurricane is forecast all are removed from the rigs. Even an ordinary storm may be fatal. We passed over a rig that had been upset a few days previously. It had completely turned turtle and nine men had died, trapped beneath it. Our pilot said, "The deepest oil well in the world is here at Grand Ecaille—22,000 feet deep. There are many ten thousand to fifteen thousand feet deep. These rigs cost money. One just finished cost three million, two hundred and fifty thousand dollars to build. It will lower its legs to the bottom of the Gulf, then raise its deck to the height of a ten-story building."

Is the Conquest Complete?

The river empties into the Gulf rather ingloriously. It has lost its thunderous power and seems very tired. It comes up against the sediment that it itself has laid down. So instead of surging into the sea in one great final flood, it divides into a dozen languid channels that pick their way over the mud flats to salt water.

These channels were for hundreds of years too shallow to be navigated by ocean vessels bound for New Orleans and Baton Rouge. This problem too has finally been solved by the engineers. Two of the channels have been "stabilized"—so engineered that, with frequent dredging, they provide a thirty-five-foot-deep access to the sea.

Since the death-dealing flood of 1927, it is reckoned that scientific control of the Mississippi has prevented at least five billion dollars in losses, not counting lives.

The conquest of the river has been called "one of the most ambitious undertakings ever conceived by man." The success of this mammoth project to date has given valley dwellers a new confidence—in some cases a dangerous complacency. No doubt the river still has many tricks in its bag. Nothing but eternal vigilance will checkmate the infernal ingenuity of Old Al, the River King.

Index